W9-DII-481

STALKING THE SUBJECT
DISCARDED

STALKING THE SUBJECT

Modernism and the Animal

Carrie Rohman

Columbia University Press   New York

Columbia University Press
Publishers Since 1893
New York   Chichester, West Sussex

Copyright © 2009 Columbia University Press
All rights reserved

Library of Congress Cataloging-in-Publication Data
Rohman, Carrie.
Stalking the subject : modernism and the animal / Carrie Rohman.
   p. cm.
  Includes bibliographical references and index.
  ISBN 978-0-231-14506-0 (cloth : alk. paper) —
  ISBN 978-0-231-14507-7 (pbk.)
  1. English literature—19th century—History and criticism.
2. English literature—20th century—History and criticism.
3. Animals in literature. 4. Modernism (Literature)—Great Britain.
5. Human-animal relationships in literature. 6. Animals—
Symbolic aspects. 7. Darwin, Charles, 1809–1882—Influence.
8. Freud, Sigmund, 1856–1939—Influence. 9. Evolution (Biology)
in literature. 10. Ethics in literature. I. Title.
PR468.A56R64   2009
820.9'362—dc22   2008004864

♾ Columbia University Press books are printed on permanent and
durable acid-free paper.
This book was printed on paper with recycled content.
Printed in the United States of America
c 10 9 8 7 6 5 4 3 2 1
p 10 9 8 7 6 5 4 3 2 1

References to Internet Web sites (URLs) were accurate at the time
of writing. Neither the author nor Columbia University Press is
responsible for URLs that may have expired or changed since the
manuscript was prepared.

For my mother and late father,

and for Dale Gilmore

The gaze called animal offers to my sight the abyssal limit of the human: the inhuman or the ahuman, the ends of man, that is to say the bordercrossing from which vantage man dares to announce himself to himself. And in these moments of nakedness, under the gaze of the animal, everything can happen to me, I am like a child ready for the apocalypse, I am (following) the apocalypse itself, that is to say the ultimate and first event of the end, the unveiling and the verdict.
—Jacques Derrida, "The Animal That Therefore I Am (More to Follow)"

Contents

Acknowledgments

This book represents a sustained commitment to thinking and writing over several years during which I received invaluable support from others. First, the book would not have been possible without the unwavering patience, wisdom, and encouragement of my mentor, Cary Wolfe, who did not leave me "to twist in the wind." His intellectual generosity, his friendship, and his belief in this project are gifts for which I remain humbled and deeply grateful.

I wish to acknowledge the institutional support of the University of Pittsburgh at Johnstown in their funding of several research activities at which I received important feedback for the completion of this project. This is especially true of my fellowship at the 2005 School of Criticism and Theory at Cornell University, where I was privileged to study with Elizabeth Grosz. I am very grateful for her reading of parts of this book, for her recognition of its value, and for her entreaty to keep working.

For the sometimes intangible but nonetheless essential support that academics need in their personal and professional lives, in their thinking and creating, I owe a debt of gratitude to a number of friends and colleagues. For their immeasurable role in this particular journey, I offer my thanks to Karen Carcia, Catherine S. Cox, Kristin Czarnecki, Kristin Lyndal Garbarino, Alessandra Lynch, David Magill, Tresa McVicker, Christine

O'Connor, Maria-Cristina Saavedra, and, especially, Bryn Weller. My profound thanks to my mother, Sandy Rohman, for her truly unconditional love, to my brothers, Lance, Grant, and Clayton Rohman, and to my beloved late father, Dan Rohman, all of whom I am honored to call family. Thanks to Dale Gilmore for his early example of living deliberately and thinking expansively; he continues to inspire. And finally, for my husband, Ernie Cascino, whose love and devotion are astonishing—my deepest and most joyful thanks.

I wish to gratefully acknowledge permission from the following publications to reproduce my work and from the following institutions to reproduce the work of T. S. Eliot and D. H. Lawrence:

A segment of chapter 2 (on *The Plumed Serpent*) originally appeared in *D. H. Lawrence: New Worlds*, ed. Keith Cushman and Earl G. Ingersoll (Fairleigh Dickinson University Press, 2003).

A portion of chapter 3 (on *The Island of Dr. Moreau*) originally appeared in *Figuring Animals: Essays on Animal Images in Art, Literature, Philosophy, and Popular Culture*, ed. Mary Sanders Pollock and Catherine Rainwater (Palgrave Macmillan, 2005).

Chapter 5 originally appeared as "Revising the Human: Silence, Being, and the Question of the Animal in *Nightwood*" in *American Literature* 79, no. 1 (March 2007): 57–84. Used with permission of the publisher, Duke University Press.

"Snake" by D. H. Lawrence, "Fish" by D. H. Lawrence, from *The Complete Poems of D. H. Lawrence* by D. H. Lawrence, ed. V. Sola Pinto and F. W. Roberts, copyright ©1964, 1971 by Angelo Ravagli and C. M. Weekley, Executors of the Estate of Frieda Lawrence Ravagli. Used by permission of Viking Penguin, a division of Penguin Group (USA) Inc.

"Burbank with a Baideker" by T. S. Eliot, "Sweeney Agonistes" by T. S. Eliot, "Sweeney Among the Nightingales" by T. S. Eliot, "Sweeney Erect" by T. S. Eliot, from *Collected Poems 1909–1962* by T. S. Eliot, copyright 1963, Harcourt, Inc. and Faber & Faber Ltd.

STALKING THE SUBJECT

The task for the critic who wishes to restore the materiality of a world outside of consciousness to criticism is to find a means of addressing l'autre without reducing it to autrui: it is to find a means of thinking alterity, of constructing a critical philosophy which will eschew the solace of identity—always predictable—in the interests of an alterity for which the subject is precisely unprepared.
   —Thomas Docherty, Alterities: Criticism, History, Representation

1   The Animal Among Others

Animal Studies and the Question of Methodologies

Literary studies and critical theory are witnessing the development of a new discipline surrounding the cultural and discursive significance of animality and its relationship to Western metaphysics and humanist discourses. Whether this discipline becomes known as "critical animal studies," or the simpler "animal studies," the contours of the field are taking shape across broad fields of inquiry. From the strictly philosophical to the historical, cultural, and literary, the past five years have brought about an unprecedented amount of scholarly work on the place, meaning, and ethical status of animals in relation to our signifying practices. For those in modernist studies, the animal problem takes on a particularly charged valence since modernism comes on the heels of Darwin's catastrophic blow to human privilege vis-à-vis the species question. I'd like to begin by looking at the impact of Darwinism (and Freudianism) and the role of historicist work on animals during that period. This view will open onto my detailed discussion of the need for a theoretically sophisticated critical apparatus in work on animality in the humanities and my subsequent framing of the question of animal subjectivity in literary and cultural modernism.

What is uncontested about the historical relevance of Darwin's work is that its appearance signified one of the great ideological pivot points in the modern era. Darwin's work is often yoked with Freud's and Marx's to demonstrate the tripartite nature of the massive ideological shifts that took place in the modern age. Noel Annan puts it bluntly that Darwin's *The Origin of Species* "became the foundation of a new history of the world."[1] We are, to this day, grappling with the aftershocks and implications of Darwin's theories, as Howard Mumford Jones suggests when describing *Origin* as "crucial, a great volume in the long tradition of British empirical thought of which it is in one sense the culmination, and a volume out of which, in one sense, the current of relativism flows into our time, a current defined and canalized by Darwin."[2] Darwin's work had scientists, theologians, politicians, and eventually the average European rethinking the most elementary contours of human identity and the human connection to other sentient life.

While historians have generally agreed upon the seriousness of evolutionary theory's cultural, political, and scientific impact, there has been a proliferation of work attempting to describe *how* the theory was absorbed into Victorian thought. On the one hand, according to Annan, Darwin's work only confirms a "positivist cosmology" in which the "history of the world is the history of progress and that there was no need of supernatural intervention during the ages to account for what happened" (35). Such notions, he reminds us, had been in circulation well before 1859. On the other hand, Darwin's introduction of the idea that chance undergirds the natural order flew in the face of moral and religious concepts that held God as the irreducible Creator, a deity bestowing divine favor on Man, who was set above the rest of the animate world. Thus Darwin provides the explanatory mechanism in scientific terms that forces our understanding of the natural world well beyond religious explanations.

More specifically, as Peter Bowler points out, the question of human origins became central to late Victorian debates about evolution. The problem of humanity's link to the rest of the animal world surfaced as a recurrent and unnerving point of conflict in scientific and philosophical discussions. "By raising the possibility of such a link," Bowler explains, "the evolutionists were threatening the concept of the immortal soul and hence the traditional foundations of morality."[3] Such debates involving religious and moral concepts rehearse the anxiety surrounding the privileged place of the human in the traditional Judeo-Christian worldview. Recent historical work on the reception of Darwinism reveals that the response to such questions of human supremacy in the face of evolution's threat was more complex than has been previously understood. For instance, Bowler explains that the picture of a simplistic and "ruthless policy of 'social Darwinism' in which unfit individuals and unfit races were condemned to death or slavery in the name of progress" tends to paint a reductionist picture of the Victorians' need to see a moral purpose in the process of evolution (180). Nevertheless, Darwin himself, despite his radical reframing of human origins, held on to what can only be described as a humanist vision of creation. While he acknowledged that humans were "nothing more than highly developed animals and sought to explain our social behaviour in biological terms," Bowler suggests that Darwin was nonetheless vulnerable to the lure of social Darwinist potentialities (179).

One of the Victorians' philosophical coping mechanisms indicates how a residual humanism helped them process and mitigate evolution's challenge to human privilege. This coping mechanism consisted of an over-investment in the notion of progress. According to Bowler, "people found that they could reconcile themselves to the prospect of an animal ancestry provided that the evolutionary process was seen as a force driving nature towards a morally significant goal" (180). Again, Darwin's own views sometimes reflect the larger societal grappling with evolution's implications for the human. While he made efforts to show, particularly in *Descent of Man*, that the putatively unbridgeable gap between human and animal mental faculties can be closed, Darwin at that time still held that "the evolutionary process was the Creator's way of generating higher mental functions in the world" (183). This *understanding* of evolution suggests a teleology that, if not utterly consonant with traditional Christian views, at least provides a narrative of purposefulness to compensate for the loss of those long-held religious cosmologies.

It is crucial at this juncture to make a distinction between the actual philosophical implications of Darwin's theories and how those theories were received, reacted to, and even processed by Darwin himself. Elizabeth Grosz's recent work on Darwinism reveals just how radical Darwin's ideas really are, despite the fact that those ideas were resisted and re-situated through a number of mitigating frameworks. Central to Grosz's understanding of Darwin's complexity is the provisional and unfixed nature of the concept "species." Far from a closed or calculable process, Darwin's understanding of the development of species "uncannily anticipates Derridean *différance*" in its emphasis on "a fundamental indeterminacy" at the heart of evolutionary mechanisms.[4] If we return to Darwin's original manuscript, we discover again the conditional quality of this concept. Darwin opens the second chapter of *Origin*, "Variation Under Nature," by discussing the vagueness of the term *species*. He goes on to clarify this problem:

> Certainly no clear line of demarcation has as yet been drawn between species and sub-species—that is, the forms which in the opinion of some naturalists come very near to, but do not quite arrive at the rank of species; or, again, between sub-species and well-marked varieties, or between lesser varieties and individual differences. These differences blend into each other in an insensible series; and a series impresses the mind with the idea of an actual passage.[5]

What follows, logically, is the arbitrariness of the concept *species*. Darwin continues, "From these remarks it will be seen that I look at the term species, as one arbitrarily given for the sake of convenience to a set of individuals closely resembling each other, and that it does not essentially differ from the term variety, which is given to less distinct and more fluctuating forms" (108). As Grosz points out, Darwin's work is "a science [that] could not take the ready-made or pregiven unity of individuals or classes for granted but had to understand how any provisional unity and cohesion derives from the oscillations and vacillations of difference. The origin can be nothing but a difference!" (21). Grosz's discussion of Darwin further emphasizes how antiteleological his ideas actually are. It is primarily the reception of Darwin's work that translates it into palatable notions of hierarchy and morally driven development.

A similar return to Darwin's *The Descent of Man* reveals the fascinating juxtaposition between Darwin's radical undermining of human privilege and his own need to rhetorically cushion this unprecedented blow. His third chapter, "Comparison of the Mental Powers of Man and the Lower Animals," continues to be an astonishing read given how exhaustively the uniqueness of human emotional and mental capacities is dismantled. Despite the fact that Darwin repeatedly introduces his subtopics with such qualifiers as this on the question of self-consciousness, "It may be freely admitted that no animal is self-conscious, if by this term it is implied, that he reflects on such points, as whence he comes or whither he will go, or what is life and death, and so forth," his rejoinders always undermine the ultimate ability to draw hard and fast distinctions between the human and the nonhuman: "But how can we feel sure that an old dog with an excellent memory and some power of imagination, as shewn by his dreams, never reflects on his past pleasures or pains in the chase? And this would be a form of self-consciousness."⁶ The chapter continues in extraordinary detail and use of example to tackle the emotional, social, linguistic, and even religious capacities that demonstrate how "there is no fundamental difference between man and the higher mammals" (86). The center of Darwin's argument here and throughout much of the text is that man resembles the apes more closely than apes resemble other species. He also relies upon an intellectual and moral morphology resulting in the conclusion that man's body *and mind* are descended from animals, a particularly unsettling notion. Perhaps the most significant conclusion, then, in *Descent* is Darwin's well-known claim that "the difference in mind between man and the higher animals, great as it is, certainly is one of degree and not of kind" (151).

Despite the fact that Darwinism contains what could be considered the most radical philosophical blow to anthrocentrism in the modern age, that blow was not immediately or consistently registered. In fact, social Darwinism itself, with its clinging to traditional notions of power and the development of civilizations, can be understood as a reinstantiation of human privilege projected onto racial and gendered taxonomies. Harriet Ritvo reiterates this sentiment in her own discussion of Darwin's influence by noting that the basis for human superiority was considered not so much eliminated as reframed in the late nineteenth century: "Clearly, if people were animals, they were the top animals, and with God out of the picture, the source of human preeminence lay within."⁷

The Victorian attitude toward Darwinism clearly included an attempt to maintain a humanist worldview, despite the deconstructive implications of evolutionary theory. Surprisingly, even after Darwin's stunning claims about human origins, we can say that compensatory theories of progress and cultural superiority allowed for a relatively uninterrogated notion of the human to remain in place, at least in the immediate aftermath of Darwin's work. What the literature of the late Victorian and modernist era reveals, however, is the lurking anxiety that this view of human privilege cannot be maintained.

The threat to humanism manifested in Darwin's work at the end of the nineteenth century is matched only by the implications of Sigmund Freud's theories at the turn of the twentieth. The publication of *The Interpretation of Dreams* in 1900 marked the beginning of another period of radical challenge to Western notions of human ontology. Freud's discussions of infantile sexuality, aggression, the death drive, and unconscious desires undercut many traditional philosophical framings of human being and knowing in the West.

Importantly, Freud's work is constructed within a Darwinian framework. This connection is clearest in his use of the recapitulation theory that links the development of the individual mimetically to the development of the species as a whole. Put in biological terms, the theory holds that "ontogeny recapitulates phylogeny." Lucille Ritvo devotes an entire chapter of her book *Darwin's Influence on Freud* to a discussion of this idea in Freudianism. She notes that Freud adds a very specific notion of recapitulation to the 1919 edition of *Interpretation of Dreams* where he writes: "Dreaming is on the whole an example of regression to the dreamer's earliest condition, a revival of his childhood. . . . Behind this childhood of the individual we are promised a picture of a phylogenetic childhood—a picture of the human race, of which the individual's development is in fact an abbreviated recapitulation influenced by the chance circumstances of life."[8]

This understanding of human development implies that childhood can be understood as consonant with early human history and even with human prehistory, something I will discuss later as it appears in *Totem and Taboo*. Freud implicitly evokes our animal heritage when he notes that children have not yet learned to estrange themselves from the rest of the animal kingdom, a distinction he believes comes later in the development of the human individual. A child, he notes, "can see no difference between his own nature and that of animals . . . he will transfer an emotion of fear which he feels for his human father onto a dog or a horse, without intending any derogation of his father by it. Not until he grows up does he become so far estranged from animals as to use their names in vilification of human beings" (qtd. in L. Ritvo, 76). Even more explicitly, Freud believed that traces of humanity's animal origins were still embedded in the individual's mental and physical structures. Ritvo notes Freud's postulation that the "early efflorescence [of sexual life] which comes to an end at about the fifth year and is followed by what is known as a period of latency (till puberty) . . . leads us to suppose that the human race is descended from a species of animal which reached sexual maturity in five years" (qtd. in L. Ritvo, 77). Here the influence of evolution is striking. As we know, it is not just childhood that is conflated with the "primitive" in Freud's work, it is also the unconscious. Ritvo reminds us that the unconscious in Freudianism acts as a repository of archaic forces and impressions, a repository continuously affecting the individual's conscious life. Emanuel Garcia has noted in this regard that "the phylogenetic endowment of the psyche, which constitutes a 'nucleus of the unconscious,' is a legitimate area of psychoanalytic investigation."[9] In a general sense, then, Freud's vision of the human individual includes the struggle to transcend one's animality, which is understood to reside in the unconscious, in childhood, and in the death drive and the libido. Garcia discusses the latter point in *Understanding Freud* when he asserts, "Amid the rich depiction of life that one finds in Freud's work, in all its sexual and emotional variety, there hovers ever-present the image of man the organism, fated to die, the prey of natural laws no less than his animal brethren" (144). I will return to a discussion of Freud shortly, particularly to his vision of the human relationship to animality in *Civilization and its Discontents,* to the role of the unconscious, and to Deleuze and Gauttari's critique of the Oedipal rubric in *A Thousand Plateaus.* What is important to note here is that even the Freudian blow to human preeminence was mitigated by the expectation that the Oedipalized adult could, at some level, transcend his individual and ancestral "childhood," his own animal nature.

To date, scholarly work on animals in British culture before the contemporary era has usually been undertaken within a historicist framework. Harriet Ritvo's *The Animal Estate* is exemplary of such studies. Ritvo examines the relationship between human and animal in Victorian Britain with an eye toward the symbolic transference of social prestige and order implicit in various breeding and taxonomic practices. According to Ritvo, controlling animals in nineteenth-century Britain gave people in an "exploitative culture" an indirect way to enact domination without overtly professing it (6). Metaphorically, she explains, the taxonomic ordering of the animal "kingdom" ran parallel to imperialist ideologies and hierarchies: "Thus the animal kingdom (that standard phrase was itself part of the metaphor) was generally compared to the lesser ranks of a domestic commonwealth" (17). Moreover, the naturalist's mastery of wild and "exotic" animals at this time ran parallel to England's massive colonial project that was well underway across the globe. Domesticated animals also served significant ideological functions according to Ritvo. The classical avatar of fidelity, the domesticated dog, "epitomized the appropriate relationship between masters and subordinates" (20). This metaphorical association helps explain Ritvo's larger claim that breeding as a cultural

practice symbolized leadership and social prestige, dominance and superiority. Breeding reinforced modes of control and power that were
both internal to British society and characteristic of its broader political
agendas.

Ritvo's contribution is particularly helpful in its theorization of species discourse *as* it buttresses human social and cultural formations. Indeed, this is her project's primary focus, as she notes in her introduction:
"Interactions with animals often reflected traditional understandings and
deeply held convictions. Examining these interactions can clarify underlying and seldom-stated assumptions of English society, or it can identify areas of unexpressed tension" (3). Ritvo's project thus scrutinizes the
discourse of animality and breeding in order to more fully reveal and articulate Victorian values. That is, her careful examination of naturalism,
breeding practices, and the emergence of zoos provides a particular lens
upon human assumptions and anxieties. What such projects do not accomplish, in turn, is the interrogation of the human *qua* human vis-à-vis
the animal. Of course, this is not their aim. In our particular theoretical moment, however, characterized as it is by emerging poststructuralist
reexaminations of how the "human" has come to attain and reproduce
cultural meaning, the question of the animal in late nineteenth- and early
twentieth-century Britain must be reframed from a number of theoretical
vantages.

In particular, historicist readings have proven inadequate to the task of
illuminating the complexities of the subject's relation to animality within
and beyond symbolic codes. Cynthia Marshall's discussion of psychoanalysis and historicism sheds light on this broader question of methodological
approach. Marshall argues that psychoanalytic theory, unlike historicism,
is able to focus "attention beneath the surface of a text, it locates slippages
and gaps in subjects' alignment with the shaping symbolic or ideological
structures and reads this misalignment as evidence of competing desires
in the nascent subject."[10] In this sense, psychoanalytic approaches can
"unsettle or denaturalize" standard portraits of subject formation (1211).
Moreover, psychoanalytic theory acknowledges various forms of negation
in which the content of a repressed idea enters consciousness only in in-
verted form (1213). Thus, as Marshall notes, the subject's complexity can
be explored through mechanisms such as projection and transference. In
fact, these rubrics of negation are particularly crucial to an investigation
of the discourse of species within humanism, since animality has his-

torically been disavowed in the Judeo-Christian West. I do not intend to overinflate the value of psychoanalytic theory for this project since I will approach my subject from a variety of critical discourses. Rather, Marshall's discussion confirms my general point that historicist approaches alone are inadequate to the task of theorizing the subject's entwinement with animal ontology in relation to symbolic systems, or as she concludes: "Historicist criticism by itself has proved unable to delve beneath the surface of symbolic constructions to identify the tensions, desires, anxieties, and discontents that contribute to the changes in forms of subjectivity and in social systems" (1214).

The problem of the animal in twentieth-century literature and culture requires a sophisticated theoretical examination that pays attention not only to the discursive categories of human and animal, but also to the production of values attached to that binary and the ethical charge of such constructions. In this regard, as we shall see, animal studies emerges from the legacy of poststructuralism and its attendant analysis of subject-formation, at the same time that its interest in the radically "other" pushes the recent "turn to ethics" in literary studies beyond the familiar boundaries of the human.

Animals in Theory

In broad critical terms, those interested and invested in the discourse of humanism are currently faced with a kind of reckoning, a coming to terms with theories of alterity. What is usually identified as poststructuralist, postmodern, or antirepresentationalist theory across the humanistic disciplines has been invested for some time now in re-theorizing the Cartesian subject of consciousness—the self-present, autonomous Western human—in relation to its various "Others." The range of these debates is wide and by now quite familiar to readers of literary and cultural criticism. Feminist theorists have identified and interpreted the productive reiteration of a marginalized feminine principle in a variety of complex discourses, and in recent years queer theorists have linked the heteronormativity of the subject to these cultural otherings. So too the dynamics of race and identity are central to postcolonial work, which outlines the subject's formation through racialized symbolic codes. In light of the vast assemblage of such postmodern investigations into Western subjectivity,

Thomas Docherty locates the ethics of postmodernism in a Levinasian summons, one which issues from the face of the other and calls for "a just relating to alterity, and for a cognition of the event of heterogeneity."[11]

While Docherty's point is a keen and important one, his use of Levinas reveals a residual and intractable problem that often remains embedded within postmodern humanisms: the crucial problem of the animal. Levinas can be situated within a long tradition of Western metaphysics that sustains the privileging of human consciousness and being by abjecting the animal.[12] His complex theory of alterity rests upon the notion that the face of the other opens the ethical relation, a relation between humans: "The Other faces me and puts me in question and *obliges* me by his essence qua infinity."[13] Levinas theorizes his complex concept of the face primarily in *Totality and Infinity* and the later *Otherwise than Being*, and the nuances of his theory have been widely discussed by philosophers and critics. According to Bernhard Waldenfels, the face can be understood as an "emblem" of the other's difference or alterity.[14] It is bewildering and strange: its ethical provocation manifests itself to us as a rupture or an invasion. This unsettling quality emerges in Waldenfels's description of the experience of otherness or alterity itself: "The face we are confronted with can be understood as the turning point between the own and the alien where a certain disposition takes place" (65). We will return to the notions of dispossession and rupture when we discuss Derrida shortly.

Within this interruption or *traumatism*, the face of the other lays a claim on me. I am interpellated or called into responsibility by the face of the other. Levinas describes this appeal or solicitation in *Totality and Infinity*: "The being that expresses itself imposes itself, but does so precisely by appealing to me with its destitution and nudity—its hunger—without my being able to be deaf to that appeal" (200). What seems a somewhat surprising turn from this point in Levinas—especially when we stop to consider concepts such as destitution, poverty, and nudity—is that this manifestation of otherness, this fundamental ethical appeal, is irrevocably linked with the ability to speak.

This ethical call cannot issue from the nonhuman face for Levinas, who defines alterity as exclusively human in its inseparability from the linguistic exchange between interlocutors. "Discourse," he writes, "is thus the experience of something absolutely foreign, a *pure* 'knowledge' or 'experience,' a *traumatism of astonishment*. The absolutely foreign alone can instruct us. And it is only man who could be absolutely foreign to me—" (73). And more specifically, "The face speaks. The manifestation of the face is already discourse" (66). John Llewelyn reaffirms the exclusivity of Levinas's ethical universe, a universe reserved for those gifted with speech: "In the metaphysical ethics of Levinas I can have direct responsibilities only toward beings that can speak, and this means beings that have a rationality that is presupposed by the universalizing reason fundamental in the metaphysics of ethics of Kant."[15] Levinas goes so far as to link the face with the transcendental signifier, the Judeo-Christian word or *logos* that binds the human to the divine in a number of religious and philosophical registers: "This infinity," he writes, "stronger than murder, already resists us in [the] face, is [the] face, is the primordial *expression,* is the first word: 'you shall not commit murder'" (199). This narcissistic framing of ethicality as embedded within human language capacities ignores the profound philosophical dynamics of the human relation to nonhuman others, especially to nonhuman animals. Moreover, as Richard Beardsworth explains in *Derrida and the Political,* Levinas's notion of alterity presupposes a certain accountability because the other is contained within an exclusively human ethical schematization.[16] Thus, despite Levinas's opening gesture in *Totality and Infinity* toward "*something else entirely,* toward the *absolutely other,*" (33) the alterity to which Levinas and, consequently, Docherty refer is not the radical alterity of the animal other, but the relative alterity of the human other. This alterity remains, as we shall see, familial, fraternal, and perhaps mostly, calculable.

But if we are to take the postmodern relation to alterity seriously, then we are summoned by another face: the face of the animal. The deconstruction of—the asking after the interestedness of—the humanist subject has recently ushered in a small but vigorous branch of theoretical work on animality, on the discourse of species. Cary Wolfe, for example, characterizes the necessarily posthumanist framework of such studies as a "rethinking of the notion of the human *tout court*—a project that fields outside of cultural and social theory have been vigorously engaged in over the past two decades."[17] Wolfe notes that work in cognitive science, field ecology, and animal rights philosophy has deeply problematized the "humanist habit of making even the *possibility* of subjectivity coterminous with the species barrier" (43). If scientists and philosophers have begun to rethink the traditional human/animal binary, literary critics have been slow to recognize the necessity for doing so.

By bringing to bear recent theories of animality upon literary modernism, this study reveals animality as a fundamental locus of identity construction and complication throughout the period. Indeed, the specter

of the animal profoundly threatens the sovereignty of the Western subject of consciousness in modernist literature, and our understanding of
that literature is incomplete without accounting for this complex threat.
My aim is not only to recast the modernist subject with reference to animality, but also to situate several major ideological discourses within the
period in relation to the species problematic. Imperialism, for instance,
and the developing discourse of psychoanalysis are deeply interested in
the boundary between human and animal. Indeed, the coherence of the
imperialist subject, like that of the Freudian subject, often rests upon the
abjection of animality. Thus, in the interests of a specific theorization of
the animal in modernism, the chapters that follow trace the displacement
of, confrontation with, and recuperation of various animalities across the
period. Modernist texts variously reentrench, unsettle, and even invert a
humanist relation to this nonhuman other.

My discussion of modernism and the animal can be situated in the
wake of postcolonial criticism, which has dominated studies of British
modernism in recent decades. Pioneering works like Edward Said's *Ori-
entalism* (1978) ushered in a new era of criticism that privileged the categories of race and gender in an effort to rearticulate our understanding
of imperialist binaries. Much of this work remains interested in exposing
modernism's latent power agendas, particularly those embedded in co-
lonialism and imperialism. As Marjorie Perloff has noted, postcolonial
work has resulted in a redrawing of the modernist map to include feminist and minority work, while modernism was traditionally construed as
"work almost exclusively *of* men *for* men. . . . And further: modernism
pertained to *white* men, indeed white Christian men."[18]

Postcolonial critiques worked to illuminate the dialectic between Western subjectivity and the non-Western "other," a disenfranchised other
whose projected alterity served to stabilize European imperialist identity.
Marianna Torgovnick's *Gone Primitive* (1990), for instance, was widely
read as an exposé of primitivism's cultural work in the modernist aesthetic. Torgovnick, like Edward Said in his work on imperialism and exoticism, gives primacy to the racial and sexual binaries used by writers
to codify the primitive. She maintains that European primitivism often
rehearses a self-serving set of dichotomies that defines native peoples al-
ternately as "gentle, in tune with nature, paradisal, ideal—or violent, in
need of control."[19] Modernist writers deploy the primitive in an ambivalent, self-serving discourse of otherness, whose object is both excessively
desirable and deeply threatening, ideal and abject.

While Torgovnick notes that Western ambivalence toward the racial-ized "savage" was frequently rooted in the post-Darwinian evolutionist premise that a continuum exists between civilized and savage, she fails to address the ways in which animality often underlies this dynamic. A similar elision appears in the more recent postcolonial work of Anne Mc-Clintock, whose insightful 1995 study *Imperial Leather* reads gender as a constitutive category of imperialism. McClintock's work establishes a link between the British investment in domesticating women and in con-trolling the racial other at the turn of the twentieth century. While Mc-Clintock discusses the appropriation of Darwinism by European anthro-pologists to determine the rank of human races, she does not recognize the discourse of species as fundamental to these imperialist otherings. For instance, although McClintock points clearly to the feminization of natives in various images from the period, she does not theorize the animalization of native populations so striking in many of her book's images. Such omissions reveal how the animal subject does not garner significant theoretical attention from most critics investigating mecha-nisms of othering.

Most threatening about the modernist evolutionary view of the primi-tive is not simply that the civilized might be connected to the primitive, but that the civilized are organically linked *to the animal*. This more profound by-product of primitivist logic is registered in the human/animal binary, which, despite its centrality to modernist literature, remains largely unad-dressed by our body of criticism. Confronting modernism's relationship to the animal puts us as readers and critics into largely uncharted territory. We are accustomed to examining discursive relationships between races, genders, or classes in modernism. And while such accounts are crucial to theorizing a marginalized "other," it is important to recognize that they limit themselves to the realm of the human. The discourse of animality, on the other hand, presents a unique set of theoretical concerns.

The profound philosophical stakes of this discourse are most clearly signaled by Jacques Derrida's increasing attention to the animal problem in the late 1990s and the last years of his life. In his interview with Jean-Luc Nancy, "Eating Well," Derrida outlines his broad focus of discussion as the "reinterpreted, displaced, decentered, re-inscribed" Western subject in recent critical theory and pointedly troubles the repeated and rehearsed cordoning off of animal subjectivity within the classic codes of philosophi-cal inquiry.[20] Derrida worries the recalcitrant humanism of Western meta-physics wherein,

> The animal will never be either a subject or a *Dasein*. It doesn't have
> an unconscious either (Freud), nor a rapport to the other as other,
> no more than there is an animal face (Levinas). . . . The discourse
> of the subject, even if it locates difference, inadequation, the dehis-
> cense within auto-affection, etc., continues to link subjectivity with
> man. (105)

For Heidegger—who figures predominantly in Derrida's critique here
and in his book *Of Spirit—Dasein,* variously understood as Being, world-
making, the privilege of questioning, or the spiritual, separates the human from the rest of the living in general. Derrida insists that we put such
attributions of the subject to test, that we commit ourselves to "ceaselessly
analyzing the whole conceptual machinery, and its interestedness, which
has allowed us to speak of the 'subject' up to now" (109), and he explains
that the central significance of self-presence, which structures Western
notions of the subject, must be vigorously investigated, especially because
the technicities of language are not, in Derrida's estimation, limited to
the human realm: "Such a vigil leads us to recognize the processes of *différance,* trace, iterability, ex-appropriation, and so on. These are at work everywhere, which is to say, well beyond humanity" (109). We will return to
this question of languaging shortly. What Derrida begins to suggest here
is that the phenomenological attributions of the human are wrongfully
denied as attributions of nonhuman animals.

  Such interrogations lead to Derrida's theorizing of the sacrificial structure that situates Western subjectivation in relation to the animal other.
This structure is dependent upon the hierarchical opposition between
"man" and "animal," and it organizes the cultural and discursive justification of violence against animals: "it is a matter of discerning a place
left open . . . for a noncriminal putting to death" (112) of entities that fall
into the category "animal." The prevailing schema of Western subjectivity itself, then, is extended by Derrida to include carnivorous virility and
thus becomes "*carno-phallogocentrism.*" Derrida adds the prefix *carno* here
to indicate his further delineation of the Western subject he had already
identified as "phallogocentric." Just as that subject is identified with phallic privilege (phallocentrism) and with the metaphysics of presence (logocentrism), so too it is associated with carnivorous sacrifice. In short, the
acquisition of full humanity in the West is predicated, among other processes, upon eating animal flesh.[21]

This valorizing function of meat-eating has been explained in a different register by Nick Fiddes in his book *Meat,* which is premised upon the idea "that the most important feature of meat . . . is that it tangibly represents human control of the natural world. Consuming the muscle flesh of other highly evolved animals is a potent statement of our supreme power."[22] This putative transcendence over nature also posits the nonanimality of the human carnivore, and, as Bataille's *Theory of Religion* suggests, works to remove man from the realm of the thing. Eating meat defines the animal as always-having-been a thing, and conversely, it defines man as never-having-been a thing. Thus Derrida explains, "The subject does not want just to master and possess nature actively. In our cultures, he accepts sacrifice and eats flesh." For this reason, Derrida explains, in Western cultures the head of state could never be a vegetarian since "The *chef* must be an eater of flesh" (114).

Derrida's formulation of this sacrificial subjectivity points to the broad figure of animality as, to borrow Judith Butler's words from *Bodies That Matter,* the constitutive outside of humanism, that which "must be excluded for that economy to posture as internally coherent."[23] And Butler's work is to the point because her claim that the production of the subject always works through a discursive exclusion resonates so clearly with Derrida's notion of sacrifice. Butler's primary argument holds that we are not always-already given as sexed human beings but must *become* human by being encoded through the cultural norm of gender. That is, the framework of gender brings us into being. Robert McKay has pointed out that Butler fails "to extend the critique of heterosexism" outward toward the discourse of species, but she does make reference to the animal as inhabiting the realm of the outside.[24] Butler's ideas about a realm of abjection clearly apply to the problem of animality in humanism. In short, becoming human requires passing through a field of discourse that defines the human subject as not-animal.

Butler is not the only feminist theorist interested in the homologous disavowal of the feminine and the animal in Western discourse. Carol Adams has theorized the specific parallel between the objectification of the female body and the animal body in her book *The Sexual Politics of Meat.* Therein Adams explains that women and animals are often subjected to the same cycle of objectification, dismemberment, and renaming, and she argues that the slippage between symbolic and real dismemberment or violence must be accounted for, in part, through this species-gender dialectic. Thus the overlapping significances of terms like *chick* and the persistent popularity of the Playboy Bunny. In fact, even Derrida articulates a certain compatibility between the discourses of gender and species when he notes in "Eating Well" that "Authority and autonomy . . . are, through this schema, attributed to the man (*homo* and *vir*) rather than to the woman, and to the woman rather than to the animal" (114). Of course, the two positions vary, and one would need to parse Derrida's schema in tandem with that of Adams in order to examine their disjunctions concerning the question of female versus animal status.

In short, the autonomy of the human subject, the sovereignty of humanness, is dependent upon our difference from animals, our disavowal of them, and the material reinstantiation of that exclusion through various practices such as meat-eating, hunting, and medical experimentation. But this hierarchical formulation is complicated by the fact that the human and animal cannot be decidedly unmoored since *Homo sapiens* are materially embedded in the physical world and subject to mortality. Indeed, the human being is constituted as both a primate body linked to material necessity and a "human" mind that tends to abstract itself from those conditions, to imagine its own transcendence. This study, then, investigates humanism's response to a threat that issues from beyond the human, but also, oddly, from within it. Indeed, the disavowal of the animal engages an interspecies relation that reveals humanity's perceptions of and relations to a nonhuman subjectivity at the same time that it reveals the human relation to self. It is in part because of this slippage that the discourse of species can operate as a privileged site of the posthuman.

The problem of nonhuman animal subjectivity, unlike the problem of artificial intelligence, for instance, is also uniquely vexing in its *organic* liminality, as is the intractable mystery of animal consciousness. Animals figure somewhere between *Dasein* and inanimate matter, but locating their ontological position is fraught with uncertainty. Indeed, in *Of Spirit* when Derrida examines Heidegger's classic formulation of the animal as "poor in world" he fixates on the ambivalence of this designation: "Its privation means that its not-having is a mode of having and even a certain relation to having-a-world. . . . The animal *has* and *does not have* a world."[25] This fundamental undecidability of animal being, this unknown quantity which is both foreign to the human and yet coterminous with it, surely helps to explain Cary Wolfe and Jonathan Elmer's remark that "the animal poses grave definitional and practical threats to the discourse of humanism."[26] The difficulty that confronts us in determining an ontological place for the animal is echoed by Bataille, who claims that the animal "opens before me a depth that attracts me and is familiar to me" but at the same time *"is unfathomable to me."*[27] Given this observation, it seems apt to reformulate Derrida's reading of Heidegger in terms of the human, which both has and does not have an animal *Umwelt*.

Bataille's paradox reminds us that the confrontation with the animal other is one of radical alterity that consequently requires an acute awareness of the politics and ethics of difference. To be sure, the easy categorization of nonhuman species into the designated signifier *animal* already does a reductive violence to the multiplicity of life forms outside the human. Though the pragmatics of this move are obvious, particularly in a study such as this one, the totalizing force of the designation enables a monolithic categorization of the nonhuman that ignores the very real and vast differences among species. More subtly, and perhaps more dangerously, this categorization works to foreclose recognition of the *individual* animal, unless that animal is incorporated into the West's pet economy.[28]

The animal's otherness is especially acute because it does not speak our language.[29] Unlike the racialized and sexualized, sometimes voiceless, subalterns that have been the subject of recent work in modernist studies, the animal literally cannot talk back to our objectifying codes. This makes the animal irreducibly other within the very terms and values of humanism itself. Consequently, Jean-François Lyotard has called the animal "a paradigm of the victim."[30] In *The Differend*, Lyotard theorizes the ethical aporia in which "the plaintiff is divested of the means to argue and becomes for that reason a victim" (9). The animal is the paradigmatic victim because it lacks even the possibility to name its injuries within humanist parlance.[31] It is therefore no surprise that the discourse of animality has remained mostly absent from critical discussions of modernism, for the marginalized other in this case cannot speak for itself and has no constituency of "organic intellectuals" in Gramsci's sense. We must insist, however, that these questions should not be invested in "returning" or "giving" language to the animal. Rather, as Derrida points out, it is necessary to dismantle the humanist relation to language by recognizing linguistic modalities outside the human.

This recognition is precisely what Derrida continues to investigate in "The Animal That Therefore I Am," where he insists again that the linguistic functions of the trace and *différance* cannot be limited to human modalities of communication: "Animality, the life of the living . . . is generally defined as sensibility, irritability, and *auto-motricity*, a spontaneity that is given to movement, to organizing itself and affecting itself, marking, tracing and affecting itself with traces of its self. . . . No one has ever denied the animal this capacity to track itself, to trace itself or retrace a path of itself."[32] Meditating on the implications of the autobiographical, then, Derrida acknowledges that the difference between such animal linguicity and the formal marks of the *cogito ergo sum* may seem "an abyss" (417), but the barrier is none the less breached. The technicities of signification cannot be reduced to a strictly human code.

Indeed, in Derrida's work on the problem of the animal, we have both an extended critique of the premium placed on "human" language capacities in drawing the species barrier *and* his intensive examination of the ethical significance of privation, inability, and mortality. "The Animal That Therefore I Am" marks an unprecedented high note in Derrida's attention to animality, wherein he suggests that the problem of the animal ("the wholly other, more than any other") may in truth be our most pressing ethical quandary in ongoing critical discussions of alterity and justice (380). As Wolfe notes in *Animal Rites*, "Derrida is struggling to say . . . that the animal difference is, *at this very moment*, not just any difference among others; it is, we might say, the most different difference, and therefore the most instructive—*particularly* if we pay attention . . . to how it has been consistently repressed by contemporary thinkers as otherwise profound as Levinas and Lacan" (67).

Derrida spends much of this essay asking after the gaze of the animal, a gaze that returns us immediately to Levinas's ethical figure of the face. By privileging in this piece the face-to-face moment between human and nonhuman animal, Derrida radically forestalls Levinas's trenchant position on the face as immanently human. He writes, "nothing will have ever done more to make me think through this absolute alterity of the neighbor than these moments when I see myself seen naked under the gaze of a cat" ("The Animal That Therefore I Am," 380). This sentence alone presses Levinas's notion of ethicality and the face well beyond its human limits. Derrida seems to challenge Levinas directly when he writes:

> The animal is there before me, there close to me, there in front of me—I who am (following) after it. And also, therefore, since it is before me, it is behind me. It surrounds me. And from the vantage of this being-there-before-me it can allow itself to be looked at, no doubt, but also—something that philosophy perhaps forgets, per-

haps being this calculated forgetting itself—it can look at me. It has
its point of view regarding me. (380)

The cat looks at me and, Derrida insists, *addresses* me. However asymptot-
ically, Derrida approaches the assertion throughout this discussion that animals clearly have a face. Derrida describes himself as hostage to the gaze
of his, individual and not symbolic, house cat. He returns again and again
to the fact that he himself is caught *naked* with this cat gazing at him, at
his body, and even at his very sex. When Derrida insists that "Nudity is
nothing other than that passivity, the involuntary exhibition of the self"
(380), he expands the Levinasian ethical universe to include—or at least to
profoundly question the exclusion of—the nonhuman animal.

   Giving primacy to the concepts of dispossession, poverty, and the incalculable, Derrida reinscribes Levinas's theses on his own terms, showing
how these concepts cannot be restricted to human subjectivity. Waldenfels makes reference to the ineffability of the face in Levinas when he explains that "the nakedness of the face, which is extended to the nakedness
of the whole body, does not mean that there is *something behind* the masks
and clothes the other wears, it rather means that the other's otherness
eludes every qualification we may apply." This elusiveness, he continues,
is due to an "'essential poverty' which makes the poor and the stranger
equal to us" (71). When Derrida describes the animal gaze in "The Animal
That Therefore I Am," we cannot help noticing that it presents a more
radical incalculability than the human face. The animal gaze is "vacant
to the extent of being bottomless, at the same time innocent and cruel
perhaps, perhaps sensitive and impassive, good and bad, uninterpretable,
unreadable, undecidable, abyssal and secret" (381). This undecidability
of the animal gaze mirrors the difficulty of placing the animal, ontologically, within the metaphysical tradition, just as Heidegger claims that the
animal is not world-making, nor without world, but rather—and prob-
lematically as Derrida reveals—"poor in world." But more poignantly,
I believe, Derrida implies in such moments what many of us have felt
while reading Levinas's description of the face: that the qualities of this
ethical relation are not only descriptive of our experience of animal others, but are sometimes *more true* of the ethical call that issues from animals, the call that obliges us into responsibility. This is related, I think,
to Cary Wolfe's question: "Why should not the supremely moral act be
that directed toward one such as the animal other, from whom *there is no*

hope, ever, of reciprocity?" (*Animal Rites,* 199). In addition to insisting upon this remaining-incalculable of the ethical relation, Derrida also turns to the animal's inability, vulnerability, and capacity for suffering when he recounts Jeremy Bentham's classic question concerning animals, "Can they suffer?"

Animality is thus a critical "unknown" in many registers. It presents, I think, a unique theoretical and ethical challenge to literary critics and to students of literature and culture. Animality should be understood as a privileged site of alterity that probes the postmodern relation to otherness beyond the easy boundaries of human fraternity. Its foreignness to the canonical treatment of humanism is, as Derrida has shown, maintained through disavowal. Humanity's identity formation through difference from the animal, predicated as it often is upon a humanist relation to language, is arguably the most intractable of humanist dogmas. This is why Derrida remarks in his discussion of Heidegger on language and the animal that, "Every time it is a question of hand and animal . . . Heidegger's discourse seems to me to fall into a rhetoric which is all the more peremptory and authoritarian for having to hide a discomfiture. In these cases it leaves intact, sheltered in obscurity, the axioms of the profoundest metaphysical humanism: and I do mean the profoundest" (*Of Spirit,* 11–12). Indeed, the structuring of humanist identity through the abjection of animality continues to elicit defensive and reactionary dismissals of the species problem for critical theory. What this threat reveals, of course, is the deeply unquestioned marginalization of the animal in Western philosophy.

This marginalization has been theorized as "speciesism" in animal rights philosophy, as an automatic discrimination against another being based solely upon its species. It is important to note that the dialectic between speciesism and humanism has remained structurally consistent in the West for centuries. Marjorie Spiegel, in her comparison of human and animal slavery, references the West's Judeo-Christian heritage and the Genesis story as traditional justifications for subduing the animal. But, as Akira Mizuta Lippit points out, our systematic disenfranchisement of animals can be traced back to Aristotle, who used language capacity as a criterion of moral worth that excluded the animal. Descartes' philosophical treatment of animality is especially notable; he compared animals to machines and insisted they have no capacity for reason. "It is Descartes," Lippit explains, "who most deeply instilled in the philosophical tradition the idea that the capacity for reason and consciousness determines the ontological universe."³³ This tradition of according subjectivity to man and not the animal is precisely the one inherited by Heidegger and Levinas, as Derrida explains, whose discourses inform his formulation of "carno-phallogocentrism." In his essay "Force of Law," Derrida connects the sacrifice of the animal to the core operations of subjectivity and justice: "In our culture, carnivorous sacrifice is fundamental, dominant, regulated by the highest industrial technology, as is biological experimentation on animals—so vital to our modernity . . . carnivorous sacrifice is essential to the structure of subjectivity," and, he claims, to the operations of justice and the law.³⁴ For Derrida in "Eating Well," traditional Christian dogma has remained central to the West's speciesist discourse. By identifying the profoundly humanist interpretation of the commandment "Thou shalt not kill," Derrida notes that the predominant discourses of the Western philosophical tradition *do not sacrifice sacrifice*." He explains, "'Thou shalt not kill'—with all its consequences, which are limitless—has never been understood within the Judeo-Christian tradition . . . as a 'Thou shalt not put to death the living in general'" (113). In short, the structure of Western culture has remained consistently built upon the bedrock of animal sacrifice.

Modernism and the Discourse of Species

While the operation of speciesism within humanism has remained largely consistent in the West, the animal problem becomes particularly acute for British modernism. The transhistorical dynamics of species discourse under humanism are refracted at this historically specific moment through the lenses of evolutionary theory, British imperialism, antirationalism, and even the discourse of psychoanalysis. Early twentieth-century British literature is marked by a certain crisis in humanism vis-à-vis the animal. As Bradbury and McFarlane have noted, the early twentieth century was a world reinterpreted by Marx, Darwin, and Freud, in which evolutionary theory and advances in technology created a doubly threatening specter for the modernist subject. Western identity was pitched somewhere between "natural" bodies and "artificial" bodies, between animals and machines, naturally given ontological differences and historically contingent and exterior techné. To be sure, the repercussions of Darwinism at the turn of the century are far-reaching. While evolutionary theories and concepts were circulating in Europe throughout the eighteenth and nineteenth centuries, the publication of Darwin's *On the Origin of Species* in

1859 lends unprecedented scientific credence to these fundamental concepts. The onset of modernism thus coincides with the proliferation of Darwin's story of human origins, which indicates that the human being can be understood as a highly evolved animal. Darwin's radical linkage of the human species and other animal life forms irrevocably problematized the traditional humanist abjection of animality. Darwin posits—and provides an explanatory mechanism for—the fundamental interontology of human and animal.

The deeply threatening nature of Darwinism is registered in the rapid development of social Darwinisms, the revamping of social hierarchies that valued a given culture or gender according to its perceived distance from the animal in the chain of evolutionary progress. These hierarchies line up with an imperialist chain of being that animalizes the colonized other in an attempt to purify the European subject of its Darwinian heritage. But our critical discussions of race and imperialism rarely understand how these otherings are given force through the discourse of species. Therefore, in chapter 2, I discuss the modernist displacement of animality onto socially marginalized groups and read these disavowals in connection to imperialism in turn-of-the-century Britain. Conrad's classically modernist *Heart of Darkness,* for instance, depends as much upon its configurations of the animal as it does on its racial assumptions. In fact, the novel's well-documented dynamics of race, which de-center Kurtz, the figure of European *logos* in the narrative, are enabled by Conrad's collocation of the African and the animal.

The Darwinian crisis is not only registered through imperialist otherings in modernism, but it also enters into a complicated dialectic with psychoanalytic theory. The discourse of species in modernism is specifically framed by this dialectic between Darwinism and Freudianism, which further explains the centrality of the human/animal dichotomy in literature of the period. Indeed, the development of psychoanalysis in the early twentieth century should be contextualized as a logical response to the humanist crisis set in motion by evolutionary theory. But this response is complex because Freudian ideology links the human with the animal *and* distances itself from that linkage, as I will show. Psychoanalysis stages what Žižek would call an "impossible" convergence of ontological opposites, in the human and animal, a convergence that modernism makes possible for the first time. And subsequently Freud's work, like modernism itself, must try to contain and control that unthinkable linkage. Psychoanalysis functions like modernism itself in terms of the animal: it acknowledges the uncertainty of the species barrier but must constantly cope with that acknowledgment.

Broadly speaking, Freud aligns the unconscious with animality throughout his work. In *The Interpretation of Dreams,* for instance, he writes that the unconscious should be taken as "the starting-point of dream formation," a process that he labels "regressive" in character (580–81). He goes on to note that dreams reveal vestigial remnants from humanity's archaic past. Lippit, whose recent book *Electric Animal* understands technology as a gesture of mourning for absented animals, discusses this correspondence between the deep recesses of human memory and the animal world in Freud. According to Lippit, Freud appropriates Darwinian thought when he outlines the recapitulation theory in which "Every organism repeats the stages of its evolution, reenacting, as it were, the history of the species in the process of its individuation" (Lippit, 164). Implicit in this Freudian trajectory, of course, is the initial and then reiterated disavowal of neurotic animality in order to become and remain human.

Freud is clearest on this requisite abjection of animality for the human psyche in *Civilization and its Discontents,* where he outlines his theory of "organic repression." Here Freud imagines early man's transition from a quadruped to a biped and the various results of this rising up from an animal way of being. Walking upright brings about the rejection of formerly stimulating smells—particularly blood and feces—and the consequent transition from an olfactory mode of sensing to a specular one. These repressions of organicism result in the onset of cleanliness, the family structure, and ultimately human civilization. Wolfe has pointed out the central aporia in Freud's theory, which takes the human as both consonant with and essentially different from the animal. According to Wolfe, "the human being who only becomes human through an act of 'organic repression' has to *already* know, before it is human, that the organic needs to be repressed, and so the Freudian 'human' is caught in a chain of infinite supplementarity, as Derrida would put it, which can never come to rest at an origin that would constitute a break with animality."[35] What's more, Freud's theory of organic repression can be read as an originary narrative of the formation of the human unconscious that outlines the initial attempt to suppress instinctual drives out of the conscious mind—a mind that is coded as human—into a separate psychic region that remains aligned with the animal. In other words, Freud's narrative suggests that an attempted rejection of humanity's own animality created the human unconscious. This process would explain Freud's hypothesis that

"Perversions regularly lead to zoophilia and have an animal character" (qtd. Lippit, 126).

Writ small, psychoanalysis views the humanized psyche as one that recites the disavowal of its Darwinian heritage, of its own animal nature. This view clarifies Deleuze and Guattari's critique of psychoanalysis in *A Thousand Plateaus* where animality operates as a privileged figure for the multiplicity of the unconscious. Deleuze and Guattari explain Freud's repression of multiplicity, of "becoming-animal," with reference to the famous Wolf-Man case that revealed a specific attachment to multiplicity in the psychotic mind. But Freud misreads this insight: "No sooner does Freud discover the greatest art of the unconscious, this art of molecular multiplicities, than we find him tirelessly at work bringing back molar unities, reverting to his familiar themes of *the* father, *the* penis, *the* vagina, Castration with a capital C . . . (on the verge of discovering a rhizome, Freud always returns to mere roots)" (27). Freud is unwilling to understand certain modes of experience outside of the Oedipal explanatory rubric. Such modes, "a circulation of impersonal affects, an alternate current that disrupts signifying projects as well as subjective feelings," for instance, or "an irresistible deterritorialization that forestalls attempts at professional, conjugal, or Oedipal reterritorialization" are the becomings-animal elaborated by Deleuze and Guattari (233). Freud explains these "unnatural participations" (258) through the Oedipal scenario, relying upon the suturing work of the word to reify their content: "Freud counted on the word to reestablish a unity no longer found in things" (28). It is this reductive capacity in psychoanalysis that works to tame the Darwinian threat of human origins that is so resonant for modernist thinkers. Psychoanalysis, like much of the Western metaphysical tradition, wants to code the human as psychically nonanimal, as mastering its inherent animal memories that reside in the unconscious.

Nowhere is the conflict between what we might call the Darwinian subject and the Freudian subject more overt than in the work of H. G. Wells, whose texts I consider in the third chapter. In his 1937 novel, *The Croquet Player,* Wells specifically narrativizes the ideological contest between evolutionary theory and psychoanalysis. Georgie Frobisher's psychic infection by the Evil of Cainsmarsh, a fictitious region haunted by the souls of our animal ancestors, demonstrates how the Darwinian threat that logically summons the repressive powers of psychoanalysis results in a failed strategy of recontainment. In fact, the inability to humanize the animal operates as one of Wells's early themes. In his 1896 novel, *The Island of*

Dr. Moreau, the doctor's vivisected creatures embody a Darwinian night-
mare of the evolutionary continuum. Moreau's desperate attempt to rid
the world of animality through his Enlightenment fantasy of rationalization not only fails, but it also reveals to Edward Prendick the impossibility
of such a project. Prendick's experience with Moreau's trans-species creatures unsettles the traditional humanist abjection of the animal.[36] Recognizing humanity's participation in animality estranges Prendick from the
human sociosymbolic order: he cannot reassimilate into British culture
once he escapes the island. If animality is repressed by psychoanalysis,
then Wells writes the inevitable return of that repressed.

The recognition implicit in Wells's work coincides with the critique of
rationalism that surfaces during the late nineteenth and early twentieth
centuries. In *Looking Awry,* Slavoj Žižek argues that the "supreme act" of
modernism occurs when reason recognizes its own repressive force.[37] This
self-critical strain of modernism is theorized most clearly in Horkheimer
and Adorno's *Dialectic of Enlightenment,* which identifies the tyranny of
instrumental reason, the "indefatigable self-destructiveness of enlightenment."[38] For Horkheimer and Adorno, Enlightenment rationality—thinking that it excises older forms of lordship and domination—only reinscribes a totalitarian knowledge regime which rules out anything incom-
mensurate with its system. The dialectic that they theorize, of course,
resides in the duality of this reason, a reason that abolishes power *and
embodies it.* In its extreme forms, this rationality is manifested by the fascist leader who whimsically pets a child or an animal to demonstrate that
"all are equal in the presence of power, and none is a being in its own
right" (253). Instrumental reason, like Freudianism, reduces multiplicity
to unity by privileging the subject/object relation: "Abstraction, the tool of
enlightenment, treats its objects as did fate, the notion of which it rejects:
it liquidates them" (13). Abstraction, they continue, makes "everything in
nature repeatable," as do the machinations of industry.

Modernism is not surprisingly marked by an ambivalence toward industry and rationality. For a writer like D. H. Lawrence, in fact, anti-industrialism
and antirationalism are pivotal axes of thought that correspond—however
complexly—with a kind of recuperative stance toward the animal. Animality figures repeatedly in Lawrence's oeuvre, often within a redemptive economy opposed to the industrialized Western subject. *The Plumed Serpent,*
which contains a complicated species ideology that maintains and resists
the humanist species barrier, animalizes the Mexican other within a racialized projection that appears to be typical of imperialist modernism. But

the Mexican affinity with animality is privileged in this unusual text which ends in a space of undecidability between the rational and instinctual, that primitivist ur-binary that often codes the animal problem for modernists. Though ambivalent at times, Lawrence's interrogations in *The Plumed Serpent* function as a posthumanist critique of rationalist humanism deployed through the discourse of species.

Lawrence's poetry also reveals the confrontation with the animal other as a destabilization of the traditional subject-who-knows. In "Snake," Lawrence laments the voices of his education, which demand a violent rejection of the animal. More radically, the poem "Fish" first admires the being of fishes, but finally acknowledges that the profound alterity of the animal other sets a limit upon the powers of human epistemology. This portrait of the human who *cannot know* challenges the tenets of Western speciesism, though the poem narrates the restabilization of the human-as-master through violence against the animal. But the tensions in Lawrence between acknowledging, destroying, and incorporating the animal's alterity point to the complexity of the human relation to the animal.

The recuperative gesturing toward animality in Lawrence's work frames my discussion in the fourth and fifth chapters of texts that invert the traditional humanist marginalization of animality. These works are exceptional not only because they refuse to project animality onto others, but also because they encode a transvaluation of speciesist values by privileging what we might provisionally call animal consciousness. In Lawrence's *St. Mawr*, Louise Witt rejects human fraternity but refuses to abject animality from her own experience. In a similar return to the animal, Birkin in *Women in Love* imagines a utopic earth devoid of the human species yet peopled with animals. His quest for a solution to the problem of human intersubjectivity repeatedly proposes forms of animal ontology as salves for the reified, industrialized human mind.

Djuna Barnes's *Nightwood* must also be classed as a text that stages a recuperation of animality. This ornate and historically marginalized novel presents what is perhaps the most complex and atypical portrait of animality in modernist literature. *Nightwood*'s central character, Robin Vote, is marked by her silence in the text. Robin's gender is indistinct, as is her sexuality, and by the end of the novel she also seems unwilling to inhabit a human identity that occludes animality. Her character fails even to correspond with the kinds of resistant subject-positions that are typically mobilized against hegemonic norms. Robin specifically resists the power of language to name and produce a differentiated subjectivity. Thus, Barnes engages the discourse of animality to trouble the very terms of human subjectivity and the think identity outside of the conditions set by its symbolic economies. Her exceptional work underscores the profoundly liminal nature of the animal problem and reminds us of the challenges we face in understanding it.

The kind of antirationalist recuperation of animality that surfaces in many of the texts under consideration throughout this study is partially enabled by the formalist "revolution" that took place under modernism. This remapping of literary language to include the irrational and nonlinear is often explained as an eruption of psychic forces that were repressed or contained within traditional literary conventions. Just as the rise of psychoanalytic theory corresponds with the post-Darwinian species crisis in Western humanism, the modernist eruption of literary convention parallels the perforation of the humanized subject by its evolutionary connection to animality. The breakdown of traditional literary syntax, structure, and narration, the introduction of circuitous and unstable narrative devices, all these changes line up with the post-Darwinian eruption of "nonhuman," chaotic forces within humanism.

This distinctly modernist formal embodiment of the animal problem is brought into relief by considering the treatment of animality in Victorian texts. Lippit, for instance, reads Lewis Carroll's *Alice's Adventures in Wonderland* as emblematic of a literary "becoming-animal," a thematic return of animality in Western literature (136). Lippit notes that the *Wonderland* story appears in 1865, only six years after the publication of Darwin's *Origin of Species*. He examines the animalized humans in Carroll's story and theorizes the ways in which the text interrogates the ability of language to contain animality. While Darwin's influence seems clear in Carroll's work, and Lippit's analysis is thoughtful, the stability of language *remains intact for Carroll,* whose linguistic devices do not become animal at any point. Lippit is right that Carroll's work displays a *thematic* and primarily metaphorical interest in animality. But it is not until we reach the modernist rejection of traditional forms that animality is instantiated in the language as well as the thematics of canonical literature.

This is not to say, of course, that all the texts considered in this study display a linguistic becoming-animal. To the contrary, H. G. Wells's work remains solidly circumscribed within traditional formal modes. But the work of Eliot and Conrad, for instance, departs from formal traditions at different moments and in various ways. My point here is that modernism emerges as a privileged site for the discursive consideration of animality at a number of junctures. The post-Darwinian crisis in humanist identity, the production of imperialist otherings, the development of psychoanalysis, the modernist revolt against Enlightenment legacies of rationalism, the twentieth-century eruption of linguistic convention, all these dynamics shape an acute engagement with the discourse of species in literature of the period. The trajectory of this study, therefore, traces modernism's own dramatic reckoning with the animal.

Many Jews indeed had a rat's fate.
　　　　　—Anthony Julius, T. S. Eliot, Anti-Semitism, and Literary Form

Man has developed consciousness slowly and laboriously, in a process that took untold ages to reach the civilized state. . . . And this evolution is far from complete, for large areas of the human mind are still shrouded in darkness.
　　　　　—Carl G. Jung, Man and His Symbols

2　Imperialism and Disavowal

　　While recent postcolonial criticism has privileged the categories of race and gender in an effort to rearticulate our understanding of modernism's imperialist binaries, it has failed to examine the fact that these discourses frequently sought justification through the discourse of species. The displacement of animality onto marginalized groups served as a fundamental modernist thematic that sought to purify Western subjectivity and thereby discursively maintain the imperialist power dynamic. While Darwin's work suggested that species evolved through a process of competition and natural selection, social Darwinists, as Marjorie Spiegel explains, sometimes applied his ideas to colonialist apologetics, "by which ruthless behavior towards different races, classes, or species could be rationalized and justified as being only a demonstration of evolution in action."[1] Patrick Brantlinger also notes that in the late nineteenth century, Europeans often categorized Negroes as a different species, excluding them "scientifically" from the human community.[2] A common form of social Darwinism involved the animalizing of disenfranchised groups and the concomitant humanizing of imperialist power.

　　In fact, displacing animality onto marginalized groups, whether they be Jews, blacks, women, or the poor, is a common feature of modernist literature. This displacement—this scapegoating—enacts an anxious *disavowal* of Darwin's incriminating suggestion that even Western subjectivity has animal roots; it indicates that, in part, European anxiety about the animal *ballasts the imperialist matrix*.

Modernist texts thus reveal various attempts to solve the species problem through the displacement of animality onto a disenfranchised "other." These displacements occurred within an imperialist chain-of-being inspired by evolutionary theory that designated white men the superior "species" and descended through racialized others and women only to bottom-out at the level of the animal. It is proximity to the animal, of course, that gives the imperialist chain-of-being its force. A given individual or race is valued according to its perceived distance from the irrational, instinctual animal, according to its "progress" upward from animality. Spiegel does well to point out that prior to the popularization of evolutionary theories, Christian ideology was used to justify the subjugation of slaves and of animals, a relation of power that was "said to be ordained by God" (25). Darwinism, which linked the human and animal in a reversal of Christian values, was rearticulated to provide an updated vindication for speciesism and its overlap with racism.

The analysis of modernist texts in which the discourses of race, gender, and animality are mutually deployed therefore opens up a new lens with which to view the relationship between modernism and imperialist identity. The vigorous reentrenchment of Western sovereignty through the primarily racialized displacement of animality away from the European subject in the work of T. S. Eliot, Joseph Conrad, and D. H. Lawrence reveals how deeply the animal threatened a destabilization of that subject. Interestingly, modernism undergoes a *formal* identity crisis that parallels this crisis of the subject yet appears to produce less anxiety. Perhaps this is the case because the destabilization of literary convention only resituates humanist autonomy, as a rejection of tradition, for the modernist writer. The destabilization of the humanist subject through the eruption of animality, to the contrary, eradicates this kind of privilege. For writers like Eliot, and more complexly, Conrad, the animal reveals a breaking point beyond which they are not willing to let the subject go. For Lawrence, the question remains an open and vexed one throughout his work.

i

There is a certain logic underlying the appearance of animality in high modernism, and T. S. Eliot exemplifies that logic with virtuosic force in his 1920 poems. High modernism like Eliot's, and Joyce's for that matter, often employs classical literary forms and genres—the complex structures of literary art—to narrate various "low" topics formerly considered unfit for literary incarnation. This hybridization produces a kind of schizophrenia of high and low, of the sacred and profane, which gives high modernism its deconstructive penchant. Eliot's poetic vistas of classical mythology and cultural analogue are run through with the morally questionable and the culturally unfit. The animal in Western humanism, and especially in post-Darwinian modernity, exists within that realm of "low" impulses that threatens Eliot's vision of humanity and therefore bolsters it in another register, as we shall see. His poetic figurations of Sweeney in particular reveal the various ways in which Eliot filters and constructs the Euro-imperialist human through the discourse of species.

Among Eliot's quatrain poems, "Sweeney Among the Nightingales" is the most famously opaque. Robert M. DeGraaff has noted that Eliot's use of "extreme ambiguity" in this poem "makes it a happy hunting ground for explicators" and that "puzzling controversies over many of its details and images are numerous."[3] In fact, most readers of the poem mention its impenetrability before presenting their own contribution to the massive critical discourse that surrounds it. But if the poem itself stands as an obtuse testimony to allusive high modernism—which it certainly does— its characterization of Sweeney is remarkably straightforward. Indeed the opening lines of this quatrain comprise an unforgettable fragment of modernist imagery:

> Apeneck Sweeney spreads his knees
> Letting his arms hang down to laugh,
>   The zebra stripes along his jaw
>   Swelling to maculate giraffe.[4]

Eliot's Sweeney is one of the clearest animalized humans to be found in the literature of modernism. Ape, giraffe, and zebra, Sweeney is a poly-animalistic figure, and Eliot's insistence on his multiple associations with the "lower" species is exponentially damning. He is "animal" on many levels. The secondary meaning of the word *maculate* drives this point home:

while usually indicating something spotted or blotched, as a giraffe, the word can also mean impure and besmirched. Eliot's complicated poem thus opens with a very uncomplicated portrait of Sweeney: ontologically speaking, he is more animal than human.

Sweeney's animality is only amplified by his fellow café dwellers as the poem continues. The silent "vertebrate" in brown not only "sprawls" and "gapes," but Rachel née Rabinovitch, after a waiter brings in oranges, bananas, figs, and hothouse grapes, is said to "tear" at the fruit with "murderous paws." These images have not gone unnoticed by critics and are usually read as symbols of Eliot's Hellenistic rage against a culturally and spiritually barren modernity. John Ower, for instance, elucidates four levels of spiritual value in Eliot's work and argues that the animality in "Sweeney Among the Nightingales" designates "Modern man's gross materialism and spiritual degeneracy."[5]

Skeptical of such orthodox readings, Stephen Clark insists upon the treatment of Eliot's violent sexual imagery *qua* sexual imagery.[6] I want to venture a reading of "Sweeney Among the Nightingales," and other Eliot poems, vis-à-vis the animal *qua* animal. That is to say, it is possible to read Sweeney and his cohorts in this poem as markers of a post-Darwinian anxiety about the nature of the human. While some critics describe Sweeney abstractly as "the embodiment of the flesh in the body / spirit debate,"[7] others provide a more literal assessment. "The animals associated with Sweeney," argues Nancy Hargrove, "are symbolic of man's regression, of his bestial nature. The dominant animal is, of course, the ape, suggesting that man as represented by Sweeney had made little if any progress in terms of evolution."[8] Eliot's repeated use of the Sweeney-as-ape trope indicates a specifically Darwinian component to the quatrain poems. Indeed, Eliot's claim that he wished to invoke a "sense of foreboding" in "Sweeney Among the Nightingales" seems partially ironic when set against the zoo-like qualities of boredom and sterile sexuality that Sweeney exemplifies. On the other hand, Rachel has "murderous paws," and there are, of course, the nightingales to contend with—the birds of Eliot's title are usually understood as prostitutes who recall the Prochne and Philomela myth.[9] Stephen Clark carefully reads the final lines of the poem, in which Agamemnon is "dishonoured" by the defecating birds, as a misogynistic insistence that the sexual act "will always conclude in the same betrayal and desecration of the male" (175). The "liquid siftings" that end the poem mark Eliot's obscene collapse of animality and the feminine, and these siftings seem to besmirch Agamemnon for his unchecked sexual communion with women. The nightingales signal Eliot's distress over humanity's connection to animality, which he aligns with feminine sexuality. Apropos of the title, the defecating birds may indirectly suggest that Sweeney's animality stems from his sexual association with women like Rachel. Perhaps the women have contaminated him with their animal being.

Women like Rachel have also elicited critical outrage concerning Eliot's relationship to what Bryan Cheyette calls semitic discourse, which cannot be separated from the species discourse that is operative in his poetry.[10] The recent, high-pitched debates over Eliot's relationship to Jewishness, both in his texts and in his personal life,[11] signal the ongoing need to understand his work in the context of "the Jewish question," which Jonathan Freedman reminds us is central to the workings of modernism itself.[12] Cheyette's discussion of this dynamic is particularly useful as it suggests that Eliot's work is, characteristically, engaged with questions of Jewishness that need not be glossed over or, conversely, damned through the freighted charge of "anti-Semitism." Rather than use these conventional terms, Cheyette wants us to situate Eliot in relationship to semitic discourse: "In the case of Eliot, it opens up a way of thinking about his use of racial discourse which accepts that, like Joyce, he constructed the Jew as a figure of confusion; a perfect objective correlative for a modernist skepticism. But, unlike Joyce, who embraced this confusion in the figure of the 'greekjewish' Leopold Bloom, Eliot wished to impose distinct boundaries between Hebrew and Hellene, Aryan and Semite" (434). My own view of these debates rests within Cheyette's admonition to "neither excuse nor accuse." While the intense attacks on Eliot's character can seem heavy-handed, Eliot's figuration of the Jew, and the often hostile metaphoric work he puts that figure to, undoubtedly require our critical attention. My own reading should not be taken as more vitriol from the anti-Eliot camp, but it does represent a rigorous commitment to unpacking the relationship between animality and Jewishness in some of his work, a relationship that does not escape a certain ugliness.

In my view, Eliot clearly displaces the typical imperialist framework of power onto the Jew, othering Jewishness in an attempt to maintain European privilege. That othering is repeatedly figured through the discourse of species. In addition to Rachel and her "paws," Eliot crafts another overtly Jewish character in the poem. When the man "with heavy eyes" leaves the room near the poem's end, he does so only to appear through the window as "Branches of wisteria / Circumscribe a golden grin." With an obvious, though seldom mentioned, pun on circumcision, and a trite caricature of

Jews with gold fillings,[13] Eliot marks this man as Jewish. Critics disagree about whether this character is Sweeney or the silent man in brown. In either case, Sweeney's zoo is full of Jews.

Sweeney himself has been read through the lens of anti-Semitism by Rachel Blau DuPlessis, who outlines Sweeney's various associations with Irish, African, and Jewish stereotypes and relies upon a homologous association between Bleistein (in "Burbank with a Baideker: Bleistein with a Cigar") and Sweeney. She notes specifically that the two characters are depicted as apish and similarly misshapen. DuPlessis argues that Sweeney is "a multiracialized figure with sexual-social implications. He is a figure who encodes attitudes toward threatening races and groups who are (in terms the poem proposes) beneath Culture in one sense while exhibiting a lurid, complete, and tempting culture of pleasure, avariciousness, and sadism."[14] The Sweeney of "Sweeney Erect" clearly fits this characterization.

This poem's title forces the species question onto center stage: "Sweeney Erect" mimics *Pithecanthropus erectus*,[15] the ape standing upright. It also emphasizes the repeated linkage of the animal and the sexual in Eliot's work. Eliot often relies upon an easy consonance between animality and debased sexual congress. Clark notes that, in addition to the title's blatant reference to male erection, it reads like a "zoological classification that endows the narrator with the forensic detachment and control of a taxonomist" (175). Equally detached is the unforgiving irony that Eliot invokes about the human condition in this visceral poem. Standing erect is usually indicative of humanity's transcendence over animality. Freud himself hazards this explanation in *Civilization and its Discontents* when he elaborates his theory of "organic repression," the process by which our ancestors became civilized by passing from an animal state to a human state.[16] "Man's erect posture," Freud explains, "would represent the beginning of the momentous process of cultural evolution" (30). This biped stance, according to Freud, results in eventual horror at the scent of excreta and blood and the consequent transition from an olfactory mode of sensing to a primary reliance on sight.

In Eliot's poem, Sweeney's erection makes a mockery of civilized humanity because his residual, sexualized animality ontologically overrides his participation in humanity ("Gesture of orang-outang / Rises from the sheets in steam"). Thus Eliot's searingly Darwinian stanza, with its vehement anti-Romanticist overtones, reminds the reader that the essential nature of this man, and perhaps of all men, is bestial. The pun on "length-ened shadow of a man" should be clear:

> (The lengthened shadow of a man
>   Is history, said Emerson
> Who had not seen the silhouette
>   Of Sweeney straddled in the sun.)

The genius of Eliot's poetry often resides in its subtlety, in its "rhetorical and connotative displacements," as DuPlessis has called them (144). Here the word *silhouette* not only refers to Sweeney's erect penis, it also cunningly evokes the evolutionary charts which use profile imagery to trace man's development from ape to human, the charts so often associated with social Darwinism and physiognomy debates in the late nineteenth and early twentieth centuries.[17] Sweeney's shadow gives humanity away, so to speak, as never fully deanimalized.

The poem's evocation of Poe's *Murders in the Rue Morgue* must not be overlooked in this light. Poe's story of a partially domesticated orangutan who "learns" to shave himself by watching his master and then violently murders an innocent woman with his razor seems an obvious source for "Sweeney Erect."[18] As Clark notes, the unsettling transformation of Poe's ape in imitation of his master might suggest that the ape must "become human to become inhuman, [to] act out his master's secret fantasies" (179). The implicit mirror imagery in Eliot's poem therefore invokes a *mise en abyme* or endless refraction of Sweeney's species status. This infinite deferral indicates an inability to locate a stabilized human subjectivity that is not dissolved by animality. Moreover, Sweeney's seemingly banal act of shaving can be read as the necessary removal of human "fur." Facial hair serves as an inevitable reminder of our animal status. In Judith Butler's terms, Sweeney must performatively reiterate or reenact his humanity by shaving off his animality, though in Sweeney's case, the "citation" of his humanity clearly fails.[19]

Sweeney's animality is further evidenced by his sadistic copulatory encounter with a diseased female, the "epileptic on the bed" who is earlier sexualized as "This withered root of knots of hair / Slitted below and gashed with eyes, / This oval O cropped out with teeth." The *vagina dentata,* typically construed as a symbol of castration anxiety, also violently fuses female sexuality and a primal fear of consumption in the poem. It is tempting to collapse Eliot's sexualized anxieties about women, animality, and Jewishness into a generalized heterophobia detectable throughout his oeuvre. But Anthony Julius instructs readers of Eliot not to be seduced by reductive theories of Eliot's antipathies. To the contrary, Julius argues that Eliot's treatment of Jews differs significantly from his treatment of women. Despite the fact that, in Eliot, "Jews and women are often rendered as non-reflective, indeed barely sentient creatures . . . animal-like in their rank corporeality" (20), Julius believes that Eliot can "imagine a relation with women, [but] he cannot with Jews. . . . The poetry is engaged in a struggle with women. It wins a series of victories over Jews" (22).

While Eliot's misogyny is undoubtedly remarkable, Julius raises a convincing distinction. He points out the discrepancy between unknown and known quantities in Eliot. Despite the mandarin ambiguities that are a hallmark of his writing, Julius explains, "a representative Jew is captured in a few malign phrases" from Eliot's pen (27). Eliot's poetry presumes to *know* the Jew unequivocally and thereby reduces Jewishness to an object easily figured and easily dismissed. This epistemologically violent summarizing quality is enabled by Eliot's deployment of his species discourse in conjunction with his semitic discourse:

> The rats are underneath the piles.
> The jew is underneath the lot.
>   Money in furs.[20]

This fragment from "Burbank with a Baedeker: Bleistein with a Cigar" is staggeringly precise in its reduction of Jews to rats, rats who pretend to be human through displays of wealth. Of course, the fundamental degradedness of animals like rats is assumed in such trite metaphors that rely upon Western species distinctions. But the role of metaphor is crucial here and allows a flat and objectified construction of both animality and Jewishness. Bleistein, who with "A lustreless protrusive eye / Stares from protozoic slime," registers at the microbial bottom of the species scale and is representative of all Jews who, like animals, lack distinction in all its senses. The poetry makes this comparison seem obvious, and it does so with aesthetic prowess. Eliot's Prufrock describes his creator's genius all too well, for Jews are fixed in a formulated phrase, sprawling on a pin, wriggling on the wall. Jews, like the bug in "The Love Song of J. Alfred Prufrock" are arrested by Eliot's verse and displayed for all to see. They appear in a poetic zoo for the reader's "viewing" pleasure.

Jewishness and zooishness present themselves as central themes in Eliot's creative lexicon, and his putatively unfinished dramatic poem, *Sweeney Agonistes,* is no exception. Here again a violent, sexualized animality is put to work by Eliot. In this cryptic text, Sweeney appears to have developed a critical awareness of the sexualized animal qualities he embodied in the quatrain poems. Not surprisingly, he also transcends his ambiguous association with Jewishness. Eliot distinctly contrasts Sweeney with two Jewish caricatures, Klipstein and Krumpacker, who do not reach "enlightenment" in the poem. One suspects that the de-Jewing of Sweeney results from Sweeney's elevated status in Eliot's poetic oeuvre. In other words, if Sweeney embodies a superior knowledge of human fate, if he "speaks for" Eliot in this work, he cannot vaguely occupy a Jewish subjectivity, so Eliot purposefully distances him from overt Jewishness.

In this drama Sweeney, as Nancy Hargrove points out, "has had an insight into the meaningless quality of modern existence and the sinful nature of man, an insight which he tries unsuccessfully to communicate to the others" (164). Perhaps more than recognizing the "sinful" nature of man, Sweeney confronts man's inherent animality, which is again coded through the sexual by Eliot. Sweeney's epiphany is metaphorized as a cannibalistic island and later as a "crocodile isle," where life amounts to nothing more than "birth, copulation, and death," where he and Doris would be reduced to their most basic corporeal functions. Sweeney goes on to muse, after Doris wants to be a missionary on the island, that he would convert and eat her in a "Juicy little . . . missionary stew." This violent extension of the missionary position may serve as Sweeney's subconscious revenge against the castrating "oval O cropped out with teeth" in "Sweeney Erect." If Sweeney feels sexually consumed by the feminine, his fantasy of cannibalizing Doris's body violently reverses that power dynamic. Indeed, male meat-eating may be read as a compensatory displacement of the sexual dynamics of "meat" and "eater" as viewed through Eliot's economy in which the feminine devours the male genitalia. Moreover, the implied reduction of Doris to "meat," her reduction to the status of other animals eaten by Sweeney, signals a concomitant horror at the animal willingness to consume one's own species. Cannibalism, which metaphorizes humanity's horror at its unavoidable compulsion to be an eating animal, frequently registers the fear of becoming or being animal in post-Darwinian modernity, as our later discussion of Conrad and Lawrence will demonstrate. Here it does so in a sexualized register.

Sweeney Agonistes is also Eliot's most obvious dabbling in the discursive realm of primitivism. The overdetermined "tribal" songs in the poem are rife with primitive imagery that ranges from bamboo trees to penguin calls to Eliot's ever-primordial fresh egg. His chief complaint, familiar from the quatrain poems, seems to be that humanity is not, or perhaps cannot, transcend its evolutionary origins. The poem drips with the instinctual and the fecund, the sexual and the mortal. Most revealing among these considerations are Eliot's experiments in linguistic devolution throughout the poem. The first of two songs reads thus:

> Under the bamboo tree
>   Two live as one
>   One live as two
>   Two live as three
>   Under the bam
>   Under the boo
> Under the bamboo tree.[21]

This song locates a deindividuation or loss of distinction in the reproductive bottom-line of life on the crocodile isle. Two become one, two become three, as the borders of self are obliterated through sexual merging and reproduction. This deindividuation is echoed in the linguistic dissolution of "bamboo" into "bam" and "boo," two nonwords, two sounds that represent the prelinguistic, infantile vocalizations of humans which can be indecipherable from the sounds of nonhuman animals. Outside of the cultural, Sweeney and Doris are reduced to the instinctual forces which drive them (the sexual act, "bam"), and to the results of that act (the crying baby, "boo").

The final lines of the poem, spoken by the full chorus of Wauchope, Horsfall, Klipstein, and Krumpacker, narrate an anxious awaiting of knocks on the door and a menacing hangman. Just before the "knocks" that end the poem, Eliot's chorus chants, "Hoo ha ha / Hoo ha ha / Hoo / Hoo/ Hoo." These sounds not only echo the "boo" of the earlier song, but they also seem to imitate a monkey's call. In a radical break from his typically highbrow style, here Eliot attempts to literalize his writing of unconscious drives. Rather than symbolize depravity through another classical allusion, Eliot uses "Hoo ha ha" to signify the visceral underbelly of the human that Sweeney had embodied and now explains, the animal self that, in Freudian terms, must be repressed into the unconscious in order for the individual to become and remain human. Eliot's "Hoo ha ha" can be read as a "return of the repressed," an unmistakable acknowledgment of Žižek's surplus of symbolic encoding, the inevitable remainder that stands outside symbolization.

What's more, such an instance of writing animality, or writing the unconscious as I have been calling it, is precisely a linguistic becoming-animal, a modernist erosion of traditional literary forms. Richard Sheppard's essay, "The Crisis of Language," aptly describes the explosion of literary conventions that is now taken as a classic characteristic of modernist writing. Sheppard specifically cites Eliot's essay "The Metaphysical Poets" (1921) as emblematic of the modernist discontent with a "progressive hardening and a cerebralization" of poetic language.[22] In fact, Sheppard describes this disaffection with language in terms of repression and release; like the industrialized city, language acts as a "surface hiding a forgotten substratum of history and civilization, or else of unorganized and festering psychic energy" (326). Consequently, the experimental modernist writer "attempts to liberate the repressed expressive energies of language" (329).

Theorizing modernism's engagement with the discourse of species sheds new light on this traditional characterization of modernist form. The twentieth-century eruption of animality, often encoded as the eruption of the unconscious, parallels the modernist explosion of linguistic convention. Modernists attempt to "defeat the censorship which the surface areas of the personality, the conscious intellect and the will, had imposed upon the profounder levels of the psyche" (333) by forging a "new" literary language that engages these repressed potentialities. In a sense, through their famed discontinuous and irrational speech, modernists write their own animality, which cannot be represented by traditional literary forms. Eliot's linguistic representation of animality—his "Hoo ha ha"—can only be marked as literature in this modernist world where literary convention is rejected and revamped, where it is opened to unconventional forces.

This exclusively modernist (and subsequently postmodernist) possibility is made clearer when one considers the primarily metaphorical representation of animality in Victorian literature. Bram Stoker's *Dracula* (1897), for instance, provides a fascinating Victorian codification of species anxieties framed by the monstrous Count Dracula. The count serves as a hyperbolic instance of "survival of the fittest" ideology since he lives for centuries by feeding off the strength of other human bodies. He takes on various animal forms, including lizard, bat, and wolf, and his cross-species monstrosity must be recontained by Stoker's narrative, which kills him off in a dramatic dénouement. Animality is represented through traditional metaphor in Stoker's gothic tale, and while the novel's sometimes lurid content is remarkable, its linguistic strategies are staid. Traditional narrative strategies do not register the eruption of animality through the eruption of language: modernist literature is the first to do that.

Anthony Julius makes the point that Eliot was particularly adept at putting anti-Semitism to artistic use (again, this is a term Cheyette would avoid): "His anti-Semitic poetry draws imaginatively on anti-Semitism's discursive repertoire" (11). One is tempted to imagine the contours of speciesism's discursive repertoire, vast and largely unaccounted for as it stands in our critical lexicon. For Eliot, at any rate, who is acutely attuned to the "wasteland" of modern culture in post-Christian Europe, who is threatened by the new woman and her sexuality, and who knows what Darwin has to say about humanity's heritage, animals operate within his last vestige of intellectual certainty. Just as his poetic grounding in classical mythology erects a protective metaphysical fortress, Eliot's species discourse shows, literally, that he is sure of something. The easy deployment of a violent, sexualized animality to other the Jew and sometimes the woman retains the classic Western hierarchy of being that Eliot so desperately wishes to rejuvenate. These epistemological economies secure for him—and thus for the European imperialist—the position of intellectual master. Rachel Blau DuPlessis suggests that Eliot feels displaced "from inheritor to disinherited" within his modernist world, and that he consequently registers this displacement in the Sweeney figure (147). More to the point, Eliot *reestablishes* his inheritance of power through these tropes of knowing that transfer displacement to animalized Jews and women. One senses this immediately when reading Eliot; his work is masterful but harbors frequent moments of violence and of desperation.

ii

The innovative, layered narration of Conrad's *Heart of Darkness* echoes the layered nature of the imperialist subject that the novel reveals. While Conrad's style cultivates ambiguity, some criticism too easily overlooks the obvious. Frederick R. Karl, for instance, issued this vague prognosis in his early psychoanalytic reading of the novel: "The story is concerned with hidden terrors in the normal heart, with the attractions of the unspeakable which we all experience, with the sense of power we wish to exert or identify with, ultimately with the underground existence each sentient being recognizes in himself."[23] In recent years, the most concrete critical readings of the novel offer the specific dynamics of race and/or gender as points of entry into these "hidden terrors." What remains unsaid is the pivotal nature of the animal in *Heart of Darkness*. Indeed, it is an Africanized *animality* that propels Kurtz into his own ontological darkness in Conrad's narrative.

Some earlier criticism has hinted at the centrality of the animal in Conrad's text. In 1975 Cedric Watts insisted that "*Heart of Darkness* has a more richly Darwinian atmosphere than any other major work of fiction."[24] One of the text's early and often-cited lines makes its evolutionary tapestry immediately evident: "'And this also,' said Marlow suddenly, 'has been one of the dark places of the earth.'"[25] Despite its industrial and scientific advances, Marlow implies, England was once a primitive place like the Congo, a landscape of "marshes, forests, savages, precious little to eat fit for a civilised man" (9–10). Conrad's words seem carefully chosen to accentuate a continuity, rather than a rupture, between the present moment and the past. Rather than using the simple past tense to have Marlow say, "this also *was* a dark place," Conrad chooses the present perfect *has been*, which suggests a chronological immediacy that makes the darkness palpable, nearly present. This suggestion serves to undermine the Victorian emphasis on progress in evolutionary theory that maintained man's distance from his animal past. In fact, Stephen Kern points out in *The Culture of Time and Space* that thinkers like Darwin and Freud helped to create a fundamental shift in the way Westerners understood the persistence of the past: "As Darwin assumed that remnants of the past are indelibly inscribed in organic matter and triggered miraculously in the proper order to allow embryos to recapitulate all that has gone before, so Freud maintained that every experience, however insignificant, leaves some trace that continues to shape psychic repetitions and revisions throughout life."[26] Kern goes on to argue that the persistence of the past and its shaping of the present moment was a major philosophical consideration in the early twentieth century.

Marlow evokes this interimplication of past and present as he conjures the image of a Roman citizen finding himself suddenly hemmed in by "utter savagery . . . all that mysterious life of the wilderness that stirs in the forest, in the jungles, in the hearts of wild men" (10). An obvious foreshadowing of Marlow's imminent journey toward Kurtz, this description is anything but "inconclusive" (11). On the contrary, Marlow's musings erect the struggle between civilized and savage and suggest man's confrontation with his evolutionary past. That past will descend rapidly toward a racialized animality as the text unfolds.

The problematics of race in *Heart of Darkness* have been repeatedly probed by postcolonial critics since the late 1970s, when Chinua Achebe vehemently raised objections to Conrad's treatment of blackness in the text. Achebe famously argued that "Joseph Conrad was a thoroughgoing racist" who used Africa "as a metaphysical battlefield devoid of all recognizable humanity."[27] But if Africa lacked humanity for Conrad, what did it conversely embody? Achebe himself comes close to recognizing Conrad's species ideology when he formulates an implicit answer to this question: the text imagines Africa as "the antithesis of Europe and therefore of civilization, a place where man's vaunted intelligence and refinement are finally mocked by *triumphant bestiality*" (252; emphasis added). And, in fact, Africans are imagined as so many animals in Conrad's classic literary masterpiece. Indeed, the racial ideologies of the text turn centrally on the discourse of species because Kurtz's devolution depends upon his identification with the African *as animal*. This identification, in turn, is leveled at European values in a kind of deconstructive mitigation of imperialism throughout the text, and yet, this deconstruction is premised on the repeated alignment of African and animal. Thus, while Achebe's critique alerts us to the racial problematics of the text, it does not flesh out the text's discourse of animality upon which its racial dynamics depend.

The West's specific cultural alignment of African slaves with nonhuman animals is painstakingly demonstrated by Marjorie Spiegel in *The Dreaded Comparison: Human and Animal Slavery*. Spiegel identifies various convergences between the discourses of race and animality that undergird a frighteningly systemic network of oppression. Historically, both slaves and animals have been deemed irrational, objectified as property, branded, shackled, experimented upon, and frequently abused to the point of death. For Spiegel, the traditional Christian justification for subduing and dominating nature is recodified in the late nineteenth century because of Darwin's theories: "From the misconstrued concept that humans are evolutionarily better than animals it easily followed . . . that whites could be evolutionarily superior to blacks." In the name of social Darwinism, then, progress through violence against others was sometimes justified as "an evolutionary birthright" (21). It was a person or ethnicity's proximity to the animal, of course, that gave this imperialist chain of being its force.

The imperialist coimplication of race and animality surfaces early in *Heart of Darkness* as Marlow travels toward his company's station. Sailing with a group of strangers, Marlow explains that "the oily and languid sea, the uniform sombreness of the coast, seemed to keep me away from the truth of things." His only "contact with reality" comes when a boat paddles by filled with singing, shouting black men. This sight stirs him from his delirium: "They had faces like grotesque masks—these chaps; but they had bone, muscle, a wild vitality, an intense energy of movement that was as natural and true as the surf along their coast" (17). The face, the most recognizably human characteristic, does not read for Marlow when it is black. These men have faces "like grotesque masks"; in other words, they don't seem to have faces at all. According to Emmanuel Levinas, the face of the other is the fundamental source of ethics that commits one to the fraternity of human kinship.[28] Rather than feel connected to the human *being* of these men, Marlow is attracted to them in a purely materialist register. Their physicality and their "wild vitality" place them in the same category with trees and rocks, as "natural" as their own coastline. Interestingly, Marlow describes the encounter as comforting because it confirmed "a world of straightforward facts" that would later be unsettled (17). Those facts subtly imply that Africans—unlike Europeans—are ruled by instinct alone and exist outside the matrix of human culture, like animals.

One of Conrad's most conspicuous images of African animality is often quoted in critical apologies for his political intentions. Hugh Mercer Curtler, for instance, wants us to consider the portrait of Europe that Marlow's experience presents, especially as he "arrives in the Congo to find upturned and rusting machinery in the midst of a verdant wilderness into which black people crawl to lick their wounds and escape their white 'masters' who beat them for no reason."[29] Curtler refers to one of the most disturbing image sequences in the text, which, it is true, paints a sordid picture of what Edward Said calls the practice of empire:[30]

Six black men advanced in a file toiling up the path. They walked erect and slow, balancing small baskets full of earth on their heads, and the clink kept time with their footsteps. Black rags were wound round their loins and the short ends behind *waggled to and fro like tails.* . . . Black shapes crouched, lay, sat between the trees, leaning against the trunks, clinging to the earth, half coming out, half effaced within the dim light, in all the attitudes of pain, abandonment, and despair. (Conrad, 19–20; emphasis added)

This passage seems intentionally ambiguous. Does Marlow consciously equate the men with animals, whose rags wag behind them like tails? After all, they register as "raw matter" in Marlow's lexicon (19). Or does he perceive that they are they *being treated like animals* by the machinery of imperialist conquest? Perhaps Marlow does both. His earlier equation of Africans with uncivilized nature may be already troubled by this sequence in which he senses injustice and wrongdoing. The straightforward "fact" of Africans' animality is beginning to be unsettled.

Marlow is again disturbed in this early, gruesome scene when he passes another group of "acute angles" who are "scattered in every pose of contorted collapse, as in some picture of a massacre or a pestilence." He is particularly "horror-struck" as "one of these creatures rose to his hands and knees and went off on all-fours towards the river to drink" (21). In the manner of an animal, the "creature" laps water out of his hand and then sits up in the sunlight, unable to keep his head from falling forward. This is not the first time that Marlow will be confronted with a man who crawls on all fours: Kurtz, the most unsettling character in Marlow's narrative, will eventually assume the same position near the end of Conrad's story.

Hints of evolutionary regression abound in the text as Marlow begins his final journey up the River Congo, toward Kurtz's African station. "Going up that river," Marlow reports, "was like travelling back to the earliest beginnings of the world, when vegetation rioted on the earth and the big trees were kings" (35). Africa thus functions in the text as a placeholder for prehistoric times, a present-day repository of the past. Marlow corroborates this reading as he continues:

> You lost your way on that river . . . till you thought yourself bewitched and cut off for ever from everything you had known once—somewhere—far away—in another existence perhaps. There were moments *when one's past came back to one,* as it will sometimes when you have not a moment to spare to yourself; but it came in the shape of an unrestful and noisy dream remembered with wonder amongst the overwhelming realities of this strange world of plants and water and silence. And this stillness of life did not in the least resemble a peace. It was the stillness of an implacable force brooding over an inscrutable intention. (35–36; emphasis added)

Marlow provides a detailed description of the organic persistence of a seemingly collective evolutionary past as it presses itself upon one's present consciousness. The passage intimates a Jungian return of repressed instinct from the unconscious. According to Jung, "Consciousness is a very recent acquisition of nature, and it is still in an 'experimental' state. It is frail, menaced by specific dangers, and easily injured."[31] Dreamlike and strange, the reality of Marlow's animal heritage rises from some unconscious source that is triggered simultaneously by the "overwhelming realities" of nature and of silence. Marlow is particularly unsettled by silence, by the profound lack of human speech. Historically, language has been used as proof of *Homo sapiens'* superiority over other species. As Jeffrey Moussaieff Masson and Susan McCarthy plainly put in this speciesist perspective, "We speak; we reason; we imagine; we anticipate; we worship; we laugh. They do not."[32] This humanist relation to language is, of course, precisely what Levinas privileges in his discourse on the ethical imperative of the "face-to-face." In this passage, silence acts as a leveling force since it signals Marlow's undifferentiation from the plants, the water, the "implacable force" of raw materiality.

The few pages that follow this dreamlike initiation are so rife with humanist crisis that they overwhelm the reader. Marlow induces a progressive destabilization of human identity when he mentions the cannibals who have been enlisted to work for him. Cannibalism itself undermines the sovereignty of the human by objectifying human flesh as edible and therefore reducing man to a thing. Georges Bataille theorizes this objectification or thing-ification in his *Theory of Religion:*

> An animal exists for itself and in order to be a thing it must be dead or domesticated. Thus the eaten animal can be posited as an object only provided it is eaten dead. Indeed it is fully a thing only in a roasted, grilled, or boiled form. . . . Concerning that which I kill, which I cut up, which I cook, I implicitly affirm that *that* has never been anything but a thing. To cut up, cook, and eat a man is on the contrary abominable. . . . And despite appearances, even the hardened materialists are still so religious that in their eyes it is always a crime to make a man into a thing—a roast, a stew.[33]

Conrad cleverly reemphasizes the corporeal bottom-line that cannibalism insists upon when Marlow interjects, "after all, they did not eat each other before my face: they had brought along a provision of hippo-meat which went rotten and made the mystery of the wilderness stink in my nostrils" (36). The hippo meat metonymically refers to human "meat" in the text, and Marlow's men will eventually throw the hippo flesh overboard because its stench nearly makes them lose "their precarious grip on existence" (42). This rotting flesh signals the sailors' anxiety about being "meat" themselves, about being reduced to an edible object, which makes them no different from other animals who are routinely killed for food. While the hippo flesh serves as an unsettling, racist metaphor for Africa's connection to animality, and its stench operates as a reminder of man's fleshness, the violent deaths of the hippos are repressed from the text as it focuses on the contours of human identity. In a complicated displacement, the hippo flesh as symbolic substitution for cannibalism also acts to validate violence against blacks as it constructs their barbaric propensities in contrast to the European "human."

That human becomes radically destabilized for Marlow as he approaches Kurtz and is ambushed by African warriors in a now classic scene of existential terror. Finding himself and his crew "on the edge of a black and incomprehensible frenzy," Marlow explains: "We were wanderers on a prehistoric earth, on an earth that wore the aspect of an unknown planet. We could have fancied ourselves the first of men taking possession of an accursed inheritance, to be subdued at the cost of profound anguish and of excessive toil" (37). The evolutionary anxiety in this passage is remarkable since it puts into words the problem of humanity's transformation from its animal past—its "accursed inheritance"—to its civilized state. Conrad suggests that Marlow and his men find themselves in a historically reminiscent scene that reenacts "man's" ancestral struggle to transcend his animal nature, a nature that is textually embodied by Africa and Africans and that is so horrific and powerful as to require "profound anguish" and "excessive toil" to conquer. Conrad's descriptions become more precise as the scene continues and as Marlow meditates upon the "monstrous" Africans: "No they were not inhuman. Well, you know that was the worst of it—this suspicion of their not being inhuman. It would come slowly to one. They howled and leaped and spun and made horrid faces, but what thrilled you was just the thought of their humanity—like yours—the thought of your remote kinship with this wild and passionate uproar" (37–38).

The philosophical paradox presented to Marlow at this juncture resides in the epiphany that Africans are both like himself *and* not like himself: they howl and leap and spin. Africans serve as the collocation of the human and animal here, and Marlow is forced to acknowledge his "remote kinship" with animality. The undecidability, in Derridean terms, of the

Western "human" at this historically specific juncture is at issue in Marlow's suspicion. His identity crisis reflects the struggle of the modernist subject to register its own Darwinian heritage just as the conflation of Africans and animals encodes imperialism's specific refraction of that crisis. Eventually, of course, a similar consonance of the human and animal is manifested in Kurtz, and Marlow's understanding of his own humanity will be more radically undermined because he cannot distance himself racially from Kurtz.

Marlow looks to the power of language to shore up humanist identity throughout Conrad's narrative. Bette London identifies the ways in which Marlow uses masculinity and narrative authority to displace his textual "identifications with the feminine and non-white" in the name of colonial orthodoxy.[34] London explains that Marlow relies upon voice and speech to turn moments of personal weakness in the story into "displays of narrative prowess" (246). Similarly, it is language itself, both spoken and written, that allows Marlow to renounce humanity's participation in animality. When Marlow asks his fellow sailors to consider their own responsiveness to the Africans' savage uproar, he insists that they too can comprehend it: "And why not? The mind of man is capable of anything— because everything is in it, all the past as well as all the future." But this admission causes an anxious breakdown in the narrative, and Marlow feels the need to reassert some more stable "truth": "Very well. I hear, I admit, but I have a voice too, and for good or evil mine is the speech that cannot be silenced" (38). Speech, for better or worse, acts as a refuge for Marlow at this moment. In a similar yet textually self-referential moment, Marlow finds solace in the Towson book on seamanship, which he finds in an abandoned post along the river. He admits that "to leave off reading was like tearing myself away from the shelter of an old and solid friendship" (40). In fact, he finds it especially remarkable that the notes in the book's margins are written in cipher. Implicitly, then, the exclusively human capacity for high-order language games delights Marlow and temporarily reassures him that human civilization has lifted itself beyond its speechless, primitive lineage. Conrad troubles this assurance when, later in the text, Marlow discovers that the cipher is actually Russian. However slightly, Marlow has misconstrued man's facility with language.

Some critics perceive a traditional association between words and Western, masculinist power in the text. Johanna M. Smith considers the problem of language in her feminist reading of *Heart of Darkness*, arguing that Conrad's narrative attempts to silence women like Kurtz's African mistress in order to contain and control them: "As Marlow creates these women to symbolize the enigma of the jungle," she claims, "his ideological project is to distance and control both mysteries."[35] Smith's reading suggests that language, stolen from women in the text, instantiates patriarchal hegemony and its desire to control the feminine. But a close look at Kurtz's relationship to language reveals the novel's implicit critique of the power of words, not its unmitigated entrenchment of traditional *logos*.

Kurtz is associated with a form of "pure" language throughout much of Conrad's text; he is metaphorized as a *disembodied* voice, as linguistic virtuosity let loose from its mortal coil. Kurtz is not someone to converse with, but someone to listen to. "The man presented himself as a voice," notes Marlow (48). Marlow experiences Kurtz as the quintessential humanist, an eloquent man of letters, distinguished in the most human of faculties: "The point was in his being a gifted creature and that of all his gifts the one that stood out pre-eminently, that carried with it a sense of real presence, was his ability to talk, his words—the gift of expression, the bewildering, the illuminating, the most exalted and the most contemptible, the pulsating stream of light or the deceitful flow from the heart of an impenetrable darkness" (48).

Language is traditionally believed to transcend the body, transcend mortality, transcend the animal. Marlow's description of Kurtz's gift with words stops nothing short of describing what Derrida calls "logocentrism," the privileging of speech over writing based on its association with *real presence*, a kind of "nonexterior, nonmundane . . . originary speech itself shielded from interpretation."[36] But this passage points out that the "gift" of speech is deceiving; it is in fact a kind of fantasy as Derrida argues. Language's ability to transcend the body is called into question because of Kurtz's participation in animality. One is reminded of the way in which T. S. Eliot's "Hoo" insists upon this participation. Eliot's formal innovations literalize the impurity of language that Kurtz symbolizes. As the novel continues, Kurtz's voice is irreducibly linked to the materiality of the mouth.

Of course, the voice can function as a kind of "missing link" between substance and symbolization since it is a physical phenomenon that "produces" and enacts signification. In fact, the perverse consumption manifested in African cannibalism earlier in the text has its Western parallel in Kurtz. Upon seeing Kurtz for the first time, Marlow notes, "I saw him open his mouth wide—it gave him a weirdly voracious aspect as though he had wanted to swallow all the air, all the earth, all the men before him" (59). Kurtz's verbal prowess is thus negatively aligned with excessive orality—the infantile, instinctual, and imperialist desire to consume the other and destroy it by making it literally part of himself. Consumption, in fact, is the highest form of power over the other: when you eat something or someone, you not only eradicate the other's autonomous being, but you do so by literally subsuming it into your own corporeality. The other's ontogeny is destroyed *in order* to support your life force. There is a kind of omnipotence inherent in every act of eating which renders the eater god-like.

Kurtz's mouth reveals the extreme contradiction of human orality: the human mouth eats flesh and recites poetry, it dissolves food and discusses philosophy. For Marlow, Kurtz's "pulsating" words embody this participation in the material, even in the cannibalistic. Marlow is consumed by Kurtz's words, which issue from his devouring mouth. The visceral quality of mouths is acknowledged by Bataille in *Visions of Excess,* where he discusses the mouth as a privileged site of animality: "The mouth is the beginning or, if one prefers, the prow of animals . . . the overwhelmed individual throws back his head while frenetically stretching his neck in such a way that the mouth becomes, as much as possible, an extension of the spinal column . . . *in the position it normally occupies in the constitution of animals.*"[37] In sum, speech, Kurtz's most human quality, does not escape the animal.

But the problem with Kurtz, finally, is not that he cannot transcend animality—it is, conversely, that he indulges in it. The details of Kurtz's deviant behavior surface throughout the story and have become familiar to readers of modernist literature. Kurtz establishes himself as a god-like leader among the African tribespeople, he surrounds his hut with the shrunken heads of presumed enemies, and he takes an African mistress. Most notoriously, something causes him "to preside at certain midnight dances ending with unspeakable rites" (50). While many readers have speculated about the content of these rites—cannibalistic, perhaps sexual—it is the something *that causes* Kurtz's behavior that remains insufficiently examined by critics, and Marlow is rather straightforward in his explanation of this cause: "But the wilderness had found him out early, and had taken on him a terrible vengeance for the fantastic invasion. I think it had whispered to him *things about himself* which he did not know" (57; emphasis added).

The cause, therefore, of Kurtz's abominations issues from both his primitive surroundings and from within his own being or psyche. Žižek's work goes a long way in elaborating the "things about himself" that underpin Kurtz's pathology. Throughout *Enjoy Your Symptom,* Žižek theorizes the Lacanian "Real," which is usually glossed as "enjoyment" but which has several philosophical variants, including the Kantian Thing:

> The subject "is" only insofar as the Thing (the Kantian Thing in itself as well as the Freudian impossible-incestuous object, *das Ding*) is sacrificed, "primordially repressed." . . . This "primordial repression" introduces a fundamental imbalance in the universe: the symbolically structured universe we live in is organized around a void, an impossibility (the inaccessibility of the Thing in itself). The Lacanian notion of the split subject is to be conceived against this background: the subject can never fully "become himself," he can never fully realize himself, he only ex-sists as the void of a distance from the Thing.[38]

As Cary Wolfe and Jonathan Elmer point out, the subjectivization described by Žižek turns fundamentally on the Enlightenment "desubstantialization of the subject, its 'purification' from its substantial origin in nature, the animal, the bodily, the contingent, in what Kant calls, in *The Critique of Practical Reason,* the 'pathological.'"[39] This Thing, according to Žižek, this surplus which resists symbolization, "represents what the subject must renounce, sacrifice even, *the part in himself* that the subject must murder in order to start to live as a 'normal' member of the community" (125; emphasis added). What Kurtz has done, it seems, is spy the Kantian Thing within himself.

The wilderness acts upon Kurtz as an epistemological reminder of his own repressed animality. Marlow makes this process clearer when he laments, "I tried to break the spell, the heavy mute spell of the wilderness that seemed to draw him to its pitiless breast by the awakening of forgotten and brutal instincts, by the memory of gratified and monstrous passions" (65). Marlow speaks these words near the end of the text when he attempts to save Kurtz from one of his unspeakable midnight rituals. Kurtz is most clearly associated with animality in this climactic scene when Marlow realizes, "He can't walk—*he is crawling on all fours*—I've got him." Kurtz, like the dying African who crawls to water early in the text, is literally and figuratively lowered to an animal state. His apparently purposeful regression is reinforced when Marlow looks toward the nearest fire: "A black figure stood up, strode on long black legs, waving long black arms across the glow. It had horns—antelope horns, I think—on its head. . . . 'Do you know what you are doing?' I whispered. 'Perfectly,' he answered raising his voice for that single word; it sounded to me far off and yet loud like a hail through a speaking-trumpet" (64).

Carole Stone and Fawzia Afzal-Khan have noted that Kurtz maintains his "whiteness" as he becomes symbolically blacker in the text. They argue that "in becoming 'blacker,' he does not lose his western norms of behavior at all."[40] What is more, Kurtz seems to maintain his humanness at the same time that he descends into an animal existence, which is why his appropriation of Africanness is an imperialist fetish. Kurtz operates in the text as the collocation of the human and animal for the Western subject. He is quintessentially human—master of the word and of his world—at the same time that he is quintessentially animal—indulging in unspeakable instincts—which indicates that the two modes of being are ontologically consonant, inseparable even. Impossibly, Kurtz closes the Žižekian "void," the foundational gesture that produces subjectivity by renouncing animality, though this closing eventually kills him.

It is crucial to emphasize, however, that it is Kurtz's *identification with Africa* that occasions the surfacing of his own Thing. This process of identification marks the text's deep racialized structure, which is not mitigated by the fact that Kurtz's racial and species hybridization unsettles boundaries between black and white, human and animal. That unsettling of the white, European "human" still depends upon the racist premise that Africans embody a savage animality. The text, in a sense, "has it both ways" since it implicates the European as savage but does so by maintaining the profound animality of the African. Therefore, we might say that the heart of Conrad's tale resides in its racialized deployment of the discourse of species to trouble the contours of Western humanism as it is symbolized in Kurtz. And that troubling is narrated through Marlow's own struggle to maintain his humanist identity despite Kurtz, whose actions are "withering to one's belief in mankind" (66), a mankind that is ultimately coded as European.

The most central repression of animality in Conrad's text is perhaps the most overlooked: the ivory trade. The colonial practice of acquiring and marketing the tusks (teeth) torn from elephants' bodies also resides at the heart of Conrad's darkness. Frederick R. Karl has argued that ivory operates as an aesthetic reminder that "beauty for the few is gained with blood of the many" (128), but Karl is referring to the many humans who died in the ivory trade. Smith comes closer to acknowledging the central violence of the ivory trade when she notes that Kurtz's mistress is adorned with elephant tusks that "connect her with the victimized jungle being invaded in the company's quest for ivory" (185). Whether Conrad intended ivory to symbolize aesthetic commodification or imperialist invasion, the embodied correlative of "ivory" must not be overlooked in this case: the elephants' bodies from which the tusks issue are completely elided from the economics of the narrative. Carol Adams has theorized this kind of elision as it applies to animals who are killed for food and for their fur and leather. According to Adams, animals become "absent referents" through butchering and through linguistic renaming.[41] This transformation occurs, for instance, when a live cow is killed and renamed "beef" or more generally "meat," and the renaming "permits us to forget about the animal as an independent entity" (40), as a being which experiences its own life. In Conrad's narrative, the violence done to elephant bodies is repressed from the text, and the elephant tusks are renamed "ivory." Elephants become the absent referents of this story, yet their bodies propel the confrontation between European and African. Ironically, as I have already shown, that confrontation partly challenges the very ideology of difference between human and animal that justifies human violence against animals.

The repressed centrality of these animal bodies in the text points to the larger dynamics of commerce and imperialism that suffuse Conrad's story. Just as the elephants' bodies are raped for their teeth, African bodies are stripped of their cultural identity by imperialist conquest. Indeed, Africa's material body is invaded by the European: the very real violence against elephant bodies in the ivory trade parallels the colonialist violence done to Africans. Of course, the speciesist ideology, which justifies violence against elephants, also justifies violence against Africans, as Conrad's tale reveals. Animals, and those we animalize, are indispensable in Western ethical codes that maintain the sovereignty of the "human." This operation is precisely our culture's "place left open . . . for a noncriminal putting to death," which Derrida discusses in "Eating Well."[42] These violences surely hover amidst "the horror" that burdens Kurtz's final hour.

iii

D. H. Lawrence must also be numbered among the modernist writers who deploy the discourses of species and of race to explore the contours of the human. At times Lawrence's exploration of the species problem unsettles conventional definitions of the human, but at other times his work reinstantiates the traditional humanist subject position through violence against animals. When his investigations engage the dynamics of race, like Eliot's and Conrad's work, they illuminate the workings of the imperialist imagination. Lawrence's *The Plumed Serpent* (1926) provides a studied meditation on the discourse of animality and its relationship to consumption. Specifically, this work contains a complex species economy that maintains *and* resists the distinction between human and animal by foregrounding connections between eating and power. Lawrence represents the unspeakable confrontation with animality as Kate's fear of cannibalistic incorporation by the Mexican other, who is figured as an animal other throughout the novel. By registering this fear of the dissolution of self, Lawrence thematizes the modernist anxiety that Darwin set in motion, that we are, in short, more similar to nonhuman animals than we are different from them. In fact, the species boundary rivals the racial one in Lawrence's imagination and emerges as one of his fundamental axes of thought.

Lawrence's species ideology is particularly Nietzschian in its nostalgia for the preindustrial and precivilized man. In his earliest work, *The Birth of Tragedy*, Nietzsche outlines the polar, aesthetic categories "Apollonian" and "Dionysian," which frame his analysis. On one side of the divide, the Apollonian position is characterized by symbolism and reason or "philosophical calmness."[43] On the other side, the Dionysian partakes of "self-forgetfulness" as man is reunited with nature (26). Nietzsche's description of a Dionysian revelry is telling: "In song and dance man exhibits himself as a member of a higher community: he has forgotten how to walk and speak, and is on the point of taking a dancing flight into the air. His gestures bespeak enchantment. Even as the animals now talk, and as the earth yields milk and honey, so also something supernatural sounds forth from him" (27).

Ironically, Nietzsche figures this return to the animal as something beyond nature (supernatural). Dionysian reunification with nature seems to set men apart and above the Apollonian thinkers who "do not divine what a cadaverous-looking and ghastly aspect they present" (26). The value judgment implicit in Nietzsche's dichotomy favors the Dionysian, for Apollo breeds a deterioration that Nietzsche will name later.

The sickness that haunts *The Birth of Tragedy* is exorcised in Nietzsche's *On the Genealogy of Morals*. At the outset of his second essay, "'Guilt,' 'Bad Conscience,' and the Like," he delineates the required developmental steps that humans must have taken in order to become conscionable: "This precisely is the long story of how *responsibility* originated. The task of breeding an animal with the right to make promises evidently embraces and presupposes as a preparatory task that one first *makes* men to a certain degree necessary, uniform, like among like, regular, and consequently calculable."[44] Most important here is what brings humanity to its orderly state, the process of "morbid softening and moralization through which the animal 'man' finally learns to be ashamed of all his instincts" (67). At this point, Nietzsche has no qualms about claiming humanity as primarily animal. His placement of the word "man" in quotation marks is particularly radical, as it indicates a linguistic and cultural constructedness that separates humans from other living creatures.

Nietzsche later argues that responsibility was ushered in after a fundamental shift in human history that resulted in man's "forcible sundering from his animal past" (85). Consequently, the responsible person is the person estranged from his "own ineluctable animal instincts," which have become suppressed (92). Ultimately, then, Nietzsche opposes the civilized to a naturalized humanity that supposedly came before it. Accordingly, what modern people have embraced are "all the *unnatural* inclinations, all those aspirations to the beyond, to that which runs counter to sense, instinct, nature, animal" (95).

Lawrence explores the potential rekindling of "real animal instincts" throughout his oeuvre, but especially in *The Plumed Serpent*. The novel's opening chapter introduces animality as a compelling trope when the Irish protagonist, Kate, dares to experience the last bullfight of the season in Mexico City. She considers her own dread of the event to be justified when the bloody spectacle registers as a "half-hearted ceremonial rape."[45] To Kate's chagrin, a bull continually pushes "his sharp, flourishing horns in the horse's belly, working them up and down inside there with a sort of vague satisfaction."[46] In Kate's estimation, this display reveals more about humans than animals: she is shocked by "human cowardice and *beastliness*, a smell of blood, a nauseous whiff of bursten bowels!" (16). For Kate, the Mexican's abuse of animals reveals a lack of humanity that is metaphorized through abject corporeality, in blood and excrement. She is overcome by the animal nature of human "civilization."

By contrast, her American friend Owen delights in the scene. He insists that viewing the bullfight is viewing "Life" (16). Owen figures as the voyeuristic European primitivist who, according to Marianna Torgovnick, takes pleasure in observing the primitive with "a scientific eye."[47] Owen

is guilty of exoticism because he seeks to be enticed by otherness. Lawrence's anti-American sentiment surfaces here as Villiers is represen-
tatively "cold and abstract" (12). He is like the mechanical gadgets that
American capitalism produces. But Lawrence repeatedly figures Villiers
as "primitive" and "bird-like" (12), and thus Americans appear to embody
both the civilized *and* the ancient, the mechanistic and the natural.

While Kate is contrasted to birdlike Villiers, her own desire to become
a bull "for five minutes" (26) to seek revenge against sadistic bullfight-
ers signals another dissolution of species boundaries. Her cross-species
identification subtly but clearly registers a desire to "become-animal" in
Deleuze and Guattari's sense.[48] But anxieties about incorporation begin
to emerge alongside questions of species as this scene progresses. Kate
appears to recognize the violence inherent in Derrida's carnophallologo-
centric schema as she staunchly disapproves of her friends' enjoyment
and decides that the two Americans are veritable vultures, "picking over
the garbage of sensations, and gobbling it up like carrion birds. At the
moment, both Owen and Villiers seemed to her like carrion birds, repulsive" (27–28).

In the novel's opening chapters, then, Kate's relationship to Mexico
and Mexicans remains primarily abstracted. The bullfight causes her to
perceive a Mexican affinity with death and decay that is uncivilized and
abject. While this spectacular physicality is beastly to her, American voy-
eurism also has cannibalistic implications. Thus, both the European and
its other seem primitive at the outset of *The Plumed Serpent* because they
participate, to varying degrees, in unclean forms of consumption. The
Mexican is steeped in a violent animality and the American consumes that
exotic otherness in a voracious appropriation of "Life," or the "natural."

It is not surprising that eating is a prevalent metaphor in Lawrence's
species rubric. In "Reflections on the Death of a Porcupine" (1925), Lawrence outlines a hierarchy of power based on species lines. He insists that
"the life-species is the highest which can devour, or destroy, or subjugate
every other life-species against which it is pitted."[49] As might be expected,
Lawrence places European men at the top of this gastropolitical hierarchy,
descends through various races, and ends by classifying nonhuman animals. Such systems, which were used to justify Social Darwinism in the
late nineteenth century, stratify a certain slippage between nonwhites and
nonhuman animals.

In *The Plumed Serpent*, non-Europeans are often animalized, represented as further down on the evolutionary chain than Westerners. For

instance, when Cipriano, the Indian general who becomes Kate's husband late in the novel, joins a tea party after the bullfight, the two peruse a
collection of "Aztec things, obsidian knives, grimacing squatting idols in
black lava" (39). These pieces disturb Kate, who admits that the centerless
nature of Mexico oppresses her. Having said so, she looks into Cipriano's
"black, slanting, watchful, calculating eyes" and sees something childish
but "at the same time something obstinate, and mature, a demonish maturity, opposing her in an animal way" (40). Here the primitive, the Mexican, and the animal are all conflated in Kate's imagination.

As the novel progresses, the dark other is more clearly represented as
the animal force in Lawrence's world. For Kate, Mexico itself is the dark
antithesis of Western culture. When she looks out across the Valley of
Mexico, her impressions are unsettling: "Superficially Mexico might be
all right. . . . Until you were alone with it. And then the undertone was
like the low, angry, snarling purring of some jaguar spotted with night. . . .
And on the bright sunshine was a dark stream of an angry, impotent
blood, and the flowers seemed to have their roots in spilt blood. The spirit
of place was cruel, down-dragging, destructive" (49–50).

Mexico is metaphorized as a bloodthirsty, threatening jaguar waiting to
pounce upon Kate and presumably consume her. Even a nearby church,
the symbolic seat of charity and welcome, appears with "its barred roof
humping up like some crouching animal." The fear of consumption is
apparently all too familiar for Kate, who, as she confronts these frightening impressions, remembers why she had come to this "high plateau
of death" in the first place. Ironically, she was propelled by another kind
of death: "Over in England, in Ireland, in Europe, she had heard the *con-
summatum est* of her own spirit" (50). In Mexico, however, death and consumption are material, rather than spiritual, concerns.

Not surprisingly, Mexicans themselves are experienced as so many
creatures from Kate's perspective. Many "eat food so hot with chile it
burns holes in their insides. . . . They live in houses that a dog would be
ashamed of" (65). Some Mexican men harbor a "cold, mud-like antago-
nism as they stepped cattishly past" and are poisonous "like scorpions."
The drunks of Mexico City register even further down on Kate's chain of
being with their "faces of pure brutish evil, cold and insect-like" (76).

Mexican women fare just as poorly in Kate's assessment. They present "images of wild submissiveness, the primitive womanliness of the
world," and they are also "somewhat reptilian" with the "dark eyes of half-

created women." It is clearly the undifferentiated identity or self in these women that repels Kate, for she repeatedly notes their "queer void insolence! Something lurking, where the womanly centre should have been; lurking snake-like" (77). Ironically, Kate is frightened by the kind of consciousness she ultimately seeks in Mexico. She has fled Europe and its individuated humanism, but she cannot yet accept the "void" that she considers her primitive, animal alternative.

Kate's growing intimacy with Cipriano, her future husband, allows her to study him with a certain intensity, and she spies this same racialized animality in him:

> The movement of his hand was so odd, quick, light as he ate, so easily a movement of shooting, or of flashing a knife into the body of some adversary, and his dark-coloured lips were so helplessly savage . . . that her heart stood still. There was something undeveloped and intense in him, the intensity and the crudity of the semi-savage. She could well understand the potency of the snake upon the Aztec and Maya imagination. Something smooth, undeveloped, yet vital in this man suggested the heavy-ebbing blood of powerful reptiles, the dragon of Mexico. (67)

Once again, an emphasis on incorporation emerges here. Kate watches Cipriano eat, focusing first on his hand, which exhibits an instinctual tendency to kill, and then on his mouth and "savage" lips. In keeping with the conflation of the primitive and the animal, Kate compares Cipriano to a snake that is ready to strike. His glittering eyes threaten her just as the crouching Mexico has, and she feels "as the bird feels when the snake is watching it" (67). Rather than figuring as a rapacious predator, the bird becomes quarry in Kate's imagination as she finishes her dinner.

Lawrence's animalizing characterizations seem at first to rehearse a familiar theme: humans have a developed sense of self that other animals lack, or Europeans have a more demarcated identity that elevates them above nonwhites. But Lawrence is ambivalent about his caricatures. For instance, this seeming regression to animality in Cipriano is both threatening and precocious; his animal way is characterized as a "demonish maturity" (40). On some level, then, Cipriano is wiser than Kate; he sees through the ruse of Western individuality and spies some primal multiplicity or intersubjectivity that Kate cannot perceive.

Indeed, Lawrence's novel, like his earlier works of long fiction, troubles Western notions of individuality. As Jürgen Habermas explains, the philosophical discourse of modernity "turns centrally on the critique of subjectivistic rationalism."[50] That is, absolute self-consciousness, inherent in the "atomistic and autonomous, disengaged and disembodied" subject, is under attack in the late nineteenth and early twentieth centuries (ix). Lawrence is clearly skeptical of this Western legacy of a reason-centered identity. When juxtaposed with Kate, in fact, a character like Cipriano seems to figure outside the economy of Western individuality.

His literary resistance to a rigid notion of self allows Dolores LaChapelle to entitle her book on Lawrence *Future Primitive*. According to LaChapelle, Lawrence longs for a time beyond industrialized modernity that will once more recognize humanity's connection to nature and disallow rationalistic notions of self. In Thomas Lyon's introduction to *Future Primitive*, he notes that LaChapelle and Lawrence both long for a less fragmented subjectivity: They grieve "over the loss of place brought about by the economics of the industrial growth society. The world in which a mountain stood wild and had its full being, was trembling with sacred potential: a human being could realize that mountain, could transcend the limited sense of self through whose perceptual filters the mountain had seemed likewise separate and alone."[51]

For LaChapelle, Lawrence desires this intersubjective connectedness to the natural world since he himself was able to feel the "old ways" of animistic culture in which all natural entities contained a spiritual charge.[52] In the passage at hand, for instance, a mountain is not utterly other than a human being; they share some basic ontology. In Cipriano, then, this intersubjective awareness is animal-like and yet sophisticated. Unlike Kate, he is able to see beyond the subjectivistic rationalism that Horkheimer and Adorno call a new kind of barbarism.[53] We will see, however, that Lawrence's allegiance to individuality is not so easily relinquished as LaChapelle would have it.

The problem of the self becomes exponentially exacerbated for Kate as the novel continues, and her dilemma points out the connection between individuation and incorporation. Thinking about her fear of the "centreless" Mexicans, Kate undergoes an epiphany about human subjectivity. She recognizes her illusion about the self: "She had thought that each individual had a complete self, a complete soul, an accomplished I. And now she realised as plainly as if she had turned into a new being, that this was not so. Men and women had incomplete selves, made up of bits assembled together loosely and somewhat haphazard" (105). Kate recognizes individuality as a kind of fiction and believes the self to be multiple and fragmentary. By recognizing this multiplicity, Kate relinquishes a founding Western premise, but in doing so, she is immediately plagued by fears of incorporation, fears that echo the cannibalistic themes of T. S. Eliot's "missionary stew" and Conrad's insatiable Kurtz: "In the great seething light of the lake, with the terrible blue-ribbed mountains of Mexico beyond, she seemed *swallowed* by some grisly skeleton, in the cage of his death-anatomy. She was afraid, mystically, of the man crouching there in the bows with his smooth thighs and supple loins like a snake, and his black eyes watching" (106; emphasis added).

The loss of autonomous selfhood renders Kate susceptible to a kind of identity imperialism; if her own borders of self are not distinct and encompassing, she feels absorbed by others against her will. This absorption is almost always figured in terms of animal predation. Thus Lawrence implies that the crossing of ego boundaries is instinctual but dangerous. Indeed such crossings are particularly dangerous for Westerners who cling to Cartesian notions of identity that privilege a transparent and absolute self-consciousness.

On the other hand, Lawrence questions the possibility of intersubjectivity, of overcoming the boundaries of identity. He is particularly skeptical when the problem of selfhood is scrutinized through the lens of sexuality, one of Lawrence's recurring considerations. Kate has noticed that Ramón and Cipriano share a kind of passion that includes "the recognition of each other's eternal and abiding loneliness," and she begins to consider the passion between men and women. Then, rather than envisioning her own engulfment by another, she theorizes unbreachable selves: "Men and women should know that they cannot, absolutely, meet on earth. In the closest kiss, the dearest touch, there is the small gulf which is none the less complete. . . . They must bow and submit in reverence, to the gulf. Even though I eat the body and drink the blood of Christ, Christ is Christ and I am I, and the gulf is impassable" (252). Here Lawrence seems to posit an essential, individual identity. Even eating the "flesh of my flesh," as evidenced by the reference to consuming the body of Christ, cannot bridge the impassable gap between two persons. Only one process can bridge the gulf between selves, but in explaining this phenomenon, Lawrence waxes ambiguous. To "meet in the quick," he explains, "we must give up the assembled self, the daily I, and . . . meet unconscious in the Morning Star. . . . But without transfiguration we shall never get there"

(253). Such passages make Lawrence's ambiguity more evident. He both confirms and resists the sovereign individual: he believes and disbelieves in the melding of identities. Thus, Don Ramón's pronouncement on the indecipherability of sexual relationships reflects this paradox. He tells Kate, "in these matters, one never knows what is half way, nor where it is. A woman who just wants to be taken, and then to cling on, is a parasite. And a man who wants just to take, without giving, is a creature of prey" (271).

Lawrence follows this theory to the letter, and his conclusions have long since commanded the outrage of feminist critics. As it turns out, the parasitic engulfment of men occurs primarily at the moment of female orgasm, when "the great cat, with its spasms of voluptuousness and its lifelong lustful enjoyment of its own isolated, isolated individuality," takes without giving. According to Lawrence, women like that "played with love and intimacy as a cat with a mouse. In the end, they quickly ate up the love mouse, then trotted off into a full belly and a voluptuous sense of power" (438). Here the anxiety about selfhood translates into castration anxiety. The discourses of gender and species are mutually deployed as feminine sexuality is animalized and the woman is tritely figured as the *vagina dentata*. Thus, Kate's fear of being devoured seems displaced by Lawrence onto feminine sexuality.

When confronted with the possibility of becoming a god in the new Aztec pantheon orchestrated by Cipriano and Ramón, Kate unfailingly returns to the dilemma of self and other, of distinction and incorporation. Cipriano begins to call her by the Aztec goddess's name, "Malintzi." Since naming is always central to identity, Kate revolts against this perceived usurpation. Resisting Cipriano's proposal to become his bride, Kate insists, "You treat me as if I had no life of my own. . . . But I have." When she is unable to fully answer Cipriano's query about who gave her this life, she simply retorts, "I don't know. But I have got it. And I must live it. I can't be just swallowed up" (370).

Of course, the new gods of Mexico, Ramón and Cipriano, insist upon the centrality of consumption as homage to their power when they preside over a human sacrifice near the novel's conclusion. In an elaborate ritual, they order the execution of two men and a woman who betrayed Ramón and attempted to kill him. The scene is clearly modeled after Aztec sacrifices that attempted to slake the endless blood-thirst of the sun god, as Bataille explains in *The Accursed Share*. These sacrifices usually concluded with the consumption of human flesh. While readers might anticipate a cannibalistic end to this violent scene, Lawrence sublimates any "real" cannibalism, which comes rather as a disappointment, given the rhetoric of the novel. When Ramón says, "Give me the blood of the three, my brother Huitzilopochtli," he does not drink it himself. Instead, he chants, "Darkness, drink the blood of expiation. Sun, swallow up the blood of expiation" (381). The sacrifice exaggerates the surrender of self, the utter elision of subjectivity, which Kate seeks out and resists.

For Ramón and Cipriano, the plumed serpent, Quetzalcoatl, appears to resolve the tension that Kate cannot put to rest. Quetzalcoatl is the god of both ways: mind and body, self and loss of self, earth and sky. This god makes manifest the overlap of species, both bird and snake, and Lawrence's characters, who "become" Aztec gods in the novel, also become nonhuman animals.

In many ways, Quetzalcoatl embodies the binaries or paradoxes that primitivism itself rehearses. John Humma has noted that the eagle and snake serve "one [as] our higher, the other our lower consciousness."[54] What is perhaps most profound for this analysis is the way in which a bizarrely cross-bred animal is elevated to a spiritual level. Most animal manifestations in the novel remain only on the physical level. But the great bird-snake is the chief of gods, and such transgressing deification implies a fundamental tainting of Western abstraction. In other words, the spiritual is never purely spirit: it is always connected to the snake, to the grounded materiality of the body. One is reminded here of Lawrence's poem "Snake," in which a serpent drinking at the narrator's water trough is variously experienced as god-like and repugnant, as an inspiration and a horror.

Despite its frequently posited status as Lawrence's most ambitious failure, then, The Plumed Serpent is an unusual and complex text for the consideration of species ideology in the modernist imagination. While Lawrence appears to rely upon an outmoded, imperialistic equation of racial and animal otherness in the novel, his European and Mexican characters are depicted in a complicated ideological framework that troubles the distinction between human and animal consciousness. Moreover, Lawrence's somewhat fantastic use of the Quetzalcoatl myth places his characters in a liminal reality beyond Western individualism where animality becomes the privileged mode of being. As a result, the interrogation of rationalist humanism in The Plumed Serpent can be read as a posthumanist critique deployed through the discourse of species. Though this critique is ambivalent at times, Lawrence's use of the animal as a symbol of salvation from Western culture is exceptional because it destabilizes the West's traditional hierarchizing of human over animal as a matter of course. Thus, as the novel ends with Kate's unresolved dilemma between remaining in the consciously mythologized world of Quetzalcoatl and returning to the individuated life of the West, it seems clear that Lawrence's contradictions bespeak a refusal to choose between the spirit and body, the rational and instinctual, the human and animal.

The least that can be said is that the psychoanalysts, even Jung, did not understand, or did not want to understand. They killed becoming-animal, in the adult as in the child. They saw nothing. They see the animal as a representative of drives, as a representation of the parents. They do not see the reality of a becoming-animal, that it is affect in itself, the drive in person, and represents nothing.
—Gilles Deleuze and Félix Guattari, A Thousand Plateaus: Capitalism and Schizophrenia

3   Facing the Animal

The displacement of animality onto marginalized others operates as an attempted repression of the animality that stalks Western subjectivity in the modernist age. Indeed, the development of Freudian psychoanalysis in the early twentieth century should be recognized as a logical response to the threats of evolutionary theory. The concept of the unconscious in Freudian psychoanalysis operates as a modernist codification of the problem of animality in the human person. Freud himself hazards an explanation of humanity's rise from its animal heritage and theorizes that our repression of organicism simultaneously deanimalizes us and makes us human. Animality is consequently equated with neurosis in psychoanalytic terms since one must repress it in order to become, and remain, human. Historically, then, we might say that Darwinism releases the specter of animality for British modernists, while psychoanalysis attempts to capture and tame it. Freud offers a "cure" for animality's presence in the human psyche. In fact, modernist literature often enacts this dialectic between Darwinism and psychoanalysis, which helps to explain the centrality of the human/animal dichotomy in literature of the period.

We have seen in the previous chapter that some modernist texts project animality away from the Western subject. In contrast, other texts insist upon the inevitable return of animality for the European. Rather than deny animality by displacing it, these texts either recognize that humans and animals are ontologically similar or acknowledge the confrontation with animals as one of radical alterity that fundamentally unsettles the "human" itself. In other words, these works resist the desire to repress the Darwinian story of origins, which includes the European in its narrative.

H. G. Wells is among the first modernist writers to thematize clearly the post-Darwinian uncertainty the human subject's stability in relation to its species status.[1] While Wells's account of this confrontation is partly racialized in *The Island of Dr. Moreau,* it is most directly a study of humanity's animal nature rather than its racial nature. Though anxious, his account asserts the coincidence of human and animal and suggests that the denial of one's animal nature cannot be sustained. Through Moreau's character, Wells exposes the repression inherent in an Enlightenment project of transcendence that attempted to deanimalize the human subject. That is, the text suggests that humanity's repression of animality is a violent impossibility.

Wells specifically narrativizes the dialectic between evolution and psychoanalysis in his novel *The Croquet Player,* which depicts British socialites' inability to exorcise the organic persistence of our animal past in their psyches. This text details an inescapable contagion of the mind that issues from the ubiquitous, vestigial presence of man's evolutionary ancestors. Characterized as a haunting and as a contagion, animality in *The Croquet Player* defies the powers of repression—in a specifically psychoanalytic register—and remains as an increasingly infectious spook.

For D. H. Lawrence, the confrontation with nonhuman animals in *Birds, Beasts, and Flowers* reveals another revision of traditional definitions of the human. Lawrence exposes the "voices" of Western humanism that encourage the violent sacrifice of animality, and he catalogues the human struggle to overcome those powerful ideological forces. At times, Lawrence's poetry acknowledges the radical alterity of the animal other and deconstructs the typical humanist subject-who-knows by framing the limits of human epistemology. While the poems sometimes restabilize the traditional humanist subject position through violence against animals, Lawrence's musings are valuable because they record the tension experienced by the modernist subject about the animal's alterity and its consequent troubling of the "human."

i

While Derrida outlines a kind of transhistorical Western "carno-phallogocentrism," Slavoj Žižek helps us understand the specific construction of the Enlightenment subject in its distancing from animality, or its "desubstantialization."[2] According to Žižek, the "'official' image of the Enlightenment—the ideology of universal Reason and the progress of humanity, etc." is rooted in the Kantian version of subjectivization:

> The subject "is" only insofar as the Thing (the Kantian Thing in itself as well as the Freudian impossible-incestuous object, *das Ding*) is sacrificed, "primordially repressed". . . . This "primordial repression" introduces a fundamental imbalance in the universe: the symbolically structured universe we live in is organized around a void, an impossibility (the inaccessibility of the thing in itself). (180)

This repression of the Thing, which for our purposes is homologous to animality, constitutes the reason-driven subject of the Enlightenment, and, as Žižek explains, parallels the splitting of the Lacanian subject that renders it a barred and crossed-out subject. The "official" Enlightenment subject is one that represses its own animality or Thingness, and, because of this repression, circulates around a void. This purified notion of the human subject is profoundly threatened by Darwin's evolutionary theory, which emerges in the late nineteenth century, as we have already seen. Darwin's insistence that differences between humans and other animals are differences of degree rather than kind radically problematized the traditional humanist abjection of animality, particularly in its purified Enlightenment form.

As evidenced in the previous chapter, animality is recurrently coded in figures of ingestion and cannibalism throughout modernist literary texts. *The Island of Dr. Moreau* further corroborates this insight. The reader meets Edward Prendick, the novel's protagonist, and two other sailors shipwrecked from the *Lady Vain* as they float helplessly without provisions and without promise of rescue. Prendick describes this initial crisis in terms of hunger and thirst: "We drifted famishing, and, after our water had come to an end, tormented by an intolerable thirst, for eight days altogether."[3] Prendick and his companions find themselves bereft of the basic comforts of human society and physical sustenance: they are confronted with mere physical survival, the need to eat and drink. Their predicament immediately compromises humanity's claim to the transcendence of animal instincts as the three men agree to draw lots and determine who will be the cannibals among them and who will be the victim. Though Prendick's companions struggle with one another and roll overboard before anyone is eaten, human nature is already marked in the novel as fundamentally physical, instinctual, and even aggressive.

Cyndy Hendershot points out that Prendick, as the novel's "representative of masculine British civilization," is set apart from the other men in the raft because he resists the initial proposal of cannibalism,[4] but the text immediately undercuts Prendick's status as nonprimitive when he is picked up by Moreau and company. Moreau's assistant Montgomery gives Prendick some "scarlet stuff, iced," and Prendick notes, "It tasted like blood, and made me feel stronger" (5–6). Here Prendick's basic physical need to eat and drink is realigned with cannibalism and therefore animalized. A few lines later, Montgomery assures the weakened protagonist that some mutton is boiling and will soon be ready to eat. When the mutton is brought in, Prendick is "so excited by the appetising smell of it" that he is no longer disquieted by the puma's incessant growls from the deck (7). Wells's emphasis on the olfactory further underscores Prendick's animal needs. Cary Wolfe and Jonathan Elmer have noted that Freud, in *Civilization and its Discontents,* associates the acquisition of humanity with a decreased reliance on smell and an increased sense of sight: "Freud's fantasy of origins tells us, then, that the human animal becomes the one who essentially *sees* rather than *smells.*"[5]

Of course, as Derrida has theorized, eating animal flesh is structured as a highly civilized activity in the West, as enacting the very autonomy and civilize-ation of the European subject. But Wells's text troubles the distinction between eating the flesh of sheep and eating the flesh of people through its alignment of the carnivorous and the cannibalistic. Thus Prendick's consumption of flesh and blood indicates the coincidence of human civilization and instinctual animality. In this way, the text highlights the Law's justificatory reification of what Derrida calls in his essay "Eating Well" a "non-criminal putting to death" that is served up for dinner, a Western cultural practice that symbolically maintains the human through the destruction of animals for food (112). Wells's text takes pains to emphasize the bloody realities of British cuisine. By foregrounding Prendick's animal response to animal flesh, the text reveals the inherent contradiction of "carnivorous civilization." Within the first few pages of the novel, then, Wells

upernatural. In other words, Moreau's science is desperate to extermi-
ate animality by creating and policing the boundaries of rationalist hu-
nanism. Moreau reveals this fundamental motivation to Prendick when
he admits, "Each time I dip a living creature into the bath of burning pain,
I say: this time *I will burn out all the animal*, this time I will make a rational creature of my own" (89; emphasis added). Wells's portrait of Moreau
insists upon the constructedness of the rational Enlightenment subject by
suggesting that the transcendence of the rational human requires a cer-
ain intense and artificial technology, a burning out of the animal portion
f human nature. The process, of course, is displaced here onto Moreau's
suspecting subjects, who are animals.

This fictional program of purification depends upon the newly articu-
l theories of mutation and natural selection that were made available
lls in the late nineteenth century by theories of evolution. That is,
he idea of species mutability emerges, Wells can fashion a character
d with the final humanization of all biological creatures. Moreau
Prendick, "These creatures you have seen are animals carven and
into new shapes. To that—to the study of the plasticity of liv-
—my life has been devoted" (81). The mutability of species was
hat compromised humanity's claim to sovereignty over other
e evolution was considered scientifically sound. And Moreau
firms this dethroning of the human when he tells Prendick,
e educated. The mental structure is even less determinate
. . . . Very much indeed of what we call moral education
cial modification and perversion of instinct; pugnacity is
rageous self-sacrifice, and suppressed sexuality into re-
(82). Wells appears to draw directly from Nietzschian
passage that explains morality as a repression of in-
tlines a similar theory in *On the Genealogy of Morals*,
he process of internalization, that "all those instincts
man turned backward *against man himself*."[9]
g may be educated reveals the ideological kernel of
humanizing fantasy—a fantasy that combines pre-
nt doctrines of perfectibility with post-Darwinian
hat all creatures can be elevated beyond their
s can be finally humanized. Horkheimer and
deeply totalizing gesture when they elaborate
ghtenment reason and its connection to fas-
itarian," they explain.[10] The "official" narra-

codes the eating of flesh as an animal practice. Prendick's "civilized" status
is undercut by his desire to feed on other animals, a desire that becomes
one among several primary markers of animality in the novel.

This early troubling of Prendick's status as human is promptly mirrored in the appearance of M'Ling, Moreau's most beloved Beast Person who Prendick perceives as a misshapen black man moving with
"animal swiftness" (9). As Hendershot points out, M'Ling serves as an
obvious point of conflation between imperialist racism and Darwinian
theories of evolutionary superiority. Not yet realizing that M'Ling is one
of Moreau's animals-made-human, Prendick experiences this creature
within a psycho-mythological register:

> I had never beheld such a repulsive and extraordinary face before,
> and yet—if the contradiction is credible—I experienced at the
> same time an odd feeling that in some way I *had* already encoun-
> tered exactly the features and gestures that now amazed me. After-
> wards it occurred to me that probably I had seen him as I was lifted
> aboard, and yet that scarcely satisfied my suspicion of a previous
> acquaintance. (10)

Prendick seems to recollect M'Ling's disquieting face through an unconscious source that is chronologically anterior. In Jungian terms, M'Ling
triggers Prendick's collective unconscious. Jung maintains that archetypes or primordial images recur in dream symbolism because the mind,
like the physical body, represents a museum with "a long evolutionary
history behind it. . . . I am referring to the biological, prehistoric, and unconscious development of the mind in archaic man, whose psyche was
still close to that of the animal."[6] Prendick's vague recognition of M'Ling,
like most recognitions in the novel, says more about him than about the
Beast Man because it indicates his own evolutionary kinship with animality. This recognition is mythologized in a subtle yet instructive reference to biblical tradition when Prendick turns to view the schooner's
deck. He is astonished to see, in addition to staghounds and a huge puma
"cramped" in a small cage, "some big hutches containing a number of
rabbits, and a solitary llama . . . squeezed in a mere box of a cage. . . . The
dogs were muzzled by leather straps. The only human being on deck was
a gaunt and silent sailor at the wheel" (11). In the parable of Noah's Ark,
humans and animals are equalized by the wrath of God infused into nature and find themselves literally in the same boat. The parable implicitly

deconstructs the superiority of man over animal by insisting upon their mutual corporeal needs. The Ark is an apt allusion for the beginning of Wells's tale, which, according to Anne Simpson, calls for humankind's "deep investigations of the nature of self-awareness."[7]

M'Ling functions as the ironic precursor to Prendick's lesson on Noble's Island, which undoes humanism's fundamental species tenet, that humans are ontologically distinct from nonhuman animals. Prendick's confusion over the status of M'Ling's humanity sets the stage for his imminent tutelage. Looking toward M'Ling through the darkness, Prendick is astonished when "it" looks back with shining green eyes. "The thing came to me," notes Prendick, "as a stark inhumanity. That black figure, with its eyes of fire, struck down through all my adult thoughts and feelings, and for a moment the forgotten horrors of childhood came back to my mind" (18). For Jung, the childhood mind is more connected to the "deeper instinctive strata of the human psyche," which adults have learned to control and repress (36). This narrative moment of terror also recalls Freudian theory, which implicitly claims that the repression of one's animality must be learned because, as children, we are not repulsed by our own physicality.[8] Ultimately, then, Prendick is poised to *unlearn* one of the basic lessons of human subjectivization: to be a person one must not be an animal.

Moreau's apology for his experimental vivisections comes late in the novel, after Prendick has misunderstood the Beast People as humans who have been scientifically devolved into protoanimals. Of course, this misrecognition underscores the text's deep implications for human identity: Moreau's vivisections, which humanize animals, vividly register the inverse fear that humans already have animal qualities. This textual dialectic mirrors the double-edged nature of evolutionary theory as it was received in the late nineteenth and early twentieth centuries. That is, while much emphasis was placed on the progressive capacities of evolution for human cultures at that time, our shared heritage with other animals resulted in anxieties about regression and atavistic "leftovers" in the human person. Moreau's response to such threats is a grandiose humanizing project that aims ultimately to eradicate animality from the sentient world. And while Moreau remains captivated by his own romance, Prendick learns by the novel's end that this kind of purification is an impossible fantasy.

The deeply disturbing nature of this eventual collapse of human subjectivity is narrativized in the ninth chapter, subtitled "The Thing in the Forest." In order to escape from the shrieks of the puma being vivisected

in Moreau's enclosure, Prendick ventures out to explore his island home. He is surprised to discover what, at first, is an indistinguishable figure that "bowed its head to the water and began to drink. Then [Prendick] it was a man, going on all-fours like a beast!" (42). This "animal" (50), this "grotesque half-bestial creature" (42), will be identified the text as the Leopard Man, but in this scene, Prendick cannot its nature and struggles to comprehend the creature's true appearance. His anxieties are heightened when he stumbles rabbit with its head torn off, the most recent victim of the on all fours. The rabbit is covered with flies, its blood therefore serves as an excessive depiction of predation what Žižek would term the "life substance" (22) Wells's terminology is perhaps most notable in rates the terrifying and various ways in whi him. The creature easily coincides with the reads as that which must be primordial the split subject of Lacanian discourse the Thing metaphorizes the Subject' abjected animality. This reading dick vacillates between the cert ing him and the suspicion tha anxious imagination: "I was hand. I thought at first it silence save for the ever again there was an ec ninth chapter serve animal within, a cape from the ultimately im human sul to escape master stitu

r
hu
reasona
of rationaliza
the animal subjec

tive of the Enlightenment proposes that matter will be mastered by scientism, systematism, and rationalist empiricism. The animal represents the human subject's internal resistance to rationality and symbolic law, so Moreau, as a perverse Enlightenment "father," wants to make all creatures reasonable.

Despite Moreau's impassioned lecture on species transformation and the plasticity of forms, Prendick objects to the suffering Moreau inflicts upon his victims. At this objection, Moreau launches into a long discussion of physical pain and the need for rational man to transcend it. "So long as visible or audible pain turns you sick," he maintains, "so long as your own pains drive you . . . I tell you, *you are an animal*, thinking a little less obscurely what an animal feels" (83; emphasis added). Here the scientist emphasizes the corporeal bottom line, the moment of pain in which materiality triumphs and the mind is conquered by the flesh. This is the moment in which humanity's embodiment cannot be denied, yet denial is precisely what Moreau recommends. Moreau refuses to see that his own violent experimentation is akin to the very "animal" drives he works against. As Horkheimer and Adorno say of the animal experimenter: "It shows that because he does injury to animals, he and he alone in all creation voluntarily functions as mechanically, as blindly and automatically as the twitching limbs of the victim which the specialist knows how to turn to account" (245). Moreau continues his argument by drawing a knife and carefully inserting it into his own leg. His indifference to the blade is meant to demonstrate his transcendence of animal sensitivity to pain, which he argues can be "ground out of existence" by evolution (84). Again, Moreau aspires to epitomize the rationalist subject in his utter indifference to *matters* of the flesh: "This store men and women set on pleasure and pain, Prendick, is the mark of the beast upon them, the mark of the beast from which they came. Pain! Pain and pleasure—they are for us, only so long as we wriggle in the dust" (84–85).

At the end of Moreau's explanation, Prendick remains, to a certain degree, horrified by the humanizing experiments. He shivers at his new-found understanding of Moreau and finds himself in a "stagnant" mood. Prendick's ambivalence reflects his persistent inability to rationalize the cruel means and questionable ends of the vivisections. Throughout the text, Wells emphasizes the extreme violence Moreau resorts to and therein provides a rare fictional representation of animal suffering in medical experimentation. Moreau's rationale reinforces the text's suggestion that actual violence against animals is a displaced violence that vainly attempts to exorcise animality from the human psyche. What's more, the text also intimates, through its portrait of animal suffering, that attempts to de-animalize humanity are fundamentally violent. Before Prendick knows of Moreau's procedures, he is driven from the compound by the puma's "exquisite expression of suffering," which sounds "as if all the pain in the world had found a voice" (40). Obliquely, then, the text bears witness to the inherent violence of the humanizing process which creates Lacan's split subject, a process which forces the individual to renounce its ani-mal nature, its connection to the natural world, and its instinctual desires and to reinforce this disavowal through violence against nonhumans. As I have already noted, Žižek explains in *Enjoy Your Symptom* that La-can's subject is predicated upon the primordial repression of the Kantian Thing, which "introduces a fundamental imbalance in the universe: the symbolically structured universe we live in is organized around a void, an impossibility (the inaccessibility of the Thing in itself) . . . the subject can never fully 'become himself,' he can never fully realize himself, he only ex-sists as the void of a distance from the Thing" (181). The violence of this "compromise formation" (Žižek, 22), in which the subject becoming hu-man must disavow its animality, is literalized in the text by the scream of the puma as Moreau forces its renunciation of animal being in order to shape its "humanity."

If Moreau's experiments characterize the attempted renunciation and purification of animality, his creations also catalogue the inevitable failure of these processes. Moreau is motivated to eliminate the perpetual regres-sion of his Beast People to an animal state. He admits to Prendick that his creatures are unable to maintain their humanlike repression of ani-mal instincts, so he works harder to perfect his craft; "I have been doing better; but somehow the things drift back again, the stubborn beast flesh grows, day by day, back again" (87). Hendershot reads the "beast flesh" as Wells's codification of sexual perversion, which was often attributed to non-European natives in imperialist narratives (5). But a close reading of Moreau's continued description suggests that the beast flesh cannot be reduced to sexuality alone. Rather, it stands for a multifaceted human participation in animality. At this point, Moreau's description is a thinly veiled denunciation of human behavior:

And least satisfactory of all is something that I cannot touch, some-where—I cannot determine where—in the seat of the emotions. Cravings, instincts, desires that harm humanity, a strange hidden codes the eating of flesh as an animal practice. Prendick's "civilized" status is undercut by his desire to feed on other animals, a desire that becomes one among several primary markers of animality in the novel.

This early troubling of Prendick's status as human is promptly mirrored in the appearance of M'Ling, Moreau's most beloved Beast Person who Prendick perceives as a misshapen black man moving with "animal swiftness" (9). As Hendershot points out, M'Ling serves as an obvious point of conflation between imperialist racism and Darwinian theories of evolutionary superiority. Not yet realizing that M'Ling is one of Moreau's animals-made-human, Prendick experiences this creature within a psycho-mythological register:

> I had never beheld such a repulsive and extraordinary face before, and yet—if the contradiction is credible—I experienced at the same time an odd feeling that in some way I *had* already encountered exactly the features and gestures that now amazed me. Afterwards it occurred to me that probably I had seen him as I was lifted aboard, and yet that scarcely satisfied my suspicion of a previous acquaintance. (10)

Prendick seems to recollect M'Ling's disquieting face through an unconscious source that is chronologically anterior. In Jungian terms, M'Ling triggers Prendick's collective unconscious. Jung maintains that archetypes or primordial images recur in dream symbolism because the mind, like the physical body, represents a museum with "a long evolutionary history behind it. . . . I am referring to the biological, prehistoric, and unconscious development of the mind in archaic man, whose psyche was still close to that of the animal."[6] Prendick's vague recognition of M'Ling, like most recognitions in the novel, says more about him than about the Beast Man because it indicates his own evolutionary kinship with animality. This recognition is mythologized in a subtle yet instructive reference to biblical tradition when Prendick turns to view the schooner's deck. He is astonished to see, in addition to staghounds and a huge puma "cramped" in a small cage, "some big hutches containing a number of rabbits, and a solitary llama . . . squeezed in a mere box of a cage. . . . The dogs were muzzled by leather straps. The only human being on deck was a gaunt and silent sailor at the wheel" (11). In the parable of Noah's Ark, humans and animals are equalized by the wrath of God infused into nature and find themselves literally in the same boat. The parable implicitly deconstructs the superiority of man over animal by insisting upon their mutual corporeal needs. The Ark is an apt allusion for the beginning of Wells's tale, which, according to Anne Simpson, calls for humankind's "deep investigations of the nature of self-awareness."[7]

M'Ling functions as the ironic precursor to Prendick's lesson on Noble's Island, which undoes humanism's fundamental species tenet, that humans are ontologically distinct from nonhuman animals. Prendick's confusion over the status of M'Ling's humanity sets the stage for his immanent tutelage. Looking toward M'Ling through the darkness, Prendick is astonished when "it" looks back with shining green eyes. "The thing came to me," notes Prendick, "as a stark inhumanity. That black figure, with its eyes of fire, struck down through all my adult thoughts and feelings, and for a moment the forgotten horrors of childhood came back to my mind" (18). For Jung, the childhood mind is more connected to the "deeper instinctive strata of the human psyche," which adults have learned to control and repress (36). This narrative moment of terror also recalls Freudian theory, which implicitly claims that the repression of one's animality must be learned because, as children, we are not repulsed by our own physicality.[8] Ultimately, then, Prendick is poised to *unlearn* one of the basic lessons of human subjectivization: to be a person one must not be an animal.

Moreau's apology for his experimental vivisections comes late in the novel, after Prendick has misunderstood the Beast People as humans who have been scientifically devolved into protoanimals. Of course, this misrecognition underscores the text's deep implications for human identity: Moreau's vivisections, which humanize animals, vividly register the inverse fear that humans already have animal qualities. This textual dialectic mirrors the double-edged nature of evolutionary theory as it was received in the late nineteenth and early twentieth centuries. That is, while much emphasis was placed on the progressive capacities of evolution for human cultures at that time, our shared heritage with other animals resulted in anxieties about regression and atavistic "leftovers" in the human person. Moreau's response to such threats is a grandiose humanizing project that aims ultimately to eradicate animality from the sentient world. And while Moreau remains captivated by his own romance, Prendick learns by the novel's end that this kind of purification is an impossible fantasy.

The deeply disturbing nature of this eventual collapse of human subjectivity is narrativized in the ninth chapter, subtitled "The Thing in the Forest." In order to escape from the shrieks of the puma being vivisected in Moreau's enclosure, Prendick ventures out to explore his island home. He is surprised to discover what, at first, is an indistinguishable figure that "bowed its head to the water and began to drink. Then [Prendick] saw it was a man, going on all-fours like a beast!" (42). This "animal-man" (50), this "grotesque half-bestial creature" (42), will be identified later in the text as the Leopard Man, but in this scene, Prendick cannot decipher its nature and struggles to comprehend the creature's trans-species appearance. His anxieties are heightened when he stumbles upon a dead rabbit with its head torn off, the most recent victim of the "man" who goes on all fours. The rabbit is covered with flies, its blood scattered about, and therefore serves as an excessive depiction of predation, consumption, and what Žižek would term the "life substance" (22). In light of Žižek's work, Wells's terminology is perhaps most notable in this section. Prendick narrates the terrifying and various ways in which "the Thing" (46) pursued him. The creature easily coincides with the Kantian Thing, which Žižek reads as that which must be primordially repressed in order to produce the split subject of Lacanian discourse (Žižek, 181). Prendick's flight from the Thing metaphorizes the Subject's haunt by *das Ding*, by repressed and abjected animality. This reading is especially compelling because Prendick vacillates between the certain knowledge that the "other" is following him and the suspicion that his fears issue from within, from his own anxious imagination: "I was tormented by a faint rustling upon my right hand. I thought at first it was fancy, for whenever I stopped there was a silence save for the evening breeze in the tree-tops. Then when I went on again there was an echo to my footsteps" (47–48). This Thing in Wells's ninth chapter serves as the animal without who ignites anxiety about the animal within, and though this chapter ends with Prendick's narrow escape from the creature, the novel will demonstrate that such an escape is ultimately impossible because the animal cannot be extracted from the human subject. As Žižek maintains in reference to the subject's attempt to escape the Thing, "The problem, of course, is that this endeavor [to master the Thing] is ultimately doomed to fail since the imbalance is constitutive" (183).

Moreau's project, while ostensibly aimed at the transformation of animals, is in fact directed squarely at this constitutive imbalance in the human subject. His strident and repeated attempts to make animals reasonable represent an extreme legacy of the Enlightenment project of rationalization in its drive to purify the human subject—and even the animal subject—of all connections to the irrational, the bodily, the supernatural. In other words, Moreau's science is desperate to exterminate animality by creating and policing the boundaries of rationalist humanism. Moreau reveals this fundamental motivation to Prendick when he admits, "Each time I dip a living creature into the bath of burning pain, I say: this time *I will burn out all the animal,* this time I will make a rational creature of my own" (89; emphasis added). Wells's portrait of Moreau insists upon the constructedness of the rational Enlightenment subject by suggesting that the transcendence of the rational human requires a certain intense and artificial technology, a burning out of the animal portion of human nature. The process, of course, is displaced here onto Moreau's unsuspecting subjects, who are animals.

This fictional program of purification depends upon the newly articulated theories of mutation and natural selection that were made available to Wells in the late nineteenth century by theories of evolution. That is, once the idea of species mutability emerges, Wells can fashion a character obsessed with the final humanization of all biological creatures. Moreau informs Prendick, "These creatures you have seen are animals carven and wrought into new shapes. To that—to the study of the plasticity of living forms—my life has been devoted" (81). The mutability of species was precisely what compromised humanity's claim to sovereignty over other animals once evolution was considered scientifically sound. And Moreau implicitly confirms this dethroning of the human when he tells Prendick, "A pig may be educated. The mental structure is even less determinate than the bodily. . . . Very much indeed of what we call moral education is such an artificial modification and perversion of instinct; pugnacity is trained into courageous self-sacrifice, and suppressed sexuality into religious emotion" (82). Wells appears to draw directly from Nietzschian philosophy in this passage that explains morality as a repression of instinct. Nietzsche outlines a similar theory in *On the Genealogy of Morals,* where he discusses the process of internalization, that "all those instincts of wild, free, prowling man turned backward *against man himself.*"[9]

The notion that a pig may be educated reveals the ideological kernel of Moreau's "benevolent" humanizing fantasy—a fantasy that combines pre-Darwinian Enlightenment doctrines of perfectibility with post-Darwinian theories of mutability—that all creatures can be elevated beyond their animality, that all creatures can be finally humanized. Horkheimer and Adorno critique this sort of deeply totalizing gesture when they elaborate the repressive forces of Enlightenment reason and its connection to fascism: "Enlightenment is totalitarian," they explain.[10] The "official" narrative of the Enlightenment proposes that matter will be mastered by scientism, systematism, and rationalist empiricism. The animal represents the human subject's internal resistance to rationality and symbolic law, so Moreau, as a perverse Enlightenment "father," wants to make all creatures reasonable.

Despite Moreau's impassioned lecture on species transformation and the plasticity of forms, Prendick objects to the suffering Moreau inflicts upon his victims. At this objection, Moreau launches into a long discussion of physical pain and the need for rational man to transcend it. "So long as visible or audible pain turns you sick," he maintains, "so long as your own pains drive you . . . I tell you, *you are an animal,* thinking a little less obscurely what an animal feels" (83; emphasis added). Here the scientist emphasizes the corporeal bottom line, the moment of pain in which materiality triumphs and the mind is conquered by the flesh. This is the moment in which humanity's embodiment cannot be denied, yet denial is precisely what Moreau recommends. Moreau refuses to see that his own violent experimentation is akin to the very "animal" drives he works against. As Horkheimer and Adorno say of the animal experimenter: "It shows that because he does injury to animals, he and he alone in all creation voluntarily functions as mechanically, as blindly and automatically as the twitching limbs of the victim which the specialist knows how to turn to account" (245). Moreau continues his argument by drawing a knife and carefully inserting it into his own leg. His indifference to the blade is meant to demonstrate his transcendence of animal sensitivity to pain, which he argues can be "ground out of existence" by evolution (84). Again, Moreau aspires to epitomize the rationalist subject in his utter indifference to *matters* of the flesh: "This store men and women set on pleasure and pain, Prendick, is the mark of the beast upon them, the mark of the beast from which they came. Pain! Pain and pleasure—they are for us, only so long as we wriggle in the dust" (84–85).

At the end of Moreau's explanation, Prendick remains, to a certain degree, horrified by the humanizing experiments. He shivers at his newfound understanding of Moreau and finds himself in a "stagnant" mood. Prendick's ambivalence reflects his persistent inability to rationalize the cruel means and questionable ends of the vivisections. Throughout the text, Wells emphasizes the extreme violence Moreau resorts to and therein provides a rare fictional representation of animal suffering in medical experimentation. Moreau's rationale reinforces the text's suggestion that actual violence against animals is a displaced violence that vainly attempts to exorcise animality from the human psyche. What's more, the text also intimates, through its portrait of animal suffering, that attempts to de-animalize humanity are fundamentally violent. Before Prendick knows of Moreau's procedures, he is driven from the compound by the puma's "exquisite expression of suffering," which sounds "as if all the pain in the world had found a voice" (40). Obliquely, then, the text bears witness to the inherent violence of the humanizing process which creates Lacan's split subject, a process which forces the individual to renounce its ani-mal nature, its connection to the natural world, and its instinctual desires and to reinforce this disavowal through violence against nonhumans. As I have already noted, Žižek explains in *Enjoy Your Symptom* that La-can's subject is predicated upon the primordial repression of the Kantian Thing, which "introduces a fundamental imbalance in the universe: the symbolically structured universe we live in is organized around a void, an impossibility (the inaccessibility of the Thing in itself) . . . the subject can never fully 'become himself,' he can never fully realize himself, he only ex-sists as the void of a distance from the Thing" (181). The violence of this "compromise formation" (Žižek, 22), in which the subject becoming hu-man must disavow its animality, is literalized in the text by the scream of the puma as Moreau forces its renunciation of animal being in order to shape its "humanity."

If Moreau's experiments characterize the attempted renunciation and purification of animality, his creations also catalogue the inevitable failure of these processes. Moreau is motivated to eliminate the perpetual regres-sion of his Beast People to an animal state. He admits to Prendick that his creatures are unable to maintain their humanlike repression of ani-mal instincts, so he works harder to perfect his craft; "I have been doing better; but somehow the things drift back again, the stubborn beast flesh grows, day by day, back again" (87). Hendershot reads the "beast flesh" as Wells's codification of sexual perversion, which was often attributed to non-European natives in imperialist narratives (5). But a close reading of Moreau's continued description suggests that the beast flesh cannot be reduced to sexuality alone. Rather, it stands for a multifaceted human participation in animality. At this point, Moreau's description is a thinly veiled denunciation of human behavior:

> And least satisfactory of all is something that I cannot touch, some-
> where—I cannot determine where—in the seat of the emotions.
> Cravings, instincts, desires that harm humanity, a strange hidden

reservoir to burst suddenly and inundate the whole being of the creature with anger, hate, or fear. . . . As soon as my hand is taken from them the beast begins to creep back, begins to assert itself again. (88–89)

As Prendick discovers, the repressed beast flesh can return in many ways and requires powerful symbolic containment.

Moreau, who coincides with and *embodies* the Freudian father, or as Lacan rewrites it, the retroactively projected Name-of-the-Father, creates the Law for his Beast Folk. His prohibitive symbolic economy reads like a mock-up of the Ten Commandments as it identifies specific bestial acts that the humanized creatures must forego. The Beast Folk chant their moral code, "Not to go on all-Fours; *that* is the Law. Are we not Men? Not to eat Flesh of Fish; *that* is the Law. Are we not Men?" In addition, they are not to claw trees or chase other men, and Prendick notes how they swear the prohibition of "the maddest, most impossible and most indecent things one could well imagine" (65). These unmentionables register humanism's projected self-loathing or shame at organicism while simultaneously acknowledging the profound unknowability of animal consciousness. The Beast Folk's interrogative coda "Are we not Men?" insists upon the *instability* of human subjectivity and the concomitant need to establish and reestablish the boundaries of the human. Indeed, the Beast Folk provide a conspicuous instance of the "productive reiteration" of hegemonic norms that Judith Butler theorizes.[11] The creatures habitually gather to repeat the Law in their desperate attempt to remain human. They must constantly remind themselves of their putative humanity. Butler's work on the iterability and cultural resignification of sexed identity can be applied to the discourse of species as it operates in Wells's text. In Butler's terms, the Beast Folk speak the necessary recitation, the repeated assumption, of their identity position, "whereby 'assumption' is not a singular act or event, but, rather, an iterable practice" (108). They speak and respeak their identity; they literally rearticulate their humanity in order to maintain its integrity.

Wells continues to lay bare the precarious nature of human identity vis-à-vis the animal through Prendick's gradual demystification of the humanist version of the subject. After several months on the island, he reports becoming "habituated" to the Beast People (96). This habituation results from an uncanny resemblance between the behavior of the Beast People and Prendick's memories of human behavior. He can no longer distinguish the carriage of Moreau's bovine creature who works the launch from "some really human yokel trudging home from his mechanical labours," or the Fox-Bear Woman's "shifty face" from the faces of prostitutes he once saw in "some city by-way." Wells's mutual deployment of gender and species discourses clearly emerges here as he adds that the female creatures had an "instinctive sense of their own repulsive clumsiness" and therefore readily adopted a human regard for decorum (96).

Victorian critics have analyzed "the animal within" as a figure that is aligned with sexuality, especially feminine sexuality, in nineteenth-century literature.[12] But those analyses tend to read out animality *as such* when they treat it as primarily symbolic of human behaviors and anxieties. While animality is occasionally gendered as feminine in the text, and while masculine imperialism is clearly at issue in Moreau's attempts to create and control the "other," the novel remains irreducibly interested in the ontological boundary between human and animal. Therefore, the text's commentary on "primitive" female sexuality cannot contain its broader concern with human animality. Prendick's habituation to the Beast People signals an erosion of the symbolic abjection of animality that constitutes human identity. If humans are socialized to see animals as fundamentally other, then Prendick's socialization is wearing thin as the Beasts appear uncannily human. There appears to be a two-way trafficking of identity-deconstruction here, as Moreau's animals become partially human while Moreau and the other men seem increasingly animal. This double destabilization unmasks the unmaintainability of the species boundary. The cultural edicts of speciesism dissolve on Dr. Moreau's self-contained island, which functions as an alternative space to the *fin-de-siècle* British socius.

Prendick's habituation to Moreau's creatures serves as a precursor to his more radical moment of deconstructive clarity involving the Leopard Man. Formerly known as the Thing in the forest, the amorphous Leopard Man hunted Prendick earlier in the novel. He proves to be Moreau's most wayward creature when he is exposed as a killer and consumer of flesh. The Leopard Man has disregarded Moreau's Law and resumed his instinctual modes of behavior; he serves as a testimonial to the impossibility of Moreau's Enlightenment fantasy of producing a purely rational human specimen. When Prendick and Montgomery discover a second slain rabbit in the woods, they suspect that the Beast People are on the verge of regression and revolt. Moreau calls the Folk together and confronts the carnivorous transgression, at which time the guilty Leopard Man leaps at

Moreau. A frantic chase ensues, and the Beast People readily join the hunt for one of their own, a betrayer of the Law. In fact, the hunt allows them to indulge their "killer" instincts; the Swine-Folk squeal with excitement and the Wolf-Folk, seeing the Leopard Man run on all fours, howl with delight (106). The frenzied pursuit further unravels Moreau's humanizing project because it disregards the fifth Law: Not to chase other Men. In Freudian terms, the chase corresponds to a return of the repressed animality in the Beast People and ultimately to a similar return in the human psyche. The narrative insists upon the Leopard Man's interspecies identity at this point: "The thing was still clothed, and, at a distance, its face still seemed human, but the carriage of its four limbs was feline, and the furtive droop of its shoulder was distinctly that of a hunted animal" (106). Of course, the psychoanalytic "hunting" of animality is narrativized by Wells in *The Croquet Player*, which I will discuss subsequently in this chapter. For Prendick, the pursuit of the fugitive Leopard Man frames the novel's most pivotal recognition. Coming upon the crouched figure who stares over its shoulder at Prendick, the latter admits: "It may seem a strange contradiction in me—I cannot explain the fact—but now, seeing the creature there *in a perfectly animal attitude,* with the light gleaming in its eyes, and its imperfectly human face distorted with terror, *I realised again the fact of its humanity*" (107–108; emphasis added).

This epiphanic moment produces a surprising inversion of the traditional humanist subject position, which abjects and represses animality. In profound contrast to that abjection, Prendick's vision privileges animality as an *a priori*, necessary, and constitutive element of the human. Prendick's vision insists that the Leopard Man's animality is actually his most human quality.

Indeed, it is the Leopard Man's terror and capacity for suffering that reveal his humanity for Prendick in this scene. Moreau's Law punishes transgressors by returning them to his "House of Pain" for further rationalization. When Prendick realizes that within seconds the animal-man will be "overpowered and captured, to experience once more the horrible tortures of the enclosure," he abruptly opts for a mercy killing and shoots the creature "between his terror-struck eyes" (108). This act of mercy grows out of Prendick's awareness of the creature's terror at its imminent suffering. His identification with the Leopard Man also suggests that experiencing fear of bodily harm and of one's mortality are supremely human characteristics. In other words, being embodied, experiencing pain, having instincts and fears, these qualities mark one's humanity as profoundly as any other qualities. We are reminded of Derrida's discussion of vulnerability and inability at the heart of the living: "Mortality resides there, as the most radical means of thinking the finitude that we share with animals, the mortality that belongs to the very finitude of life."[13]

The broader implications of Prendick's privileged epiphany about the Leopard Man are almost immediately addressed in the text. The Beast People gather together after the fugitive's body is dragged away, and Prendick continues to analyze the products of Moreau's bizarre undertaking: "A strange persuasion came upon me that, save for the grossness of the line, the grotesqueness of the forms, I had here before me the whole balance of human life in miniature, the whole interplay of instinct, reason, and fate, in its simplest form" (109). Philosophical pronouncements like this one, that trouble the sanctity of humanism, characterize the remainder of the novel.

Jill Milling's analysis of science-fiction narratives involving beast-men confirms that the scientist/protagonist "who makes discoveries about the relations between humans and other animals . . . records a sense of wonder, displacement, and ambivalence resulting from these revelations."[14] Prendick's vision of humanity is permanently altered by his experience on the island. When he laments the Beast People's lost innocence at Moreau's hands, he implicitly laments humanity's denaturalization as evolved, subjectivated, rational beings. Moreau's beasts *had* been "adapted to their surroundings, and happy as living things may be. Now they stumbled in the shackles of humanity, lived in fear that never died, fretted by a law they could not understand" (109). Humanity is metaphorized as the antithesis of freedom, as a blind adherence to authority, to the Law, to the symbolic order. The human creature has lost its immanence. In these rare moments, one detects in Wells traces of a nostalgic longing to return to some originary, animal moment in history before the human emerged as fully other from its fellow creatures, before man became the "thinking animal." But for most of the novel, humanity's residual animality stalks the human and threatens its locatability.

Moreau's death at the claws of his Leopard Man confirms the futility of his project and sounds a warning to rationalist humanism that attempts to purify humanity of its animal tendencies are doomed to fail. Prendick's unsuccessful return to "civilization" echoes this defeat. Rather than feeling restored by English society, Prendick reports a "strange enhancement of the uncertainty and dread" he confronted on Moreau's island. His detailed explanation of this "delusion" warrants a sizable quotation:

I could not persuade myself that the men and women I met were not also another, still passably human, Beast People, animals half-wrought into the outward image of human souls; and that they would presently begin to revert, to show first this bestial mark and then that. . . . I see faces keen and bright, others dull or danger-ous, others unsteady, insincere; none that have the calm authority of a reasonable soul. I feel as though the animal was surging up through them. . . . [In London] I would go out into the streets to fight with my delusion, and prowling women would mew after me, furtive craving men glance jealously at me, weary pale workers go coughing by me, with tired eyes and eager paces like wounded deer dripping blood. (154–155)

At the novel's end, then, Prendick cannot reengage the basic human-ist disavowal of animality. He recognizes the undecidability of the species boundary, and there is a certain horror in that recognition. Ultimately, Prendick places himself in a liminal species category that seems more animal than human: "And it even seemed that I, too, was not a reasonable creature, but only an animal tormented with some strange disorder in its brain, that sent it to wander alone, like a sheep stricken with the gid" (156). Perhaps Prendick obliquely acknowledges the unreasonableness of Enlightenment reason here, a strange disorder in the human brain. The novel's final chapter informs us that Prendick must live as a recluse in order to maintain his sanity. He finds "hope" in an abstract sense of pro-tection that he gains from his astronomical studies, in the "eternal laws of matter" (156). Clearly, Prendick's gesture toward stability fails to recontain the anxiety released by the novel.

ii

While *The Island of Dr. Moreau* maps a blurring of species bound-aries on the physical body, *The Croquet Player* privileges the psyche as its evolutionary battlefield. The novel's narrator-protagonist, Georgie Fro-bisher, underscores the psychological nature of Wells's narrative in his opening line, "I have been talking to two very queer individuals and they have produced a peculiar disturbance *of my mind*" (emphasis added).[15] The mental disturbance of which Frobisher speaks is immediately figured as a contagion that has "infected" the croquet player despite its "fantastic and unreasonable" nature (9). Indeed, Frobisher is poised to detail the manner in which he acquired an acute disease of the mind through the recounted experiences of Dr. Finchatton. Frobisher's own confusion subtly emerges alongside these introductions when he notes that his immanent tale is "much more realistic and haunting and disturbing than any ordinary ghost story" (10). Frobisher seems to contradict himself; his story is unreasonable but realistic, fantastic but particularly disturbing. As the novel will reveal, this vacillation reflects modernism's struggle to acknowledge and control the story of human origins that Darwinism outlines.

Frobisher introduces himself in the first chapter as an expert sportsman, an archer, croquet player, and tennis devotee. Disciplined and controlled, he can "keep [his] head and temper at croquet and make a wooden ball perform like a trained animal" (11). Likening Frobisher's athletic expertise to animal training seems merely rhetorical at this juncture, indicating metaphorically his ability to subdue and control the erratic tendencies of the croquet ball. In fact, the image foreshadows the central anxiety of the novel: the *inability* to control one's animality. Wells's text will finally suggest that humans are simply trained animals, and that their training is insufficient to eradicate their deeply animal nature.

At the novel's outset, Frobisher is associated with control and a specifically class-based transcendence. The sportsman's own admission that he and his aunt "are the floating cream of humanity" (14) reinforces their distance from all things gritty, from the material detritus that gathers at the bottom of the proverbial cup. His aunt is "naturally hostile to sexual facts," and Frobisher seems unaffected by such bodily vulgarities (12–13). Moreover, Frobisher is a wealthy socialite, a man whose routine engagements consist of high culture diversions like daily tea and his aunt's social appointments. In partial contrast to Frobisher's "nerve and self-possession" (12), however, he admits to being effeminate and to having "soft hands and an ineffective will" (13). He argues, moreover, that most sporting people, who pretend to "hairiness and virility," are actually "soft" like he is (11). Gaming is not reality, Frobisher insists, and players create an imaginary realm within their "pleasant round of harmless and fruitless activities" (12).

Georgie Frobisher comes to swallow a profound dose of Darwinian reality in *The Croquet Player,* a reality that his cultivated, recreational prowess will not sufficiently tame. His original description of this psychic force, initially characterized as an evil presence or ghost, underscores his own powerlessness to subdue it: "The ghost they told me about was something . . . that began as an uneasiness and grew into a fear and became by slow degrees a spreading presence. And still it grew—in size, in power and intensity. Until it became a continual overshadowing dread. I do not like this ghost that grows and spreads, even though it does so only in the mind" (10). This "spreading presence" remains opaque in Frobisher's opening description, though its psychological quality and its contagious nature are evident.

When, in the second chapter, Frobisher recalls his encounter with Dr. Finchatton, this presence, later dubbed "the Evil" (38), is characterized as an unavoidable and ubiquitous reality that stalks its human prey. The doctor initially challenges Frobisher: "But suppose you found there were ghosts all about you. . . . 'There,' he said and waved a hand at the tranquil sea and the innocent sky" (21). Dr. Finchatton wishes to know whether Frobisher engages himself in "real thinking. About things that *pursue* and worry you and cannot be explained" (21; emphasis added). Wells's metaphor of prey and quarry aptly characterizes the precarious state of modernist subjectivity, which is stalked by the question of its own animal ontogenesis. Moreover, the ubiquitous nature of this stalker underscores its inescapable presence for Wells's characters, suggesting that the Evil issues from within rather than without. Of course, the reader soon learns that this evil force is coterminous with humanity's animal ancestry.

When Frobisher observes that Dr. Finchatton appears quite normal at first glance, he indicates a matter-of-factness about the presence of the Evil in the human person. He says of the doctor, "there was nothing about him to warn me off him. There was nothing eccentric in his manner or indeed in his general appearance" (23). Finchatton's averageness, indeed his modest good looks and his typical Englishman's dress, suggest that ordinary folk are susceptible to the Evil, though Frobisher will eventually question the doctor's mental health. In contrast to his ordinary appearance, Dr. Finchatton's tale of the "haunting" in Cainsmarsh strikes Frobisher as extraordinary. But before he recounts the remarkable tale, Dr. Finchatton describes his own difficulties within the medical profession. As a medical student he had been repulsed by dissection; he "felt too much" and "didn't like the damaged human stuff in the wards . . . it horrified me" (26). Finchatton reveals his inability to confront the non-transcendent, corporeal aspects of the human: the body, blood, death, disfiguration, and the natural decay of the human corpus. His decision to buy a small medical practice in Cainsmarsh is motivated by the desire to escape these "harsh red realities" (26). Once established in the region, he avoids newspapers because they contain war photographs, and he refuses to read books "later than Dickens" (27). This literary reference acknowledges the way in which modernist literature and Wells's own work openly thematize the "harsh red realities" inscribed in the post-Darwinian story of human identity. Wells seems to recognize that writers in the modernist era confront the species problem more squarely than earlier writers, and that their grapplings therewith unsettle the conventional tenets of humanism.

Of course, Dr. Finchatton's desperate attempt to escape these realities is met with an excess of them, which suggests in psychoanalytic terms that the more desperately one represses a "neurosis," the more violently it returns. Cainsmarsh, which is eventually revealed as the doctor's fictitious construction rather than a geographical region, functions in the text as a placeholder for the unconscious. Finchatton remarks that this region, with its lack of cultural lore, is ostensibly an improbable place for "anything you could call psychic." And yet, he muses, "It is in just such a flat, still atmosphere perhaps—translucent, gentle-coloured—that things lying below the surface, things altogether hidden in more eventful and colourful surroundings, creep on our perceptions" (29). And "creep" is the operative word in the phrase, for the text reveals that the malevolent presence in Cainsmarsh is indeed a return of repressed animality, an unleashing of what Jung has called the collective unconscious, in a specifically animal register.

But this recognition comes gradually to Finchatton, to Frobisher, and to the reader. At first, the doctor notices an unusually high suicide rate in Cainsmarsh and an abnormal incidence of "inexplicable crimes" that have no obvious motives (30). The Cainsmarsh population is especially dependent upon "opiates" and other mind-altering drugs, a dependence indicative of their attempt to control and redirect the psychological imbalances they experience. Finchatton notices his own infection by the "brooding strangeness" (30) of the place when his sleep becomes disrupted:

> I would wake up in a state of profound uneasiness, and without any physiological cause that I could trace I fell a prey to evil dreams. They were quite peculiar dreams, like none I had ever dreamt before. *They were dreams of menace, of being waylaid, stalked, and pursued and of furious struggles to defend myself,* dreams out of which I would wake shouting . . . sweating and trembling in every limb. (31; emphasis added)

As a medical doctor, Finchatton attests to the lack of a "physiological cause" for these terrifying dreams. Consequently, his troubles are catapulted into the realm of the psyche. Freud explains such psychic disruptions by suggesting that dreams function as a retrogressive link to the unconscious. In *The Interpretation of Dreams* Freud characterizes dreaming as "an example of regression to the dreamer's earliest condition, a revival of his childhood, of the instinctual impulses which dominated it and of the methods of expression which were then available to him."[16] He goes on to suggest that dreams reveal humanity's ancestral past:

> We may expect that the analysis of dreams will lead us to a knowledge of man's archaic heritage, of what is psychically innate in him. Dreams and neuroses seem to have preserved more mental antiquities than we could have imagined possible; so that psycho-analysis may claim a high place among the sciences which are concerned with the reconstruction of the earliest and most obscure periods of the beginnings of the human race. (588)

The hunting imagery in Finchatton's dream further foreshadows the imminent revelation that Cainsmarsh is an atavistic repository of the savage, animal past. Therefore, as Finchatton remains in Cainsmarsh, his unconscious mind is overstimulated, and it stalks his very subjectivity. Finchatton's "furious struggle" to defend himself in his dreams is precisely that, a desperate attempt to protect *the humanized self*—the transcendent, autonomous "I"—from its inevitable participation in the animal.

Finchatton's daytime hallucinations provide a more specific manifestation of this Darwinian intrusion on his subjectivity. He becomes "nervous and fanciful" as the unidentified stalkers in his dreams begin to take various animal forms: "I would turn convulsively under the impression that a silent hound was creeping up to attack me from behind, or I would imagine a black snake wriggling out from under the valance of an armchair" (32–33). At first, Finchatton insists to himself that these are merely hallucinations, "symptoms of relaxing mental control" (33). He begins to study his "profoundly uneasy" patients and concludes, "There was fear in the Marsh for them as for me. It was an established habitual fear. But it was not a definite fear. They feared something unknown" (34). This something, hidden beneath the surface in "Cainsmarsh," this unconscious force, is partly revealed when the doctor seeks out the counsel of Old Rawdon, one of the local vicars.

Rawdon himself appears to occupy an ambiguous position on the species grid. Dr. Finchatton is unsettled when the elderly vicar "sat down quite close to me with one long bony hand cupping his hairy ear" (37). Of course, Wells's cross-species portrait of Rawdon only parallels the explication he is poised to give Finchatton, who asks if there is something extraordinarily wrong in their part of the country. The vicar coins the moniker "The Evil" (38) in his description of Cainsmarsh's curse, a curse that causes him to fear for his reason. Folks in his district are furtive and suspicious; they are violent toward their children, and especially brutal to animals. "They beat their dogs and horses," explains the vicar, "Not regularly. By fits" (39). Apparently, the people of Cainsmarsh sense the animal "enemy" that Rawdon unveils, and they consequently displace their anxiety by brutalizing their own animals. This "enemy," according to the vicar, is no simple beast but is, rather, the collective animal ancestry of the human species, unearthed by archaeologists in Cainsmarsh, "Something colossally evil. Broken up. Scattered all over the Marsh" (40).

Vicar Rawdon voices the developing anxieties of an era in his half-mad speech to Dr. Finchatton. Graves are everywhere, he exclaims, graves of our ancestors that should be left untouched since their disturbance creates "doubts and puzzles—destroying faith" (41). In the first decades after Darwin's *Origin of Species* (1859) was published, the major debates over evolutionary theory were religious, centering on its implications for Christian theology's depiction of man as created by God *ex nihilo*. In keeping with these protestations, the vicar was "At a jump . . . denouncing Darwinism and evolution" (41). But as Rawdon's ruminations continue, they reflect the deepening of the humanist crisis in species identity that marks the early twentieth century. He begins to rant about "Giants" in a local museum who wield "murder stones" (42). Finchatton eventually understands that Rawdon refers to model dinosaurs displayed in natural history museums. Yet the vicar clearly imagines these beasts as an immanent threat to his safety. He goes on to discuss the biblical curse of Cain, and Finchatton notes that Rawdon eventually gets "the children of Cain and the cave men and the mammoths and megatheria and dinosaurs all jumbled up in the wildest confusion" (44). Rawdon's hysterical conflation of dinosaurs and men parallels the confrontation that humanism must make after Darwin, a confrontation with the interontology of the human and animal. Rawdon's diatribe recasts the most difficult "truth" of evolutionary theory, the overlap of human and animal *being*. Moreover, the novel's widespread use of infection tropes reflects modernism's anxiety about the *biological* coimplication of human and animal.

Thus Rawdon's "lunatic" rantings actually function as the Darwinian truth of Wells's text, a text that will finally insist that the human mind cannot transcend its connection to animality. Rawdon's most radical characterization of the "remote, archaic, bestial" (45) haunting in Cainsmarsh is the one that forces Dr. Finchatton to break from his narration and stare at Georgie Frobisher. Vicar Rawdon elaborates on the nature of the haunting:

It's bad enough to be haunted by Georgian ghosts, Stuart ghosts, Elizabethan ghosts, ghosts in armour and ghosts in chains. Yet anyhow, one has a sort of fellow-feeling for them. They aren't just spirits of cruelty, suspicion, and ape-like malice. But the souls of a tribe of cave men might be. . . . Grisly ghosts. . . . Yes. And yet, if cave men, why not apes? *Suppose all our ancestors rose against us! Reptiles, fish, amoebae!* (45; emphasis added)

Dr. Finchatton reports to Frobisher that upon hearing this theory he tried to laugh, but could not. Rather, he became "more saturated with terror" (45) than he had been prior to his visit with the vicar. Rawdon's suggestion is indeed a powerful one that marshals the vast history of species evolution to threaten the sovereignty of humanism. It implies that Cainsmarsh (read the unconscious) is saturated with animality. In fact, the notion that our ancestral amoebae haunt us implies an inevitable, molecular instantiation of the animal within human bodies that clearly evokes terror. Deleuze and Guattari would reference this imagery as a "becoming-animal which always involves a pack, a band, a population, a peopling, in short, a multiplicity" (239). The image of an irreducible multiplicity— our ancestral amoebae, for instance—is for Deleuze and Guattari an animal, unconscious, libidinal image that psychoanalysis wants to reduce and control because it threatens the sanctity of the individuated subject. When Dr. Finchatton admits that his medical training predisposes him to diagnose the problem as a "virus in the air or the water or the soil" (53), he reissues the equation of animality with multiplicity and with materiality. He determines not to drink water or food which has not been boiled or well-cooked.

The lesson of Wells's tale, of course, is that the material invariably infuses the psychological. Vicar Rawdon evokes the biblical metaphor "ashes to ashes" when he explains how the archaeologists' digs result in infection: "They turn up the soil, they strip things bare, and we breathe the dust of long-dead men" (43). Thus, it is as bodies, as physical animals who require oxygen to function, that the people of Cainsmarsh are infected. They inhale particles of the already-dead, particles that are emblematic of their own mortality. In the vicar's eyes, these inhalations reactivate the animal being that resides as evolutionary residue in the human psyche. Corporeality is thus understood as a weakness and a curse that activates degraded mental propensities. In keeping with the Judeo-Christian philosophical tradition that values transcendence over the corruptible and animal body, the dust of materiality taints the spirit and animalizes the mind.

Returning home from his terrifying encounter with the vicar, Finchatton experiences his own version of atavism. He sees visions everywhere along the roadside and once at home becomes drunk. Feeling compelled to confront the land itself, he flings open his door: "There crouched the marshes under the moonlight and the long low mists seemed to have stayed their drifting at the slam of the door against the wall. As if they paused to listen. And over it all was something, a malignant presence such as I had never apprehended before" (46–47). Forcing himself to brave this confrontation, the doctor tries to speak out against the Evil of Cainsmarsh, "I forget what I said. Maybe I myself went far enough back to the Stone Age to make mere inarticulate sounds. But the purport was defiance—of every evil legacy the past has left for man" (47). Like Dr. Moreau, Finchatton cannot accept the human connection to animality. In this moment, the doctor's inability to remain linguistically human is ironically emphasized as he tries to speak out against his animal ancestry. In fact, Finchatton reverts to an imagined prelinguistic past, before the organization of language, when protohumans—as animals or "cave men"—expelled "mere inarticulate sounds." His defiance against humanity's animal legacy is profoundly and satirically mitigated by his own barbaric yawp.

The text continues to dwarf the stature of contemporary human civilization in contrast to its evolutionary past. Still determined to comprehend the nature of the Cainsmarsh haunting, Dr. Finchatton visits the local museum that vicar Rawdon mentions and seeks out its archaeologist in residence. This scientist proudly exhibits the skull and remains of a "Neanderthaler," which he calls the museum's "special glory." Finchatton is immediately unsettled by this "louring beetle-browed skull, that still seemed to scowl from its empty sockets" (58). This animal/human gaze problematizes the doctor's own subjectivity and resonates with Lippit's claim that the "locus of animality itself functions as a cut that lacerates the discourse of the subject."[17] After the doctor "marked the snarling grin of its upper jaw and the shadowy vitality that still lurked in the caverns whence its eyes had once glared upon the world," he turns in astonishment to the archaeologist and exclaims, "That in our blood!" (59). Finchatton confronts what we now call the shared genetic code between humans and their primate ancestors. As Darwin's findings indicate, the genetic mutations of other animals eventually produced humans, and their biological essence still runs in our veins. More significant to Wells's novel, Finchatton's humanist worldview collapses when the scientist describes the prehuman world. Indeed, the historical primacy of creatures like the Neanderthaler reduces human history to a mere insignificance:

> His sort had slouched and snarled over the marshes for a hundred times the length of all recorded history. In comparison with *his* overlordship our later human rule was a thing of yesterday. Millions of these brutish lives had come and passed, leaving fragments, implements, stones they had chipped or reddened by their fires, bones they had gnawed. Not a pebble in the marsh, not an inch of ground, their feet had not pressed or their hands gripped a myriad times. (59)

Wells again underscores the ubiquitous nature of this ancestral specter. Just as Vicar Rawdon's amoebae image suggests a teeming multiplicity, so too the archaeologist's description insists that humanity's animal ancestors saturate the earth. The scientist continues to trouble the sanctity of the human by suggesting that these creatures left not only bones but spirits as well, which haunt the earth. And while the scientist ostensibly dismisses this possibility with a chuckle, the novel does raise the question of animal consciousness through such suggestions. The scientist's "teasing" reveals modernism's anxiety about the deconstruction of the human person traditionally viewed as the only creature with a soul.

The archaeologist's full explanation of the Cainsmarsh haunting, which explains changes in the perception of time, encapsulates one of the more profound ideological shifts of the modernist age. In *The Culture of Time and Space*, Stephen Kern outlines the late-nineteenth-century scientific arguments over the age of the earth in his chapter entitled "The Past." Kern explains that these arguments were eventually settled in 1903 by the discovery that radium salts release heat, but that the subsequent debates only emphasized the fact that on an earth that is hundreds of millions of years old, "the history of man came to appear increasingly as a parenthesis of infinitesimal brevity."[18] Prior to these scientific discoveries, the biblical past of a few thousand years had supported an anthropocentric view of the universe in Western metaphysics. In contrast, new scientific calculations of the past forever changed the privileged status of the human. Kern also briefly notes that Darwin and other thinkers of his time like Marx and Hegel "shared the idea that philosophies, nations, social systems, or living forms become what they are as a result of progressive transformations in time, that any present form contains vestiges of all that has gone before" (51). Therefore Western humanism is not only attenuated by its connection to the animal world at this time, it has also lost its claim to temporal privilege in the grandest of metanarratives.

For Wells's archaeologist, these newfound perceptions of time, both past and future, have caused the Cainsmarsh disease. He explains to Finchatton that a century earlier, men mostly "lived in the present" since they "knew nothing of the remote real past." In fact, reminders of man's evolutionary heritage—like the prized skull—were buried and forgotten, so men "lived in a magic sphere and we felt taken care of and safe" (63). Of course, scientific discoveries shattered these illusions of safety by revealing humanity's ancient lineage in a "savage" and seemingly limitless past. The scientist explains:

> We have broken the frame of the present and the past, the long black past of fear and hate that our grandfathers never knew of, never suspected, is pouring back upon us. And the future opens like a gulf to swallow us up. The animal fears again and the animal rages again and the old faiths no longer restrain it. The cave man, the ancestral ape, the ancestral brute, have returned. (64)

The scientist's impassioned speech implies that a post-Darwinian knowledge of human ancestry causes previously unearthed or repressed instincts to surge up from a collective unconscious. He impresses upon Dr. Finchatton that this savagery is "a mental thing and it had to be fought out in the mind" (64). Of course, as Kern explains, Darwin and Freud share a basic ideological assumption that remnants of the past shape the future, whether individually or as a species (42). As we have already noted, Freud suggests that the unconscious harbors traces of humanity's ancient past, and he argues that "organic repression" acts as the human-izing force that separates us from our animal instincts. What we find in this novel, then, is a dialectical tension between Darwinism and psycho-analysis that frames the very organic realities of the animal problem as primarily mental concerns. This displacement resonates with Deleuze and Guattari's critique of psychoanalysis that, they claim, names and frames neurotic animality within the Oedipal scenario in an attempt to control the uncontrollable.

The museum archaeologist hopes Finchatton will be able to "broaden his mind" to include the vast reaches of the past "where the cave man was as present as the daily paper and a thousand years ahead was on the door-step" (65). If the doctor cannot adjust mentally to this reorganization of time, though, the scientist recommends a psychotherapist named Dr. Nor-bert to Finchatton. After returning home and discovering a dog "battered to a pulp," Finchatton finds himself in a "state of horror, at nature, at the deep fountains of cruelty in the human make-up" (67). In short measure, according to his story, Finchatton seeks out the counsel of Dr. Norbert.

Dr. Norbert, or as the chapter title dubs him, "The Intolerable Psy-chiatrist," enters the scene just as Georgie Frobisher is becoming infected with the Evil through Finchatton's narrative. The croquet player admits, the "ancestral skull, lurking unseen at first in the background, had slowly become visible . . . ! It was like something being lit up behind a transpar-ency" (80–81). In Frobisher's imagination, the skull takes on skin and lips and ghoulish eyes that stare out from its sockets. "The cave man," he reports, "was becoming more and more plainly a living presence as the story germinated in my mind" (81). Thus the croquet player's own animal nature surges up from his unconscious. On the following day, Frobisher and Dr. Norbert are left alone since Dr. Finchatton is not well enough, mentally, to join them. At this juncture, the psychotherapist reveals that Cainsmarsh is a fictive construction of Finchatton's unstable mind created in order to control and mitigate his neurosis. Of course, the fact that the Evil does not reside in some geospatial location, the fact that it cannot be contained in a particular region, only magnifies its threat. These animal phantoms *are* ubiquitous because they exist in the mind. Wells's phantas-matic device serves to problematize the traditional division between mind and matter: if the animal is manifested through our unconscious, then our unconscious mind is animal. No matter how subterranean the un-conscious is considered to be, its centrality to the human psyche is clear. Thus, human *logos* is partly "contaminated" by the animal. Dr. Norbert confirms the radical nature of this implication when he rails against, "A sickness in the very grounds of our lives" (85). Norbert's phrase indicates how profound the crisis was which humanism underwent after evolutionary theory was popularized and generally accepted as accurate. The very grounds, the very foundations of humanist identity were plagued with the return of the animal.

Indeed, Dr. Norbert's agitated explanation of this psychic disruption should be remarked as the most overt and perhaps the most courageous passage in modernist literature that confronts the animal problem for humanism at that time:

> Man is still what he was. Invincibly bestial, envious, malicious, greedy. Man, Sir, unmasked and disillusioned, is the same fearing, snarling, fighting beast he was a hundred thousand years ago. These are no metaphors, Sir. What I tell you is the monstrous reality. . . . Any archaeologist will tell you as much; modern man has no better skull, no better brain. Just a cave man, more or less trained. There has been no real change, no real escape. Civilization, progress, all *that*, we are discovering, was a delusion. (89)

Norbert expresses a central anxiety of the modernist age that stems from the unmasking of man as a member of the larger animal community and from the recognition that "progress" may only represent a new form of "blind domination" (Horkheimer and Adorno, xvi). His insistence that these discoveries about humanity are "no metaphors" is especially interesting for literary studies since literature is rife with metaphorical comparisons and metamorphical exchanges between humans and animals. But such metaphors, Norbert implies, do not intend a primary ontological symmetry between their terms of comparison and thus remain systems of substitution that do not trouble the fundamental divide between animal and human. In contrast, Darwinism insists upon a demetaphorizing of the overlap between human and animal ontogeny. Consequently, the human/animal comparison so long hierarchized in Western philosophy and literature is fundamentally changed by theories of evolution. The logic of the human/animal metaphor is altered: one can no longer say with the same force that humans are like animals because humans *are* animals.

Dr. Norbert's characterization of the return of animality parallels a certain democracy of infection upon which the novel insists. The psychotherapist describes a worldwide rupture of animality in the human psyche, "A new plague—of the soul. A distress of the mind that has long lurked in odd corners of the mind, an endemic disorder, rising suddenly and spreading into a world epidemic" (86). The novel itself recapitulates a class-defying, democratic version of this story when it insists upon Frobisher's infection alongside the less-sophisticated people of Cainsmarsh. Of course, the fact that Dr. Norbert himself has battled the Evil indicates its inevitable presence even among those trained to repress it.

This democracy of animality is notable in the context of other modernist writers who, as chapter 2 describes, displace the animal onto racialized and sexualized groups. For T. S. Eliot and Joseph Conrad, for instance, such disavowal has the effect of deanimalizing the white European subject and therefore maintaining its claim to imperialist privilege. But Wells's novel refuses the scapegoating of a marginalized group and dramatically indicts the human species—or at least the English—as a whole. There is an almost courageous confrontation of the animal problem in Wells, a confrontation that acts as a leveling force for human communities. In this text, as in *The Island of Dr. Moreau,* the European is forced to acknowledge its own humanity as connected to the animal. In this way, Wells disallows the construction of imperialist privilege through the discourse of species.

Indeed, the novel vigorously mocks psychoanalysis and its inability to repress the animal, "the pursuing brute who never desists," within every human psyche (91). When Frobisher inquires about a cure, Dr. Norbert elaborates his theory of "rational insensitiveness" (72). Summoning the powers of reason and repression, Dr. Norbert instructs Frobisher, "Do as I have done and shape your mind to a new scale. . . . We have to bind a harder, stronger civilization like steel about the world. We have to make such a mental effort as the stars have never witnessed yet. Arise, O Mind of Man! . . . Or be for ever defeated" (92). The repressive philosophy of psychoanalysis in relation to the modernist animal is reflected in Norbert's invocation of the human mind. Reason, he asserts, in all its steely fortitude, can extinguish humanity's own animality. This rationalization is akin to the violent process identified by Horkheimer and Adorno in the *Dialectic of Enlightenment,* the process by which reason acts as a repressive and leveling totality.

Norbert's call to rationalism and the repression of animal instincts is immediately compromised by Frobisher's remark that the psychotherapist was now "fairly raving. There was even a touch of froth on his lips. He paced up and down and talked on and on, in a fine frenzy" (92). Dr. Norbert's attempt to suture animality within a reason-driven mind only reinstantiates his animal behavior, his own "bow-wowing" at Frobisher (94). Consequently, when he warns Frobisher that "There will be no choice before a human being but to be either a driven animal or a stern devotee to that true civilization, that disciplined civilization, that has never yet been achieved" (94–95), the reader sees through this putative choice. Wells makes it clear that being a staunch rationalist equals being a driven animal. The novel implies that rationalist psychoanalysis not only fails to repress animality, but that it actually enacts a form of animality. Repression itself is accused of being uncivilized. Ultimately, the novel insists that there is no escape from one's animal nature, which is violent and menacing.

The croquet player confirms this inevitable contagion of the human in the final pages of the novel. He admits that the two doctors have managed to "hypnotize" him and that he is unable to detach himself from the story (95). Wells's reference to hypnosis further indicts the repressive mantle of Freudianism. In *Electric Animal*, Lippit carefully outlines Freud's early interest in hypnosis and theories of animal magnetism that influenced his ideas about transference. Though Freud eventually disavows his work on hypnosis, Lippit argues that the "communicative powers of animal magnetism . . . can be said to lie at the origin of psychoanalysis" (101). And if psychoanalysis carries this Derridean trace of animality, its later efforts to exorcise the animal enact an attempted disavowal of its own deep ideology.

Even though he has avoided the doctors since Norbert's raving episode, Frobisher laments, "Yet all the same the mischief had been started in me *and it grows.* In those two brief mornings, I got myself infected, fool that I was to listen to them! And now the infection is working in me" (96; emphasis added). The reader knows, therefore, that despite his last dismissal of Dr. Norbert in the name of a croquet round, Frobisher *remains* contaminated by the Evil. Thus critics like William J. Scheick—who contends that Wells challenges the reader to participate in the mind of Man—miss the point that Wells's story reveals the therapeutic method as impossible and thus undermines the curative hope.[19] The novel's end signals the increasingly infectious haunting of Western subjectivity by its own unearthed, phantasmatic animality.

iii

Sandra Gilbert, in her careful study of Lawrence's poetry *Acts of Attention*, observes that Lawrence's poems in *Birds, Beasts, and Flowers* fail when they become "polemical essays, almost mechanical impositions of ideas on their subjects."[20] Specifically, the use of animals to elaborate some human tendency or political theory leaves the poetry stiff and forced. In "Bibbles," for instance, Lawrence's antidemocratic strivings spoil the poem's rendering of his dog. These observations implicitly explain the centrality of poems like "Snake" and "Fish" in critical exegeses of the collection. That is, when Lawrence uses humanity as a poem's ultimate reference point, the poetry usually becomes symbolic and trite. In a poem like "Fish," however, Lawrence resists anthropomorphic symbolism as he confronts the alterity of the animal other. The struggle to resist human ways of codifying the animal is thematized in the much-anthologized poem, "Snake." It is worth noting here that the more obvious sexual interpretations of the snake and fish poems as part and parcel of Lawrence's phallic and semen imagery seem thin in comparison to a more philosophical reading of the poems in their engagement with questions of animals and animality. In fact, I will argue in chapter 4 that Lawrence's recurrent reliance on sexuality is actually one particularly important current in his larger project of recuperating a kind of animal consciousness or being in the twentieth-century subject. That is, Lawrence's emphasis on the sexual should not be understood as his ultimate philosophical focus, but rather as one step in a broader recuperation of animality. Reading these two poems in terms of the animal, rather than the sexual, begins to move us toward this broader understanding of Lawrence's ideology.

The well-known poem, "Snake," opens with a swift inversion of the human/animal binary since Lawrence immediately places himself/the narrator in a secondary position to the snake:

A snake came to my water-trough
On a hot, hot day, and I in pyjamas for the heat,
To drink there.

In the deep, strange-scented shade of the great dark
    carob tree
I came down the steps with my pitcher

And must wait, must stand and wait, for there he was
    at the trough before me.[21]

Lawrence emphasizes the inferiority of his narrator's position through repetition: he must wait, must stand and wait. The snake, he explains, came *before him*. This theme of animals' evolutionary primogeniture, so to speak, is a recurring one in the collection. Animals have something over Lawrence, and over humanity; they came first and thus have a kind of originary knowledge that the latter-day human species lacks. This view of the animal displaces, almost marginalizes, the human in Lawrence's poems. It also provides a certain relief from the burden of superiority that humans bear in traditional Western species hierarchies. After describing the snake as it drinks without forcing metaphoric gestures, Lawrence affirms once again the momentary and evolutionary primacy of the snake: "Someone was before me at my water-trough, / And I, like a second-comer, waiting."

Just when human supremacy seems diminished and the snake's being exalted, Lawrence unsettles the reversal of values with a psychological intrusion which reasserts humanism's traditional speciesist injunction: "The voice of my education said to me / He must be killed, . . . And voices in me said, If you were a man / You would take a stick and break him now, and finish / him off." These are the internalized "voices" of what Derrida calls the sacrificial structure of Western humanism, the carnophallogocentric symbolic order, which defines subjectivity—especially white male subjectivity—in sacrificial relationship to otherness. Lawrence's description reduces Derrida's schema to its essential form: to be a man, you must kill the animal.

"But," replies the narrator to this call of the Big Other, "must I confess how I liked him, / How glad I was he had come like a guest in quiet, to / drink at my water-trough." A close reading of the poem reveals that the narrator's ambivalence toward the reptile is initiated by the voices of his education. Moreover, fear itself seems to issue from these same voices. At the poem's beginning, the narrator is only watchful and transfixed. The first mention of fear comes in response to those humanist injunctions: "Was it cowardice, that I dared not kill him? / Was it perversity, that I longed to talk to him? / Was it humility, to feel so honoured? / I felt so honoured. / And yet those voices: / *If you were not afraid, you would kill him!* / And truly I was afraid, I was most afraid." Accusations of cowardice incite the narrator's dread. The poem suddenly translates the confrontation between man and animal into the realm of fear and reverence. The text constructs a kind of religious subject-position in response to the snake.

The narrator's fear becomes loathing, despite—or perhaps because of—his observation that the snake "looked around like a god." As the creature slowly withdraws into the earth, "A sort of horror, a sort of protest against his with- / drawing into that horrid black hole" takes hold of the speaker. Surrendering to the precepts of humanism, he throws a log toward the snake, who convulses in "an undignified haste" and is gone:

> And immediately I regretted it.
> I thought how paltry, how vulgar, what a mean act!
> I despised myself and the voices of my accursed
>   human education.

> . . . .

> For he seemed to me again like a king,
> Like a king in exile, uncrowned in the underworld,
> Now due to be crowned again.

> And so, I missed my chance with one of the lords
> Of life.
> And I have something to expiate:
> A pettiness.

The central lesson of Lawrence's poem resides in the narrator's inability to act outside of the "accursed" voices of humanism, which are paltry in their unilateral abjection of the animal. Because he tritely enacts a small-minded, violent gesture toward the snake, the narrator despises himself. Indeed, he has diminished his own ability to experience and somehow be enlightened by "one of the lords of life." The poem ultimately implies that the Western tendency to reject and destroy the animal in turn impoverishes humanity's own animality. Lawrence would have understood this disavowal as the impoverishment of humanity's "blood-consciousness."

Christopher Pollnitz explains how Lawrence's formulation of blood-consciousness stemmed from his reading of J. G. Frazer's anthropology, especially *Golden Bough* and *Totemism and Exogamy*.[22] In a 1915 letter to Bertrand Russell, Lawrence explains the dualism between mental consciousness and blood-consciousness: "One lives, knows, and has one's being in the blood, without any reference to nerves and brain. This is one half of life, belonging to the darkness. And the tragedy of this our life, and of your life, is that the mental and nerve consciousness exerts a tyranny over the blood-consciousness . . . and is engaged in the destruction of your blood-being or blood-consciousness" (qtd. in Pollnitz, 11). It is precisely this tyranny or interference of the blood-being by the mental life that Lawrence narrates in "Snake." Lawrence goes on in his letter to insist that all creatures and plants possess this blood awareness, and that the origin of the animal totem in tribal societies results from the ancient, shared being of humans and animals. Pollnitz rightly observes that the poems of *Birds, Beasts, and Flowers,* therefore, occupy "a privileged place as touchstones of what blood-consciousness consists of" (13). Nonhuman animals, for Lawrence, possess the intuition or primal awareness that he finds lacking in his own species.

At the outset of "Fish," Lawrence attempts a description of fishness, of the being of fishes, with a clear, though subtle, envy:

Fish, oh Fish
So little matters!

Whether the waters rise and cover the earth
Or whether the waters wilt in the hollow places,
All one to you.

Aqueous, subaqueous,
Submerged
And wave-thrilled.

As the waters roll
Roll you.
The waters wash,
You wash in oneness
And never emerge.[23]

Lawrence describes fish being as oneness, or as Georges Bataille puts it in *Theory of Religion*, "immediacy or immanence."[24] Fish have a privileged experience of immanence since their milieu is contiguous, ubiquitous water. Indeed, one is tempted to suspect that Bataille had Lawrence's poem in hand when he formulated his reductionist definition of animal ontology: "every animal is *in the world like water in water*."[25] Certainly, this is the theory with which Lawrence's poem initially describes the fish: "As the waters roll / Roll you."

Fish have no sense of self, no differentiated consciousness; indeed, they have no kind of knowledge in the metaphysical sense according to the poem. Lawrence describes their emancipation from the prison house of abstraction: "Never know, / Never grasp. / Your life a sluice of sensation along your sides, / a flush at the flails of your fins, down the whorl of your / tail." Lawrence's recurring appeal to the body, to primordial, animal ways of being, and his often contradictory rejection of sexuality, find a special convergence in the fish:

> You lie only with the water;
> One touch.
>
> No fingers, no hands and feet, no lips;
> No tender muzzles,
> No wistful bellies,
> No loins of desire—
> None.
>
> . . . . .
>
> Admitted, they swarm in companies,
> Fishes.
> They drive in shoals.
> But soundless, and out of contact.
>
> They exchange no word, no spasm, not even anger.
> Not one touch.
> Many suspended together, forever apart,
> Each one alone with the waters, upon one wave with
>   the rest.

Thus, being "wave-thrilled" represents an archaic form of being, free from self-consciousness and from contact with the other; the thrill issues from that freedom in isolation. The fish is literally "In the element, / No more." There is no subject/object awareness for this creature. He experiences no separation from the "wave-mother" since the water flows around and through him (Lawrence makes clear the maleness of the fish who "ejects his sperm" into the water).

Roughly the first half of the poem, then, is a meditation on the ontology of fishes that emphasizes their unconscious, vitalistic mode of being in contrast to self-conscious and intersubjective humanity: "To be a fish! / So utterly without misgiving / To be a fish / In the waters." As in the poem "Snake," Lawrence emphasizes the evolutionary primacy of the animal other, and here he most clearly values the firstness of fish being: "Loveless, and so lively! / Born before God was love, / Or life knew loving. / Beautifully beforehand with it all." It is at this halfway mark, however, that the poem undergoes a radical shift; its second half presents a critique of itself, particularly of its ecstatic meditation on being a fish.

At this point the narrator begins to reflect upon the process of describing and naming nonhuman animals. Interestingly, the narrator suggests that understanding a water-serpent comes easily, and one is reminded again of the kingly snake who looks around like a god at Lawrence's water-trough. The stanza that follows this observation masks the poem's fundamental shift with its first word, "But":

But sitting in a boat on the Zeller lake
And watching the fishes in the breathing waters
Lift and swim and go their way—

I said to my heart, *who are these?*
And my heart couldn't own them.

This admission marks the first of many descriptions in the poem that name the limits of human epistemology. Lawrence takes pains to insist that the human mind is incapable of comprehending the fish. In order to emphasize this point, Lawrence inserts the poem's most anthropomorphic metaphor:

A slim young pike, with smart fins
And a grey-striped suit, a young cub of a pike
Slouching along away below, half out of sight,
Like a lout on an obscure pavement.

Aha, there's somebody in the know!
But watching closer
That motionless deadly motion,
That unnatural barrel body, that long ghoul nose . . .
I left off hailing him.
(Emphasis added)

Rather than contrast humans and fishes, this moment in the poem implies a similarity. Like the fish who can never know, never grasp, humans themselves can never fully grasp fishness. This epistemological limit, this inevitable lack of human knowledge becomes the poem's second major consideration. Lawrence writes, "I left off hailing him," and that is precisely what the poem does from this point forward. While the work's second half contains a few physical descriptions of the fish, it does not attempt "to be a fish" any longer, to inhabit fish ontology through the poetic imagination.

Rather, the poem insists upon the radical alterity of the fish and elaborates the narrator's profound inability to comprehend its experience. In simple yet solemn language, Lawrence writes the limits of the human intellect in its relentless drive to divine and name the animal other:

I had made a mistake, I didn't know him,
This grey, monotonous soul in the water,
This intense individual in shadow,
Fish-alive.

I didn't know his God,
I didn't know his God.

Which is perhaps the last admission that life has to
    wring out of us.
. . . .

And I said to my heart, *there are limits*
To you, my heart;
And to the one God.
Fish are beyond me.

Lawrence acknowledges the difficulty with which this admission of limitations comes to the narrator/himself, and to the larger discourses of humanism. For the Western rationalist subject to name its intellectual limit requires a relinquishing of mastery and autonomy. Lawrence's poem acknowledges that, for humanity, the subjectivity of the animal other is ultimately unknowable. Pollnitz has noted the poem's ideology of otherness: "A subject's furthest knowledge of another is that its knowledge is incomplete, that the other has a separate and numinous opening on to the unknown" (15).

This admission of epistemological limitation destabilizes the traditional humanist subject position in which human supersedes animal as a matter of course. In fact, the poem implicitly unearths and undermines the Genesis creation myth that narrates God's own appointment of man as controlling master of nature and of nonhuman animals. The fish "was born in front of my sunrise, / Before my day," notes the narrator. After hooking the fish and forcing it from its water-being, the narrator anticipates the creature's immanent death that he is causing and replies, "And my heart accused itself / Thinking: *I am not the measure of creation. / This is beyond me, this fish. / His God stands outside my God.*" The radical otherness of the fish is underscored by the hyperbolic suggestion that humans and fish are created by two wholly divergent forces, two different Gods. Their worlds do not overlap in Lawrence's cosmology. In contrast to the Judeo-Christian portrait of man as steward and cocreator of the universe, Lawrence's narrator insists, *I am not the measure of creation*. The poem undermines Western hu(man)ity's conventional vision of itself as preeminent among earthly creatures.

Though seldom noted by critics, "Fish" offers a rare poetic indictment of man's sacrificial relationship to nonhuman animals. The narrator's "heart accused itself" as he watches the fish die: "He outstarts me. / And I, a many-fingered horror of daylight to him, / Have made him die." The poetic situation suggests that the recognition of one's epistemological limitations parallels the recognition that one should refrain from destroying that which one cannot know. Deborah Slicer has argued that animal rights philosophy must move beyond the according of value to nonhumans based on their similarities to humans and begin to theorize the importance of alterity. She suggests, "There is no reason why animals' differences, independence, indifference cannot be grounds for caring, for relationships characterized by such ethically significant attitudes as respect, gratitude, compassion, fellow or sisterly feeling, and wonder."[26] Lawrence's poem moves in the direction of Slicer's theory since it regrets the sacrifice of the radically other.

　　The poem ends with the complex image of Jesus as fish: "In the beginning / Jesus was called The Fish. . . . / And in the end." Sandra Gilbert suggests that Jesus as fish represents immortality and *being* that is unencumbered by thought (172). Jesus certainly parallels the fish in Lawrence's poem as an innocent sacrifice, a being unknowable to his sacrificers. More importantly, Jesus as fish represents the broad coincidence of the animal, the human, and the divine. The poem's ending not only celebrates the erasure of species boundaries, it also, like Lawrence's work in *The Plumed Serpent,* spiritualizes the animal.

Do you think that creation depends on man! *It merely doesn't.—There are the trees and the grass and birds. I much prefer to think of the lark rising up on the morning upon a humanless world.—Man is a mistake, he must go.*

—*Rupert Birkin, in* Women in Love

4   Recuperating the Animal

If the post-Darwinian story of human origins that links human and animal being creates anxiety and ambivalence toward animality in modernist literature, it also opens up a space for critiques that trouble Western humanism and its abjection and repression of the animal. What we find amidst the anxious literary grapplings with animal being understood as a threat to the human are texts that not only refuse to project animality onto marginalized others, but that radically invert the traditional speciesist hierarchy that values human over animal as a matter of course. In other words, these texts in their privileging of the animal tend to marginalize the conventionally human, and in doing so they enact a transvaluation of humanist species values that disrupts the "human" at its core.

D. H. Lawrence is perhaps the British modernist most engaged with the species problem throughout his work. We have already seen how the tension between destroying and acknowledging the radical alterity of the animal other recurs in his writing and reveals the deeply troubling relationship between human and animal in the modernist moment. Lawrence's work also signals a deepening disgust with humanism in its rationalist mode. That is, Lawrence seems to be skeptical of the very characteristics that are cited as separating human from animal and that putatively make humans *the* superior species: reason, language, abstraction, self-awareness. Lawrence's antirationalist leanings coincide with his characters' awareness of animal- or blood-consciousness, in human and nonhuman animals. The animal in Lawrence's universe thus becomes a source for an alternative form of consciousness that can redeem a human culture faced with its own increasing mechanization and alienation, and in this regard his work serves as a classic "romantic" response to the "official" version of Enlightenment subjectivity that imagines the human as perfectible through reason.

Thus, while recent criticism has focused on the ways in which Lawrence problematizes language and sexuality, I want to focus on his troubling of the human. Lawrence champions alterity and difference both for the self and for intersubjective relationships, and the animal serves as a central figure of such otherness. His work understands animality as spontaneity, the unknowable, the bodily, and the pure. Essentially, the animal possesses the kind of *being* that Lawrence wants to recuperate in humans, a being that rejects mechanistic forms of self-consciousness and embraces radical mystery.

i

Women in Love narrates what is essentially a struggle between the debilitating predictability of rationalist consciousness and the incalculable energies of an "inhuman" being that escapes strict rational and linguistic codes. In this novel, Lawrence seems his most stridently antihumanist if we understand Rupert Birkin as representative of Lawrence's larger philosophical proclivities. Birkin is surrounded by values and behaviors divorced from organicism and from the mysteries of materially embedded *being*. He desperately seeks to free himself from the deadweight of self-consciousness by recuperating a kind of animal ontology in himself and in others. This "underground" of the conventionally human is already at issue in Lawrence's opening chapter of *Women in Love,* "Sisters." Amidst Gudrun and Ursula's discussion of men, marriage, and child-bearing, Lawrence issues this characterization of Ursula:

> The two sisters worked on in silence, Ursula having always that strange brightness of an essential flame that is caught, meshed, contravened. She lived a good deal by herself, to herself, working, passing on from day to day, and always thinking, trying to lay hold

on life, to grasp it in her own understanding. Her active living was suspended, but underneath, in the darkness, something was coming to pass. If only she could break through the last integuments! . . . she could not, not yet. Still she had a strange prescience, an intimation of something yet to come.[1]

This paragraph is remarkable because, in its initial description of Ursula's personality or state of mind, it outlines the central philosophical questions of the novel itself, questions that circulate around self-awareness, abstract knowledge, being, animality, the body. Ursula's "essential flame," her vital being or ontology, is caught, is caged if you will, because she attempts to conceive of it rationally. Because Ursula tries to grasp her life "in her own understanding," her "active living" is held at bay and remains under the surface, repressed by her reasoned analysis. She cannot yet break through the last "integuments" of intellectual self-awareness. Lawrence's use of this word—integument—reveals the centrality of the material, the bodily, and the animal in the text. An integument is an enveloping layer, especially the skin or membrane, of an organism or organ. The image thus suggests an entrapment of organicism, a constraint of the bodily and bodily energies. Because Ursula has a strange foreknowledge of something to come, the reader already anticipates the eventual release of her essential flame, accomplished by her rupture of abstract, rational self-awareness.

The debilitating tyranny of the rational is immediately rendered in Lawrence's depiction of Hermione Roddice, Rupert Birkin's long-standing lover. Hermione, the daughter of a Derbyshire Baronet, is shaped and influenced by money, class, culture, and education. But most of all, she is characterized by a tortured self-awareness. Ursula watches her walking toward the local church where the daughter of the town's mine owner is to be married. Hermione is one of the head bridesmaids, and though her outward appearance is impeccable and calm, her inner state is tumultuous: "Her long pale face, that she carried lifted up, somewhat in the Rossetti fashion, seemed almost drugged, as if a strange mass of thoughts coiled in the darkness within her, and she was never allowed to escape" (15). The prison house of rationalism and its grip on self-knowledge is most forcefully established here as one of the major themes, if not the central theme, of the novel. Hermione is "full of intellectuality, and heavy, nerve-worn with consciousness" (16); Lawrence echoes her redundant self-awareness in his syntax, writing, "Hermione *knew herself* to be well dressed; she *knew herself* to be the social equal, if not far the superior, of anyone she was likely to meet in Willey Green" (16; emphasis added). What Hermione cannot comprehend is the void in her personality that makes her feel "tortured, exposed." But Lawrence is quick to explain, "It was a lack of robust self, she had no natural sufficiency, there was a terrible void, a lack, a deficiency of being within her" (16). Hermione is not robust or natural; she has over-intellectualized her *being* and crippled it in the process.

The tension between being and rationality is central throughout Lawrence's work, and especially in *Women in Love*. Michael Bell gives considerable attention to this dynamic in his study, *D. H. Lawrence: Language and Being*. Bell theorizes a connection between Lawrence's ideology and Martin Heidegger's, particularly in terms of their mutual privileging of ontology over epistemology. The early Heidegger of *Being and Time* saw Being as "more primordial than value although openness to Being is, in his view, almost impossible within our culture largely because our very language, the inescapable medium of thought, is radically imbued with post-Socratic, especially post-Cartesian, assumptions."[2] Language, therefore, tends to mitigate our ability to experience *Dasein* or being. As Bell explains, "The point at which Being is apparent is also the point at which intellectual formulations are otiose or banal" (9). Thus Lawrence shares Heidegger's skepticism toward language and his belief that words obscure our experience of intense being. What Lawrence seems not to share with Heidegger is the notion that animals are "poor in world," that they do not partake fully of Being. To the contrary, Lawrence privileges the being of animals and seems to ascribe to them a more pure ontological mode that exists outside language that, if restored to the human animal, can save him or her from the deadening effects of advanced socialization.

Birkin's quest in the novel is indeed a quest for being, for a recuperation of something beyond the rational, and, as we shall see, beyond language. But how, precisely, can we understand this being he seeks? Many critics fixate on sexuality as the ultimate solution to the Lawrentian quest. Indeed, Hermione is subtly characterized as nonerotic; "she drifted along with a peculiar fixity of the hips, a strange unwilling motion" (15). And sexuality is without doubt a central concern in the text. But I want to suggest that a more compelling reading of the novel reveals sexuality as one important component of a larger recuperative effort in Lawrence, a recuperation of animality for the human subject.

After introducing the frustrated rationalist, Hermione, to the reader, Lawrence constructs a vivid contrast to her stultification in his depiction of the local bride and groom. When the long-awaited groom steps down from his carriage and sees his bride, he prepares himself "for the leap, to overtake her":

> "Ah-h-h!" came her strange, intaken cry, as, on the reflex, she started, turned, and fled, scudding with an unthinkable swift beating of her white feet . . . towards the church. Like a hound the young man was after her, leaping the steps and swinging past her father, his supple haunches working like those of a hound that bears down on the quarry. (19)

In contrast to Hermione's careful and studied (re)presentation of her *self*, the lovers "forget themselves" when they act spontaneously—like animals—engaged in an instinctual, sexualized chase.[3] Their sport with one another serves as the novel's early example of being or experience that operates outside the strict framework of conventional rationalism. The contrast with Hermione's reality is unmistakable, and this contrast reappears in the second chapter as Birkin's central preoccupation.

During the wedding party at Gerald Crich's family home, the elderly Mrs. Crich raises the problem of intersubjectivity and the conventions of family structure in a conversation with Birkin. Mrs. Crich complains of not knowing the people in her home, of being introduced to "Mr So-and-so" and feeling surrounded by strangers (24). What is more, her own sons-in-law call her mother, which she considers absurd: "'Now Laura's got married, there's another. And I really don't know John from James yet.'" (25). Crich's critique is a sweeping one since it signals a lack of real connection even with one's supposed intimates, with those in one's own home and extended family. Birkin's response is characteristic of the sometimes violent antihumanism he espouses throughout the text:

> "People don't really matter," he said, rather unwilling to continue. The mother looked up at him with sudden, dark interrogation, as if doubting his sincerity. "How do you mean, *matter*?" she asked sharply. "Not many people *are* anything at all," he answered, forced to go deeper than he wanted to. "They jingle and giggle. It would be much better if they were just wiped out. Essentially, they don't exist, they aren't there." (25; second emphasis added)

Thus we are introduced to Birkin's weariness with the conventionally human, especially with the type that Hermione represents, with her desire to qualify and make permanent their romantic relationship. In fact, after she initiates an intellectual discussion about nationality, race, and property—all markers of identity—during the gathering, Birkin becomes sickened with the banter: "He detested toasts, and footmen, and assemblies, and mankind altogether, in most of its aspects. Then he rose to make a speech. But he was somehow disgusted" (30). This moment reveals Birkin's weariness with the taxonomic function of language that produces hierarchies and social "values," the operation of language that "disconnects us from the world."[4] This disdain resonates with Birkin's response to Gerald Crich's quip about wanting peace of mind: "'Peace of body,'" he replies, to the contrary (30). In his discussion with Mrs. Crich mentioned earlier, Birkin links matter and being, materiality and ontology, when he explains that most people don't *matter*, because (and note the deliberate syntactical construction of the phrase) not many people *are* anything. Implicitly, Birkin is weary of what people say about themselves because their words do not correspond to what they are.

At this point, for the second time in two chapters, conventional signifying networks that fix identity like language, marriage, and familial relations are juxtaposed with figures of animality. Birkin escapes to the lawn that is bordered by gardens and a field: "The view was pleasant . . . the water gleamed and the opposite woods were purplish with new life. Charming Jersey cattle came to the fence, breathing hoarsely from their velvet muzzles at the human beings, expecting perhaps a crust. Birkin leaned on the fence. A cow was breathing wet hotness on his hand" (31). It is in this warm, watery environment, mingling with the cattle, that Birkin feels free to contradict Gerald—associated with ice, snow, and the Arctic north throughout the text—concerning the earlier hound-like chase between bride and groom. While Gerald bristles at the broaching of accepted behavior, Birkin calls the bride's flight "almost a masterpiece of good form," adding, "It's the hardest thing in the world to act spontaneously on one's impulses—and it's the only really gentlemanly thing to do—provided you're fit to do it" (32). Thus the novel introduces its recurring associations between spontaneity, antirationalism, and animality, all of which Birkin explores, in theory and in practice, throughout the text.

Like much of the philosophical subtext of Lawrence's work, the question of animality in this novel is complex and requires a patient scrutiny. Despite the massive critical focus on sexuality in Lawrence's work, the novel insists that surrendering to "crude" instinctual desire, or the "animal instincts" as sexual, will not satisfy Birkin's desires. In fact, this sexual solution is especially misguided when combined with intellectualism, as Hermione is made to demonstrate when she visits Ursula's classroom and asks if the school children, indeed if anyone, really benefits from *knowing* things in an abstract and critical manner. Birkin is immediately scornful of Hermione, thinking her questions hypocritical. "But knowing is everything to you," he accuses, "it is all your life." "Hadn't they better be *animals*," Hermione presses, "simple animals, crude, violent, *anything*, rather than this self-consciousness, this incapacity to be spontaneous." But Birkin, in this exchange, rejects Hermione's strident division between mind and instinct because, he insists, she is "merely making words." He lays bare her seeming interest in animality: "knowledge means everything to you. Even your animalism—you want it in your head. You don't want to *be* an animal, you want to observe your own animal functions, to get a mental thrill out of them. . . . What is it but the worst and last form of intellectualism, this love of yours for passion and animal instincts?" (40). Hermione ultimately wants to capture or observe animality in her consciousness, in her mind. She doesn't want to authentically experience the instinctual; she doesn't want to *be* an animal. Birkin implies that if she were to genuinely experience her own animality, she would never maintain such an abstracted interest in her own behavior. The animal, for Lawrence, escapes this kind of tortured self-awareness.

Birkin's continued vociferations clarify and refine his critique of Hermione's intellectualism. He calls her passion a lie and asserts that her will drives her, her will that must control everything it encounters: "You want to clutch things and have them in your power. You want to have things in your power. And why? Because you haven't got any real body, any dark sensual body of life. . . . You have only your will and your conceit of consciousness, and your lust for power, to *know*" (42). Essentially, Birkin accuses Hermione of filtering every experience and sensation through her rationalistic consciousness, in which she maintains power over something by being able to observe it, name it, and analyze it. This is precisely the case when she *says* "better to be an animal," and gets a certain transgressive thrill out of saying such a thing. Birkin counters that she only wants to watch her own sexual behavior in mirrors to "make it all mental." To the contrary, Birkin argues that real "sensuality" is "a fulfillment—the great dark knowledge you can't have in your head—the dark involuntary being. It is death to one self—but it is coming into being of another."

The emphasis on consciousness is important here. While sensuality is of the body, it is much more than the body: it is a "dark sensual body of life," which implies a phenomenon encompassing not just the physical, but rather the whole range of lived experience. This "sensuality" is also a question of relinquishing rationalism in the mind. When Ursula asks how one can have knowledge that is not in the head, Birkin explains that there is knowledge in the blood: "when the mind and the known world is drowned in darkness—Everything must go—there must be a deluge. Then you find yourself a palpable body of darkness, a demon—" (43). Thus Lawrence's famous philosophical framing of antirationalism— blood-consciousness—emerges in this text, and once again, I want to connect this alternative form of consciousness to animality in Lawrence's work. Blood-consciousness defines Lawrence's rejection of the overly intellectualized and his concomitant desire for a recuperation of the animal in the human.

This exchange between Birkin, Hermione, and Ursula is central to my reading of the novel's recuperation of animality precisely because Birkin accuses Hermione of not wanting to really *be* an animal. Birkin, on the other hand, attempts to reinvent his humanity through various explorations of what we might provisionally call animal consciousness or being throughout the text. As Bell points out, modernist critics have recognized Lawrence's "sense of the human personality as a process to be understood in 'inhuman' as well as 'human' terms,"[5] but the discursive role of animality in his work remains largely untheorized. It is the ontological tension between humanity and animality—a tension complicated by questions of consciousness, language, abstraction, and self-awareness— that repeatedly frames Birkin's interrogation of meaningful experience in this text. Thus Birkin's insistence that, "You've got to lapse out . . . lapse into unknowingness and give up your volition. . . . You've got to learn not-to-be, before you can come into being" (44), and his lamentation that people are "*always* aware of themselves" (45), become philosophically juxtaposed to the various depictions of animal being in the text. Animality is conversely associated with spontaneous, self-forgetful, nonmechanistic and nonrationalist modes of experience. Indeed, the injunction to learn "not-to-be" before you can come into being suggests a further implied divergence with Heidegger's work. That is, we must learn to operate outside of *Dasein* as that form of ontology restricted to the humanized subject. We must reenter the "outside" of the human in order to become fully human, because the reified human is not, and never was, itself.

As I noted earlier in this study, Lawrence's nostalgia for the animal is a logical counterpart to his vehement anti-industrialism, a sentiment perhaps more transparent in this novel than in any other. The fifth chapter, where Birkin encounters Gerald as they travel from rural England to London, highlights this rejection of the early twentieth century's rampant industrialization. Birkin's approach to the city exacerbates his antihumanism, and when he agrees with Gerald's assessment that life "doesn't centre" anymore (58), that the old ideals are dead, he sets the stage for another forceful rejection of the human:

> Birkin looked at the land, at the evening, and was thinking: "Well if mankind is destroyed, if our race is destroyed like Sodom, and there is this beautiful evening with the luminous land and trees, I am satisfied. That which informs it all is there, and can never be lost. After all, what is mankind but just one expression of the incomprehensible. And if mankind passes away, it will only mean that this particular expression is completed and done. That which is expressed, and that which is to be expressed, cannot be diminished. There it is, in the shining evening. Let mankind pass away—time it did. The creative utterances will not cease, they will only be there. Humanity doesn't embody the utterance of the incomprehensible any more. Humanity is a dead letter. There will be a new embodiment, in a new way. Let humanity disappear as quickly as possible. (59)

This is one of many passages in the novel that depict Birkin's fantasy of a utopic world devoid of the human species. Like the second portion of Lawrence's poem "Fish," the decentering of the human in this passage is radical. Birkin not only imagines the destruction of the human, he longs for it with a nostalgia for some ontological innocence that exists outside the realm of the symbolic order, of rational knowledge, and of the knowable. The "incomprehensible" functions as the privileged term in Birkin's fantastic economy, and while humanity has become far too predictable, animals partake of the mysterious and the unquantifiable. David Parker discusses the importance of the "unknown" in Lawrence's works that, he asserts, resist ideological closure.[6] In Derridean terms, then, the radical incalculability of the animal other, which may function as the most different difference in our critical discussions of alterity and justice, must also be understood as a privileged term in Lawrence's imaginative economy.

The overly mechanistic London emerges in this chapter as a figure for extreme comprehensibility, the known and predictable quality associated with mass reproduction and technology. Carol M. Kaplan notes that for Lawrence London, even more than the mining town of Beldover, "exemplifies an overindustrialized society that . . . makes its inhabitants feel that they are trapped and that their lives are devoid of meaning."[7] Even the bohemian world associated with Halliday and his artistic cadre in the city, a community that putatively represents freedom and spontaneity, is portrayed by Lawrence as "more enslaved by conventions" than the bourgeoisie that Halliday's group reviles (Kaplan, 115). As Birkin approaches London, he is approaching an extreme version of the rationalist humanism he desperately wishes to escape: "They had passed Bedford. Birkin watched the country, and was filled with a sort of hopelessness. He always felt this, on approaching London. His dislike of mankind, of the mass of mankind, amounted almost to an illness" (Lawrence, 61). Drawing himself inward, away from the "mass of mankind," Birkin asks Gerald if he feels like one of the damned, and though Gerald laughs, Birkin insists, "It is real death" (61).

Birkin's exohumanism, his privileging of that which exists outside humanist frameworks, reaches a feverish pitch as his relationship with Hermione comes to a violent end. At Breadalby, Hermione's family home in Derbyshire, Birkin's battle with Hermione over knowledge and being rages on. Birkin becomes furious when Hermione claims that learning astrological principles makes her feel "*uplifted, so unbounded————*" (85). Birkin's by now predictable response follows: "'What do you want to feel unbounded for?' he said sarcastically. 'You don't want to *be* unbounded'" (86). Ironically, Hermione's most spontaneous and "sensual" experience in the novel follows this exchange when she smashes Birkin on the head with a paperweight. In this moment of consummation her heart "was a pure flame in her breast, she was purely unconscious in ecstasy" (105). Violence, then, removes her from the constraints of humanism, if only for a moment. Indeed, hers is a potential return to instinct, the instinct to kill the other who disrupts or dismantles one's theory of self.

After Birkin insists that Hermione let him pass out of her grip, he walks straight to the open country, wandering on to "a wild valley-side, where were thickets of hazel, many flowers, tufts of heather, and little clumps of young fir-trees, budding with soft paws." And though he is barely conscious, he is aware that he wants something. Birkin takes off his clothes, shedding the raiments of culture and exposing his animal body to the earth. He desires a renaturalization amidst the nonhuman world: he wants to touch all the bushes and flowers, "to saturate himself with the touch of them all" (106). The lush descriptions that follow obsessively emphasize the *tactile,* the sense most aligned with our materiality and perhaps most distant from the specular that functions to freeze images as wholes, as entities singular unto themselves. Touch, on the other hand, "saturates": it requires interaction. A touch is sometimes difficult to isolate because it operates systematically, in a network of interconnected nerves and sensory apparatuses. It is perhaps the least linear sense; it is of multiplicity rather than identity, the sensory experience of otherness and difference. Touch is bodily. It requires that one be in bodily contact with the object in order to function, whereas one can see, hear, or smell an object that is at a great distance. Touch emphasizes our corporeality.

When Birkin's first tactile saturation amidst the primroses is too subtle and too soft for his deep need to escape the rationalism Hermione represents, he seeks out a clump of fir trees. Lawrence's description thereof warrants a sizable quotation: note the urgency of the tactile sense here as Birkin stages a sometimes masochistic bringing-into-consciousness of his body:

> The soft sharp boughs beat upon him, as he moved in keen pangs against them, threw little cold showers of drops on his belly, and beat his loins with their clusters of soft-sharp needles. There was a thistle which pricked him vividly. . . . To lie down and roll in the sticky, cool young hyacinths, to lie on one's belly and cover one's back with handfuls of fine wet grass, soft as breath, soft and more delicate and more beautiful than the touch of any woman; and then to sting one's thigh against the living dark bristles of the fir-boughs; and then to feel the light whip of the hazel on one's shoulders, stinging, and then to clasp the silvery birch-trunk against one's breast, its smoothness, its hardness, its vital knots and ridges—this was good, this was all very good, very satisfying. . . . How fortunate he was that there was this lovely, subtle, responsive vegetation, waiting for him, as he waited for it; how fulfilled he was, how happy! (107)

When Birkin emerges from the valley, he wonders at his "sanity" but decides that his kind of madness is preferable to normative social and cultural values:

"He was weary of the old ethic, of the human being, and of humanity. . . . What a dread he had of mankind, of other people! It amounted almost to horror, to a sort of dream terror. . . . If he were on an island, like Alexander Selkirk, with only the creatures and the trees, he would be free and glad, there would be none of this heaviness, this misgiving." (108)

Birkin's desire to escape the constraints of human subjectivity is continually figured as a privileging of the animal and vegetal world. In fact, Birkin's implicit desire to "be" like an animal can be understood on two levels. He wants to be *like* an animal in terms of spontaneity and freedom from extreme forms of rationalism, to mimic this quality. But he also wants to *be* as an animal *is:* in other words, he wants to be true to his own ontological integrity, which he is convinced includes much more than rote social relations and "civilized" ways of behaving. In this way the animal functions as a marker of being that is unspoiled by cultural reification and intellectual posturing. Thus Lawrence, through Birkin's character, dismantles traditional humanism by exploding it, by insisting that the "human" cannot be hermetically sealed off from animality, the body, from difference and change, from the "inhuman."

As the embodiment of a mechanistic humanism that is specifically invested in controlling and dominating animality, Gerald Crich serves as a marked contrast to Rupert Birkin in the novel. In the text's early chapters, one gets glimpses of this tendency in Gerald. He is efficient, industrious, and has a passion for discussion, and Birkin's accusation in chapter 2—"you are afraid of yourself" (33)—reveals Gerald's need to repress the unquantifiable elements of his nature. This fear is revealed at Halliday's flat in London after the host suggests that by giving up clothing entirely he would feel he was really living. Halliday continues to extol the virtues of nudism by privileging touch over vision, the same preference Birkin's escape to the firs reinforces: "Oh—one would *feel* things instead of merely looking at them. I should feel the air move against me, and feel the things I touched, instead of having only to look at them. I'm sure life is all wrong because it has become much too visual—we can neither hear nor feel nor understand, we can only see" (78). But when Maxim agrees energetically, Gerald *looks* at the naked Russian and is repulsed:

Gerald glanced at him, and saw him, his suave, golden coloured body with the black hair growing fine and freely, like tendrils, and his limbs like smooth plant-stems. He was so healthy and well-made, why did he make one ashamed, why did one feel repelled. Why should Gerald even dislike it, why did it seem to him to detract from his own dignity. Was that all a human being amounted to? So uninspired! thought Gerald. (78)

Thus the "naked" truth of human existence—that all spiritual and transcendent capacity is grounded in the primate body—puts Gerald off. What is most clever about this passage is the way Lawrence highlights the fact that it is the other's corporeality, not his own, which drains Gerald of his human "dignity." Gerald perceives his own animality refracted through Maxim's; indeed, he seems forced against his better judgment into this den of nudists where he must confront representations of his own bodily self. We can assume that, as one who is "afraid of himself," Gerald avoids any regular philosophical consideration of his own body, his contingency, his animality. His relation to self seems not just partially but *primarily* mediated through his relation with the other. Indeed, this intersubjective dependency is cited by Gudrun in the novel's closing chapters as underlying Gerald's promiscuity: Gudrun recognizes that he is not complete in himself, that he requires a constant sexualized bringing-into-being of his identity through interaction with women.

Gerald also works to disrupt Gudrun's connection to animals and animality. In the "Water-Party" chapter, Gudrun and Ursula break off from the festivities and find an isolated spot on the Crich property to bathe and have tea. Afterwards, Ursula sings to accompany Gudrun, who dances with abandon, "as if she were trying to throw off some bond, flinging her hands suddenly and stamping again, then rushing with face uplifted and throat full and beautiful and eyes half closed, sightless" (166). When the two are suddenly confronted with a group of curious Highland cattle, Gudrun insists that her sister continue to sing so she can resume her dancing:

[She] went in a strange, palpitating dance towards the cattle, lifting her body towards them as if in a spell, her feet pulsing as if in some little frenzy of unconscious sensation . . . her breasts lifted and shaken towards the cattle, her throat exposed as in some voluptuous ecstasy towards them, whilst she drifted imperceptibly nearer. . . . She could feel them just in front of her, it was as if she had the electric pulse from their breasts running into her hands. Soon she would

touch them, actually touch them. A terrible shiver of fear and pleasure went through her. (167–68)

Gudrun's near-communion with the cattle—a rare moment of abandon
which aligns her with the "electric pulse" of their nonhuman being—is
abruptly interrupted by Gerald who has discovered the sisters and calls
the animals off from a distance. Thus Gerald disrupts Gudrun's "lapsing-
out" into an ecstatic experience of animality. And Gudrun, resenting the
intrusion, responds with a "strident cry of anger" (168). What is more,
Gerald seems completely unable to comprehend Gudrun's desire to dance
with the cattle. He merely scolds her, saying that the animals can be dangerous, and, that since they *belong* to him, he is responsible for their behavior. Gudrun mocks the notion that Gerald possesses the cattle: "'How
are they yours! You haven't swallowed them. Give me one of them now,'
she said, holding out her hand" (170). At this moment, Gudrun recoils
at Gerald's mechanistic control over nature and the animal. She resents
his inability to recognize her communion, and his proprietary dismissal
of the animals involved in that experience. By the scene's end Gudrun
"felt in her soul an unconquerable desire for deep violence against him"
(170). Though at other times in the text, she is mesmerized by this very
control.

Indeed, Gerald's penchant to disavow his *own* animality tends to mes-
merize Gudrun. The opening scene of the "Coal-Dust" chapter depicts
his violent domination of an Arab mare at the coal train's crossing, as
the Brangwen sisters look on in astonishment. Gerald's horse is immediately distressed by the approaching train and by its "repeated sharp blows
of unknown, terrifying noise" (110). Over and over the horse recoils in
"terror"—the word appears five times in two pages—but Gerald meets
the animal's escalating fear with equally brutalizing restraint:

The mare opened her mouth and rose slowly, as if lifted up on a
wind of terror. Then suddenly her fore feet struck out, as she con-
vulsed herself utterly away from the horror. Back she went, and
the two girls clung to each other, feeling she must fall backwards
on top of him. But he leaned forward, his face shining with fixed
amusement, and at last he brought her down, sank her down, and
was bearing her back to the mark. But as strong as the pressure of
his compulsion was the repulsion of her utter terror, throwing her
back away from the railway, so that she spun round and round, on

two legs, as if she were in the centre of some whirlwind. It made
Gudrun faint with poignant dizziness, which seemed to penetrate
to her heart. (111)

Gerald continues to ignore the animal's instinctual fear with an "almost
mechanical relentlessness, keen as a sword pressing in to her" (111): he
"brought her down, almost as if she were part of his own physique" (112).
Thus Lawrence makes the comparison between the horse and Gerald's
own animal being transparent: he represses the mare as if she were part
of his own body. And the repression is rendered as an acute corporeal
violence. Gudrun turns pale when she sees blood on the mare's flanks:
"And then on the very wound the bright spurs came down, pressing re-
lentlessly. The world reeled and passed into nothingness for Gudrun, she
could not know any more" (112). But until this moment of lapsing, Gerald's dominance has been enticing to her.

In fact, the disparity between Gudrun and Ursula's responses throughout this scene reveals their respective relationships to animality and
its repression and, in turn, explicates the larger dynamic between the
two sisters and their lovers in the novel. Ursula implicitly undergoes a
cross-species identification with the horse and its experience of inchoate
fear. She screams at Gerald, "No—! No—! Let her go! Let her go, you
fool, you *fool*——!"; but Gudrun is mortified by this identificatory out-
burst and hates Ursula "for being outside herself. It was unendurable
that Ursula's voice was so powerful and naked" (111). This moment reveals that Gudrun shares Gerald's ties to cultural *restraint* and his dis-
comfort with energies—be they instinctual, animal, emotional, etc.—that
give the lie to such repressions. Thus Ursula's "naked" voice discomforts
Gudrun just as Maxim's bare physique unsettles Gerald. Indeed, this
scene marks Gudrun's deepening sexual attraction to Gerald, whom she
watches "with black-dilated, spell-bound eyes": his violent repression of
the horse "seemed to penetrate to her heart" (111). In the scene's aftermath, Ursula decries Gerald's desire to humanize and masculinize himself by bullying "a sensitive creature, ten times as sensitive as himself"
(113). Her condemnation of this violent disavowal parallels the openness
to nonrational forms of experience that will characterize her relationship
with Rupert Birkin. To the contrary, Gudrun interprets Gerald's repressive power through a sexualized, somewhat sadistic lens. A close reading
of her response reveals that Gudrun, rather than identify with the horse's

suffering, actually identifies with Gerald's sexual domination of the female animal:

> Gudrun was as if numbed in her mind by the sense of indomitable
> soft weight of the man, bearing down into the living body of the
> horse: the strong, indomitable thighs of the blond man clenching
> the palpitating body of the mare into pure control; a sort of soft
> white magnetic domination from the loins and thighs and calves,
> enclosing and encompassing the mare heavily into unutterable sub-
> ordination, soft blood-subordination, terrible. (113)

The central issues of power, control, the will, and repression are fore-grounded here and will continue to define the characters' struggles with their relationships to self and other. The ambivalence of this sadomasoch-istic fantasy makes it unclear whether Gudrun wants more to dominate or to be dominated. What remains certain is her attraction to dominance *as such,* and specifically to the dominance of animality and the body by a masculinized and mechanistic force.

The scene in which Gerald controls his horse is not the only one in which his dominion over animality seals his communion with Gudrun. A more intimate bond between the lovers is nurtured in the chapter titled "Rabbit." Gudrun is becoming an artistic mentor to Gerald's young sister, Winifred. When the two painters decide to make Bismarck, the family rabbit, their next object of study, Winifred warns her tutor that the animal is terribly strong and a fearful kicker. But Gudrun is undeterred, and when the rabbit is momentarily still, she reaches into its cage and grabs it by the ears. Lawrence details the animal's behavior with unusual attention to its resistance: "It set its four feet flat, and thrust back. There was a long scraping sound as it was hauled forward, and in another instant it was in mid-air, lunging wildly, its body flying like a spring coiled and released, as it lashed out, suspended from the ears" (240). Gudrun must avert her face to avoid being scratched, but her astonishment quickens into rage:

> Gudrun stood for a moment astounded by the thunder-storm that
> had sprung into being in her grip. Then her colour came up, a heavy
> rage came over her like a cloud. She stood shaken as a house in a
> storm, and utterly overcome. Her heart was arrested with fury at the
> mindlessness and the bestial stupidity of this struggle, her wrists

were badly scored by the claws of the beast, a heavy cruelty welled
up in her. (240)

At this moment of Gudrun's "rage" and "cruelty," Gerald enters to stamp
out the "mindlessness" of the rabbit, the very mindlessness that Birkin
seems to value in the novel. The struggle between Gerald and the rabbit
is depicted with nearly mythical force. The rabbit is "like a dragon" and
"inconceivably powerful and explosive": Gerald is filled with "white-edged
wrath" and with lightning quickness puts the rabbit in a stranglehold. At
the same time "there came the unearthly scream of a rabbit in the fear
of death. It made one immense writhe, tore his [Gerald's] wrists and his
sleeves in a final convulsion, all its belly flashed white in a whirlwind of
paws, and then he had slung it round and had it under his arm, fast. It
cowered and skulked. His face was gleaming with a smile" (241).

It is this violent subordination that opens up an "obscene" communion between the lovers. Gudrun is pale and looks "unearthly" because
the "scream of the rabbit, after the violent tussle, seemed to have torn
her consciousness." Gerald looks back at her with intensity, and Gudrun
"knew she was revealed" (241). Gudrun's response parallels her reaction
to Gerald's domination of his horse, but this time Gerald is aware of her
attraction to him. Gudrun is sexually roused by Gerald's sadistic suppression of animality. It is finally the death-scream of an animal that seals her
sexual attraction to Gerald.

In her study, *D. H. Lawrence and the Paradoxes of Psychic Life,* Barbara
Schapiro uses the work of Jessica Benjamin to explore both the acknowledgment of otherness in intersubjective relationships and the failure of
that differential in Lawrence's work. She notes that the breakdown of the
"assertion-recognition dialectic" results in sadomasochism as an attempt
to be recognized by the other.[8] Schapiro's work would suggest that Gudrun
and Gerald spiral into sadistic behavior because of their inability to discover real otherness each in the other. The violence of their communion
is underscored when Gudrun reveals a deep scratch in her forearm made
by the rabbit: seeing this wound, Gerald feels "as if he had had knowledge
of her in the long red rent of her forearm, so silken and soft. . . . The long,
shallow red rip seemed torn across his own brain, tearing the surface of
his ultimate consciousness, letting through the forever unconscious, unthinkable red ether of the beyond, the obscene beyond" (242).

Such valorizations of violent repression are consistent with Gerald's
further characterization in the novel as "The Industrial Magnate," as the

title of chapter seventeen dubs him. Unlike his father, Thomas Crich, who is compassionate toward his coal miners and who "wanted his industry to be run on love" (225), Gerald Crich embodies a historically specific materialism motivated by the hyper-industrialism of the age. He finds the suffering of workers ridiculous and believes in "the pure instrumentality of the individual. As a man as of a knife: does it cut well? Nothing else mattered" (223). Gerald's megalomaniacal humanism is the profound humanism of the Judeo-Christian West, a humanism which constructs man as the incarnation of divine *logos* whose purpose is to "subjugate Matter to his own ends" (223). This view establishes a kind of creation principle in the domination of the natural world: as God formed the earth and its beings, so man will control matter in His stead, in "the pure fulfillment of his own will in the struggle with the natural conditions" (223–24). Gerald longs for this divine power over nature and dreams of establishing a coal mine that operates as a perfected system, as an incarnation of his own rational will:

> He, the man, could interpose a perfect, changeless, godlike medium between himself and the Matter he had to subjugate. There were two opposites, his will and the resistant Matter of the earth. And between these he could establish the very expression of his will, the incarnation of his power, a great and perfect machine, a system, an activity of pure order, pure mechanical repetition, repetition ad infinitum, hence eternal and infinite. He found his eternal and his infinite in the pure machine-principle of perfect co-ordination into one pure complex, infinitely repeated motion, like the spinning of a wheel . . . this is the God-motion, this productive repetition. . . . And the whole productive will of man was the Godhead. (228)

Clearly, Gerald finds more than sadistic pleasure in the subjugation of horses, rabbits, and the earth: indeed, his very soul, his spiritual self-understanding at the deepest level is tethered to his will, his power to dominate matter. Gerald's view closely approximates what Horkheimer and Adorno elaborate as "rational administration," and Gerald himself is a figure of instrumentality, a thing only as valuable as its capacity to produce.[9] The failure of Gerald and Gudrun's relationship can be understood as a failure to escape rationalism and the mechanistic suppression of the unknowable, which is repeatedly linked to animality in Lawrence's text. Gerald and Gudrun insist upon having power over one another: they refuse to accept the alterity of one another as something that inevitably stands outside of their epistemological realm. The animal serves as a figure of radical alterity that is so threatening, to Gerald in particular, that he must control and repress it. But Gudrun eventually joins his battle for power. Their "tango" is especially bitter during their sexual interactions, when they vie for knowledge and control. One might say that, for Lawrence, sexuality represents the human in its most animal attitude, so Gerald and Gudrun are especially concerned to dominate one another sexually to maintain control over their own animality. In fact, Kenneth Inniss has called sex the "last form of wildness" for Lawrence.[10]

Gudrun's commitment to rationalism is revealed after her first sexual encounter with Gerald. As she awakes and realizes she is still underneath the bridge, resting on Gerald's shoulder, she recalls their communion and her "soul thrilled with complete knowledge." She is immediately concerned to possess Gerald in her consciousness: "She wanted to touch him and touch him and touch him, till she had him all in her hands, till she had strained him into her knowledge. Ah, if she could have the precious *knowledge* of him, she would be filled, and nothing could deprive her of this" (332). Lawrence signals the fatal consequences of this desire through his plot sequence: on the following day, Gerald watches in horror as his ailing father breathes a last, agonizing breath.

But it is not long before Gudrun experiences her own death-knell of sorts. When Gerald comes to her in secret after his father's death, he uses her, sexually, to escape from the mechanical emptiness that has begun to overtake his consciousness: "Into her he poured all his pent-up darkness and corrosive death, and he was whole again. . . . And she, subject, received him as a vessel filled with his bitter potion of death. She had no power at this crisis to resist. The terrible frictional violence of death filled her, and she received it in an ecstasy of subjection, in throes of acute, violent sensation" (344). And though Gerald is overcome by the "sleep of complete exhaustion and restoration" (345), Gudrun lies awake in a "state of violent active superconsciousness" (346).

It is thus a superconsciousness—an extreme investment in knowledge, power, and control—that eventually destroys their relationship and, literally, destroys Gerald. Their penchant to dominate alterity, to control otherness, turns rapidly into a death struggle between them. When they reach the German Alps, on holiday with Birkin and Ursula, Gudrun realizes that she is locked in a destructive battle with her lover: "The deep resolve formed in her, to combat him. One of them must triumph over the other. Which should it be? Her soul steeled itself with strength" (413). Their struggle ends high in the mountains after Gerald tries, but fails, to strangle Gudrun, and wanders to his death amidst the frozen slopes.

Birkin and Ursula, rather than destroying one another in a battle of wills, discover a somewhat utopic existence outside the constraints of conventional notions of identity, and Birkin's way of being sets the parameters for this experience. If Gerald's repressive superhumanism results in his demise, Birkin's "exo-humanism" determines his salvation. I have already discussed Birkin's more extant or overt resistance to rationalist humanism, but the text is filled with subtle markers that link him with what we might provisionally call animal consciousness.

Birkin's resistance to identity, to the fixity of social and interpersonal subject positions, is galling to Hermione, who clings to cultural signifiers and the distinctions they produce. In chapter 8, as Hermione entertains a group of friends at her family home, an Italian guest notices Birkin during a waltz because he does not conform to the group's behavior: "Birkin, when he could get free from the weight of the people present, whom he disliked, danced rapidly and with a real gaiety." The contessa watches him with excitement and exclaims, "Mr Birkin, he is a changer. . . . He is not a man, he is a chameleon, a creature of change" (92). And while the contessa admires this difference and flux, this inhuman creaturely propensity in Birkin, Hermione is mortified by the quality and reuses the woman's words to damn him: "'He is not a man, he is treacherous, not one of us,' sang itself over in Hermione's consciousness" (92). Birkin is linked to animality here because he rejects a stable self—a Cartesian subjectivity—and acknowledges self-difference and transformation, a certain self-alterity. Birkin's animal-like detachment is noted elsewhere in the novel. Ursula sees him from a distance as he works with a saw and hammer: "unaware of anybody's presence. He looked very busy, like a wild animal active and intent" (123). Later in the novel, Gerald bristles at his friend's lack of attachment to personal relationships: Gerald "knew Birkin could do without him—could forget, and not suffer. This was always present in Gerald's consciousness, filling him with bitter unbelief: this consciousness of the young, animal-like spontaneity of detachment" (206).[11]

Birkin's need to change, his rejection of static ego positions, is correlative to his distrust of the separating and reifying functions of what Lacan would characterize as the "castrating" fixation of identity by the symbolic, and the lack accompanying the production of the subject "I." But the novel powerfully undermines this work of language and the symbolic primarily through Birkin's distrust of it, which further demonstrates the text's recuperation of animal being. Michael Bell discusses this suspicion toward language in the novel: "When we are told of Birkin the *[sic]* 'he was irritated and weary of having a telling way of putting things' we recognise a language nausea in the author himself whereby even his own articulacy could come to seem a burden and a cheat."[12] Of course, Birkin's weariness with language only makes sense as a corollary of his privileging of being, spontaneity, detachment, and sensory modes of knowing. In fact, Diane Bonds rightly points out that Lawrence values language if it expresses the "soul or life-force of individual organisms" (8). She also discusses the obvious paradox involved in Lawrence's desire to overcome the disconnecting power of language *through writing*.

The animal, who cannot speak our language, whose "identity" and way of living function outside the dicta of human discursive frames, is thus a model for right living and right being in the text. And Ursula's inherent recognition of this privileged phenomenology of the animal eventually makes her the ideal partner for Birkin. At the beginning of the "Moony" chapter, Ursula's corresponding rejection of the human becomes clear:

> From the bottom of her heart, from the bottom of her soul, she despised and detested people, adult people. She loved only children and animals: children she loved passionately, but coldly. . . . She loved best of all the animals, that were single and unsocial as she herself was. She loved the horses and cows in the field. Each was single and to itself, magical. It was not referred away to some detestable social principle. . . . She had a profound grudge against the human being. That which the word "human" stood for was despicable and repugnant to her. (244)

The human-animal relationship also functions as a model of experiencing alterity and rational limits that Birkin wishes to reproduce in the human-human relationship. In this sense, unlike Gerald, Birkin attempts to partake in animal being, or to rejuvenate humanity's inherent animality, which escapes comprehension and naming. For Lawrence, this life-force is often associated with spirituality, as we saw in our discussion of *The Plumed Serpent*. In this text, a similar connection is made during Ursula and Birkin's lovemaking, when Ursula discovers "the strange reality of his being, the very stuff of being, there in the straight downflow of the thighs. It was here she discovered him one of the Sons of God such as were in the beginning of the world, not a man, something other, something more" (313).

Lawrence's emphasis on alterity in these descriptions of sexual contact is recurrent and reinforces Birkin's vehement protestations against psychosexual merging. After a bitter disagreement with Ursula, Birkin laments both Hermione and Ursula's need to absorb the other sexually:

> Fusion, fusion, this horrible fusion of two beings, which every woman, and most men insisted on, was it not nauseous and horrible anyhow, whether it was a fusion of the spirit or of the emotional body? . . . Why could they not remain individuals, limited by their own limits? Why this dreadful all-comprehensiveness, this hateful tyranny? Why not leave the other being free, why try to absorb, or melt, or merge? One might abandon oneself utterly to the *moment,* but not to any other being. (309)

Birkin values an ontological limit against which his own being can collide. He tries to explain this need to Ursula when he says, "I don't *know* what I want of you. I deliver *myself* over to the unknown, in coming to you, I am without reserves or defences, stripped entirely into the unknown. Only there needs the pledge between us, that we will both cast off everything, cast off ourselves even, and cease to be, so that that which is perfectly ourselves can take place in us" (147). And in keeping with this ontological limit, Birkin's most satisfying sexual conjunctions with Ursula are those in which the unbreachable difference between them is acknowledged and honored. These moments might best be described as mutual invocations of unknowability that are manifested in the body but produce an ecstatic consciousness that remains outside the linguistic and the rational. In this same chapter, when the lovers reunite after their quarrel, they seem determined to pare back their dependence on language and to communicate through silence (Bonds, 109). Birkin speaks to Ursula in a "voice that was as if laughing, because of the unblemished stillness and force which was the reality in him. She would have to touch him. To speak, to see, was nothing. It was a travesty to look and to comprehend the man there." Rather than "know" Birkin in this oculogical sense, Ursula feels she must know him in silence, through touch, where she can "mindlessly connect with him, have the knowledge which is death of knowledge, the reality of surety in not-knowing" (319). At the end of the "Excurse" chapter, then, Birkin and Ursula's lovemaking is profound because it escapes linguistic meaning and enacts difference itself: "Quenched, inhuman, his fingers upon her unrevealed nudity were the fingers of silence upon silence, the body of mysterious night upon the body of mysterious night, the night masculine and feminine, never to be seen with the eye, or known with the mind, only known as *a palpable revelation of living otherness*" (320; emphasis added). Theirs is a shared experience of alterity revealed not through reason but through corporeal awareness, the kind of awareness Lawrence associates with the animal. And Lawrence reasserts this necessary and mutual difference for the two: "she was to him what he was to her, the immemorial magnificence of mystic, palpable, real otherness" (320).

Birkin and Ursula find salvation by dismantling the repressive form of humanism that Gerald embodies, the humanism that excludes animality. Their broadening of the human to include "animal" forms of consciousness and to embrace alterity is primarily played out in a sexual register. In the "Snow" chapter, for instance, when the two are dancing together, Ursula is frightened and attracted by Birkin's quasi-"human" behavior: "Clear before her eyes, as in a vision, she could see the sardonic, licentious mockery of his eyes, he moved towards her with subtle, animal, indifferent approach." Though Ursula fears his intentions, when the two are finally alone, she yields to Birkin's "remorseless suggestivity" (412). This scene, though late in the novel, is pivotal for Ursula since she finally accepts her own animal pleasures:

> They might do as they liked—this she realised as she went to sleep. How could anything that gave one satisfaction be excluded? What was degrading?—Who cared? Degrading things were real, with a different reality. And he was so unabashed and unrestrained. Wasn't it rather horrible, a man who could be so soulful and spiritual, now to be so—she balked at her own thoughts and memories: then she added—so bestial? So bestial, they two!—so degraded! She winced.— But after all, why not? She exulted as well. Why not be bestial, and go the whole round of experience? . . . There would be no shameful thing she had not experienced.—Yet she was unabashed, she was herself. Why not?—She was free, when she knew everything, and no dark shameful things were denied her. (413)

This moment is, in many ways, the apex of the novel. With each sentence Ursula confirms the revelatory nature of Birkin's insistence that one must refuse the constraints of the "human" when they abject behaviors and experiences considered other, considered animal. To be soulful and bestial, to go the "whole round of experience," this is the inclusive Lawrentian vision of the human animal. Ursula, in this utopic moment, *is herself* because she has expanded her subjectivity to include her own animality.

ii

If *Women in Love* holds out the salvific possibility of shaping one's identity through relationship to human otherness by recuperating humanity's own animality, Lawrence moves away from that possibility in his later short novel, *St. Mawr*. This text outlines its protagonist's gradual retreat from the human "other," a retreat fueled by her connection to a particular animal. St. Mawr, a partially domesticated horse, becomes Lou Witt's model for genuine living, and she finds herself increasingly dissatisfied with her human milieu. In light of Birkin and Ursula's discoveries in *Women in Love*, this novel implies that a relation to human alterity is not radical enough to loosen the grip with which conventional humanism constricts the individual. Indeed, this text specifically considers the animal *qua* animal, rather than treating the animal as symbolic of human qualities.

Many critical discussions of the novel have treated St. Mawr primarily as a symbol of America, or of nature unspoiled by centuries of civilization. In one sense, though, symbolism is precisely the abstraction that Lawrence rails against. His characters' struggles to experience the "life in things" correspond with an avoidance of the separating quality of language and metaphor, systems that substitute meaning for meaning in a potentially infinite regression from the material embeddedness or context of the signified content. Lawrence's repeated emphasis on the bodily and its attendant experiences of the unknown also tend to attenuate the power of language and the symbolic. Thus my insistence on reading animality *qua* animality in this text—rather than animality as merely a symbol of some other concept—might be understood as a specifically Lawrentian refusal of forced abstraction.

It is particularly fruitful to read this novel in tandem with *Women in Love* since both texts examine animality as a salve to the overly mechanized state of human subjectivity in the early twentieth century. Indeed, Lou Witt suffers from many of the same ills as Gerald Crich. In particular, her relationship with her husband, Rico, serves as a crucible of the larger rationalism that she and Lawrence struggle against. Her marriage is characterized by a battle for power and domination similar to the contest between Gerald and Gudrun. Lou and Rico exhaust one another because they are held together by "a strange vibration of the nerves, rather than of the blood. A nervous attachment, rather than a sexual love. A curious tension of will, rather than a spontaneous passion. Each was curiously under the domination of the other."[13] Barbara Ann Schapiro has contextualized this recurrent issue in Lawrence's work in terms of recent psychoanalytic theory that understands the psyche more in terms of relationality than in terms of inherent drives. Schapiro emphasizes the "context-dependency" of meaning in Lawrence's philosophy and notes,

> It is precisely the retreat from connection, from our natural bonds, and from the flow of passionate life in general, that Lawrence identified at the source of modern malaise, a cultural pathology. Although he does not use the clinical term, Lawrence diagnosed modern Western society as schizoid: our culture's overvaluation of abstract rationality and autonomous individuality, he believed, betrayed an emptiness, a hollowness at the core, and a tragic incapacity for real relationship. (3–4)

Lou and Rico's attempt to dominate one another is entirely consistent with Schapiro's discussion of intersubjectivity and sadomasochism, which I have already discussed in reference to *Women in Love*. She explains sadomasochistic desire in terms of a failure in the "assertion-recognition dialectic" (9). This means that the discovery and acknowledgment of an assertive and self-sufficient other—in relational theory this other is the primary caregiver—is necessary for the optimal development of the self. Of course, this recognition of otherness is precisely what Birkin and Ursula perform in order to avoid the pitfalls of a battle of wills, of the deadly tension between Gerald and Gudrun.

Lou Witt and Gerald Crich both suffer from a mechanistic drive to have power over others, but the difference between them is stark: while Gerald is unable to recognize and escape his own mechanistic emptiness, Lou acknowledges her predicament and changes her priorities. She considers the "curious numbness that was overcoming her" and admits, "She wanted to come unwound. She wanted to escape this battle of wills. Only St. Mawr gave her some hint of the possibility" (26). Unlike Birkin who finds salvation through self-alterity and intersubjective difference, Lou will ultimately reject human forms of otherness. In fact, her experience with St. Mawr, a horse, essentially drives her further and further away from human contact.

After seeing him for the first time, she is overcome with emotion and goes home to cry, despite the fact that she "never did cry" (14). It is specifically the horse's gaze that affects Lou in her reconstruction of the encounter:

> The wild, brilliant, alert head of St. Mawr seemed to look at her out of another world. It was as if she had had a vision, as if the walls of her own world had suddenly melted away, leaving her in a great darkness, in the midst of which the large, brilliant eyes of that horse looked at her with demonish question. . . . What was his non-human question, and his uncanny threat? She didn't know. He was some splendid demon, and she must worship him. (14)

St. Mawr's intense animal being, associated with the uncanny and the unknown, initiates Lou's interrogation of her own being. The horse's de-monic "question" functions, in fact, as a terrible *questioning* and under-mining of Lou's established life. She asks herself repeatedly, what was the horse's terrible question: "*She didn't know.* He was some splendid demon, and she must worship him. She hid herself away from Rico. She could not bear the triviality and superficiality of her human relationships" (14; emphasis added). In this initial scene, then, it is the horse's unquantifi-ability that most affects Lou. The fact that she cannot explain St. Mawr's gaze, a gaze that calls her own being into question, seems to compel her "worship" of him. This animal antiepistemology will continue to drive Lou away from the predictable world of human convention.

Despite the fact that St. Mawr is a domesticated animal, then, it is his wildness—indeed his resistance to domestication—that is most valued in the text. Morgan Lewis, the horse's groom, explains that St. Mawr's jumpi-ness around Rico stems from his having been beaten in the past. By impli-cation, we know that St. Mawr has resisted human domination, a quality perfectly aligned with Lawrence's opposition to stultifying conventional humanism. But Lou is more philosophical about St. Mawr's reactions, particularly because Lewis has indicated that one must meet the horse "half-way" (18). Lou understands that this meeting requires one to partake of the horse's world in which "all things loomed phantasmagoric" (19) and in which the horse was "swift and fierce and supreme, undominated and unsurpassed" (20). This participation requires a relinquishing of "human" ways of knowing and, perhaps most importantly, a relinquishing of human transcendence or superiority over the animal. Lou recognizes accordingly that Rico could never meet this horse "half-way" since he could not acknowledge the animal's inherent value as something outside human social and economic frameworks. Therefore, St. Mawr's reactions to individual characters function as a gauge of their own humanist paralysis. Rico's eventual "accident" with the horse is already understood as an indication of Rico's extreme humanism, his inability to experience his own animality in communion with St. Mawr.

The horse's instinctual rejection of Rico is refracted, conversely, in his acceptance of Morgan Lewis, the groom who seems more than able to meet St. Mawr halfway. Lewis is not only characterized as "the attendant shadow of the ruddy animal" (17), but Lewis's own animality trumps his humanity. This fact is registered in Lewis's attachment to his beard. In fact, Lawrence emphasizes Lewis's hairiness—"with his black beard coming up to his thick black eyebrows" (22)—and notes that he looked darker than Phoenix, the Mexican-Navajo. When Lou's mother, Rachel Witt, asks about his beard, Lewis insists that he would never shave it off because it is part of him. Indeed, we are reminded of T. S. Eliot's Sweeney, who fails to recite his humanity when shaving off this furry reminder of animality in "Sweeney Erect." While Eliot harbors contempt for Sweeney's inability to perform his humanity, Lawrence—and we cannot help but remember the author's own bearded visage—seems drawn to the beard in its vestigial suggestivity. Thus Morgan Lewis clings to his beard as a physical connection to his own animality. Rachel's response confirms this implication: "I shall always remember Lewis for saying his beard was part of him. Isn't it curious, the way he rides? He seems to sink himself in the horse. When I speak to him, I'm not sure whether I'm speaking to a man or to a horse" (23). Lewis's relationship to the horse can be sharply contrasted to Gerald Crich's in *Women in Love*. While Gerald treats the horse as part of himself, he does so in order to control— and ultimately disavow—his own animality. He sinks his body and his spurs into the mare's flesh in an act of violent domination, domination of the human will over the animal instinct. But Lewis "seems to sink himself in the horse" not in order to force his will upon the animal, but rather to meet him "half-way," perhaps to foster some shared moment of ontological understanding between the human and the nonhuman animal.

Lewis is by far the character most successful in blurring species bound-aries in the text, and it is Lou and Rachel's discussion of this undecidability in him that engenders the novel's central philosophical discussion of the value of "animality" for the human person. After Rachel cuts Lewis's hair, she is jarred by an unexpected attraction to him, despite feeling that he's "just an animal" (47). Though she is normally repulsed by men she con-siders unintellectual, Rachel is curiously compelled by Lewis's hair: "A man with no mind! I've always thought that the *most* despicable thing. Yet such wonderful hair to touch. . . . I suppose one likes stroking a cat's fur, just the same. Just the animal in man" (47). When Rachel continues by calling Lewis stupid, her daughter disagrees and insists that he simply doesn't care for the same things they do.

With this distinction, Lou begins to lay out the novel's, and in some respect Lawrence's, larger theoretical precepts on animality, precepts that constitute the contours of a posthumanist philosophy. She contends that there is "something else besides mind and cleverness, or niceness or cleanness. Perhaps it is the animal. Just think of St. Mawr! I've thought so much about him. We call him an animal, but we never know what it means. He seems a far greater mystery to me than a clever man. . . . There seems no mystery in being a man. But there's a terrible mystery in St. Mawr" (48). Lou challenges the leveling power of the signifier *animal* in all its linguistic and cultural embeddedness when she says, "We call him an animal, but we never know what it means." First, as I have men-tioned previously, the word *animal* is applied to hundreds of nonhuman species, a practice that disregards differences between species and among individual creatures within a species. In other words, the term *animal* cancels out St. Mawr's horseness. It does so in part, and thus secondly, because the term *animal* in Western languages is specifically associated with deficiency, degradedness, and base qualities. The term, for Lou, does anything but indicate the valuable mystery of St. Mawr. This is in fact the pejorative sense in which Rachel uses the word when she says "he's just an animal—no mind" (47). Rachel reiterates the West's cultural assigna-tion of the animal as a creature without mind.

But Lou continues to deconstruct these assumptions. When her mother asserts that man is wonderful because he thinks, Lou insists that man's kind of thinking is "so childish: like stringing the same beads together over and over again" (48). As Carol Siegel suggests in her discussion of cultural feminism in the novel, this accusation is specifically aimed at a "culture that Lawrence identifies as sterile because it is male-dominated and consequently purely intellectual and narrowly logical."[14] If we include considerations of animality in our reading of this statement, we can say that Lou decries what Derrida calls carno-phallogocentricism in Western metaphysics, the rigid rationalism that excludes women and animals from the moral community. Lou continues to interrogate her culture's privileging of rationalism by inverting the traditional hierarchy of value that places human above animal. St. Mawr figures here as a creature unfettered by the shackles of reason, one of Lawrence's recurring Nietzschian considerations. Lou would "hate St. Mawr to be spoilt" by a human mind, and she poses to her mother a crucial question: "But what *is* real mind?" (49).

Morgan Lewis again undermines Rachel's easy distinction between human and animal. Her daughter believes that Lewis "has far more real mind than Dean Vyner or any of the clever ones. He has a good intuitive mind, *he knows things without thinking them*" (49; emphasis added). Here Lawrence attempts to define animal consciousness—in Morgan Lewis— as a nonrational epistemology, a mode of knowing that is independent of strict logic. Lewis, like animals, knows without asking, analyzing, and rationalizing. Lou continues to explain her distinctions:

> I don't want to be an animal like a horse or a cat or a lioness, though they fascinate me, the way they get their life *straight*, not from a lot of old tanks, as we do. I don't admire the cave-man, and that sort of thing. But think, mother, if we could get our lives straight from the source, as the animal do, and still be ourselves. You don't like men yourself. But you've no idea how men just tire me out: even the very thought of them. You say they are too animal. But they're not mother. It's the animal in them has gone perverse, or cringing, or humble, or domesticated, like dogs. I don't know one single man who is a proud living animal. I know they've left off really thinking. But then men always do leave off really thinking, when the last bit of wild animal dies in them. (49–50)

"Real" mind, then, is not strictly mind at all. Thinking, for Lawrence, is more than reasoning; indeed, it is also *being*, being a "proud living animal." Real mind partakes of the intuitive and the extrarational. Lou's explanation also reinforces Lawrence's reliance on the wild/domesticated binary and his recurrent disdain for domestication. In fact, Lou implies that St. Mawr is partially spoiled by domestication when she explains,

"Life doesn't rush into us, as it does even into St. Mawr, and he's a dependent animal" (49).

Like Birkin in *Women in Love,* Lou comes to disdain the domesticated human that has lost its connection to spontaneous, animal consciousness. Birkin believes he can find salvation through his relationship to Ursula because that relationship acknowledges what we might describe as an animal otherness, a "pure" living alterity in each person, and because the relationship honors bodily experience as something that cannot be framed or explained by humanist cultural discourses. What is striking about the comparison between Birkin and Lou Witt is that Lou, at least within the span of the novel, rejects the possibility of finding this ontological connection in another person. Indeed, we might say that Birkin's human otherness, though it attempts to recuperate human animality, is *not other enough* for Lou Witt, who is compelled almost singly by the horse's way of being-in-the-world. Another way of framing the comparison between the two texts is to consider the later novel as outlining a more specific idealization of animality *as such*—of nonhuman subjectivity—rather than a human participation in animal being.

It is important to ask whether Lawrence's idealization of animality *qua* animality can sometimes slip into what might be considered a nostalgia for a nobler humanity. Marjorie Garber discusses this kind of transference in her essay, "Heavy Petting," part of Diana Fuss's collection *Human, All Too Human.* Garber reads recent and historical obsessions with dogs and other animals in Western culture as an idealized projection of human integrity onto the animal. "The dog," she claims, "becomes the repository of those idealized human properties that we have cynically ceased to find among humans."[15] While Lawrence rarely projects notions of "fidelity, family, marriage . . . and unambiguousness" (32) onto St. Mawr, Garber's larger contention that the "renewed, even obsessive, popularity of anthropomorphism in science and popular culture is a sign of a desperate nostalgia for humanism" (33) opens up a possible critique of Lawrence's repeated idealization of the animal.

There are moments in the text that exhibit an attenuated form of Garber's transference. Perhaps the most obvious of these occurs when Lou detects "a great animal sadness" (75) in the horse, a consciousness of the lost nobility in man. In this moment, the horse actually takes on Lawrence's anti-industrialist sensibility and is described as a "generous creature which sees all ends turning to the morass of ignoble living" (76). In what I would call a moment of romantic weakness, Lawrence attributes to

St. Mawr an outmoded discernment of nobility: "[Lou] knew that the horse, born to serve nobly, had waited in vain for someone noble to serve. His spirit knew that nobility had gone out of men. And this left him high and dry, in a sort of despair" (76). This description is paradoxically freighted with assumptions about animals inherently longing to serve man and yet exhibiting a more enduring integrity. In fact, this explanation of the horse's bad temper serves as an idealized justification of humankind's age-old dominance of animals. Earlier in the text, Lawrence suggests that the horse simply resists domestication, that its natural wildness and sponta-neous life cannot be contained by man's control. Therefore, this passage not only slips into an idealized anthropomorphism, but it also reveals the philosophical moves that thinkers like Vicki Hearne make in order to jus-tify our domestication of certain animals like horses and dogs.[16]

It is no surprise that these idealizations sometimes occur in Lawrence's text, for whenever we describe the "other" we participate in a projection, and Lawrence *is* engaged in a philosophical quest for the best kind of *human* being that he can imagine. I have already shown how Lawrence relies on racialized stereotypes in *The Plumed Serpent* to construct an ideal animal-spiritual ontology, and *St. Mawr* contains similar racialized constructions that I have not addressed specifically in this discussion. In fact, the problem of projection and representation is a much debated one in feminist, postcolonial, and queer theory. And as I note in my intro-duction, theorizing the animal is especially dangerous because the ani-mal cannot theorize back. Having said this, however, it is important to make distinctions about these inevitable projections. Though Lawrence's text sometimes engages in idealizations that suggest a desire for a cer-tain hyperhumanism, these moments are atypical of his work. Lawrence certainly displays ambivalence toward animality throughout his oeuvre, and his texts reveal repeated tensions between respecting and co-opting the alterity of the animal other. But I want to suggest that there is a very strong current in works like *Women in Love* and *St. Mawr* that values the undecidability—the "mystery"—of animality, a current that privileges an-imal alterity in its phenomenality and in that privileging reveals that "the human" is not, never was, and indeed should not be coterminous with its rationalized self-fantasy. Lawrence tends to privilege animals because they are unrepresentative of humanist values, not because they seem to mimic them. In other words, Lawrence's idealization of the animal is not, pri-marily, what Garber calls "Dog Love"; it is rather a privileging of animality that contests the virtues of the conventional Western human.

Recent readings of *St. Mawr* have been too quick to dismiss the text's attention to the horse as humanistic fantasy. John Haegert's extended reading of the novel, for instance, collapses St. Mawr, Morgan Lewis, New Mexico, and America itself into a monolithic category of "seductive" symbols, interchangeable representations of an unspoiled nature that are ultimately deconstructed and therefore fail to provide any stable meaning.[17] In keeping with Garber's perspective, Haegert argues that St. Mawr's disappearance from the text near its end "should warn us that the proleptic pattern he initiates may be an illusion after all, or what amounts to the same thing, an all too human fiction generated by Lou's desperate need to see the familiar repeated in the strange" (80). Haegert emphasizes the characters' divergent readings of St. Mawr (as noble, evil, deviant, pure) and the text's "refusal to substantiate the symbolic value [Lou] attaches to St. Mawr or to the New Mexican landscape." He concludes with the claim that just as "St. Mawr proves to be an arbitrary and indeterminate signifier, so all of Lou's selected symbols of natural life fall far short of the power and magnificence they were meant to express" (85).

Haegert's heavily theoretical reading, which essentially sees the novel as "a crisis of the sign" (88), proffers a reductionist conclusion that specifically misunderstands the pivotal role of animality in the text. Of course, it is true that Lou's sometimes romantic notions of the horse are called into question by the text, as it is true that Lawrence recognizes the danger of projecting "one's egoistic need" (91) onto nature, but these ambivalences in the text do not render St. Mawr an "arbitrary" sign. To the contrary, the fact that St. Mawr cannot be encompassed by a totalizing meaning in the text points to the fullness, if you will, the plenitude of his meaning as animal other, as unknowable quantity, as a being radically different from the human. To put a finer point on it, the text doesn't so much refuse to provide a symbolic meaning for St. Mawr as it insists upon the radical alterity of St. Mawr *as his meaning* for Lou Witt. This refusal should not be read as a "crisis of the sign," but rather as a crisis of the *real*, an eruption of that which resists symbolization—what Žižek calls enjoyment and what Lawrence experiences as animality. In fact, it is primarily Lou's perception of St. Mawr that leads her to ask near the novel's end, "What was real? What under heaven was real?" (131).

Having said this, I must repeat that St. Mawr *is* considered a partially domesticated animal in the text, and thus his being is understood as partly tainted by human interaction. In other words, I am not arguing that St. Mawr serves only as a pure and unadulterated power that remains unquestioned in the text. But it is that in him which resists the human, which remains outside and apart from the symbolic—and yet, of course, deeply embedded in it as its "other"—that compels Lou's decision to retreat from others, to seek her aloneness in the New Mexican landscape. The indeterminacy of St. Mawr as sign, in other words, does not cancel out the important discourse of animality in the text; it reinforces it. In fact, St. Mawr's eventual absence from the text is an indication of Lawrence's awareness that his own and Lou's repeated attempts to represent the animal are futile, because the animal eludes our symbolic codes. This elusiveness is the very thing that Lawrence seemed to value in animals, and the textual relinquishing of such representations merely reinforces his understanding of the animal as a redemptive figure, an understanding that I read as Lawrence's specific kind of posthumanism that dismantles species boundaries.

By the end of *St. Mawr* Lou feels she is finished with people, with men. She "wanted relief from the nervous tension and irritation of her life, she wanted to escape from the friction which is the whole stimulus in modern social life. She wanted to be still: only that, to be very, very still, and recover her own soul" (137). This recurring association between animality and the soul in Lawrence's work is one I have already outlined in *The Plumed Serpent* and in the poem "Fish." In fact, Inniss takes note of this correspondence, explaining, "The 'animal' kingdom, then, is within us. 'Africa' or 'Mexico' are objective correlatives, correspondences, for a level of consciousness, for states of soul" (23). For Lawrence, the animal possesses a spiritual innocence shaped by negativity, that is, an innocence *from* extreme forms of rationalism that mechanize being. Animals display a kind of antiepistemology, a means of knowing that operates outside the constraints of language: they "know" without reasoning, questioning, or wondering. Theirs is a presence that mocks the logic of Cartesian self-consciousness and power. Such "soul" is not the divine *logos* of Judeo-Christian tradition; rather, it is an innocence from reason, which for Lawrence has become humanity's most crippling distinction.

Chaplin's well-known aversion to sound is thus not to be dismissed as a simple nostalgic commitment to a silent paradise; it reveals a far deeper than usual knowledge (or at least presentiment) of the disruptive power of the voice, of the fact that the voice functions as a foreign body, as a kind of parasite introducing a radical split: the advent of the Word throws the human animal off balance and makes of him a ridiculous, impotent figure, gesticulating and striving desperately for a lost balance. —Slavoj Žižek, Enjoy Your Symptom

5   Revising the Human

Djuna Barnes's *Nightwood*, like many modernist texts, sustains a commentary on the problematic status of the human subject in the early twentieth century as it straddles the legacies of Enlightenment rationalism and the revelations of Darwinism. But unlike much modernist writing, this novel refuses the disavowal of animality onto marginalized others in the service of imperialist and masculinist projections. While critics have been engaged for some time in examining the discourses of gender, race, and sexuality in the novel, Barnes's species discourse, and its relationship to language in this text, circumscribe a posthuman identity premised on a critique of the phallus. Robin Vote figures nonidentity as a form of subjectivity in *Nightwood*, where the nonlinguistic, the undecidable, and the animal serve to revise what counts as human.

Barnes's novel formulates a scathing critique of language, of that which forces the unknowable into the realm of the known. Indeed, reading this ornate and historically marginalized text engages us in deep philosophical narratives that trouble humanist subjectivities by privileging a kind of animal consciousness. Bonnie Kime Scott reminds us that the original title of Barnes's novel reveals more clearly its engagement with the discourse of species: "Djuna Barnes wrote to her writer/agent/friend Emily Holmes Coleman that, before settling upon *Nightwood* as a title for her best-known

novel, she had considered *Night Beast,* and regretted the 'debased meaning now put on that nice word beast.'"[1] This final sentiment hints at the
larger philosophical structure of Barnes's mandarin text, for, in effect, the
novel privileges the "beastly." It validates a human ontological mode that
is open to multiplicity, organicism, and perpetual change. Conversely, the
text associates traditional humanist forms of identity with alienation, dis-
illusionment, futility, and disaster.

This critique of identity is played out primarily through the dialectic of
language and silence in the novel. The word as stabilizer of identity comes
under consistent abuse, particularly through the immoderate speeches of
Dr. Matthew O'Connor and the various linguistic refusals of Robin Vote.
Robin embodies nonidentity as an authentic form of being in the text,
and her silence is a marker of this value system. She refuses to categorize
her gender or her sexuality, and by the novel's end she is unwilling to
conform to a human identity that disavows her own animal being. Robin
will ultimately transgress the symbolic as a limit upon her phenomenality. Through Robin's character, Barnes troubles the very terms of human
subjectivity by thinking identity outside the conditions set by its symbolic
economies.

Nightwood is a novel obsessively concerned with the politics of the outside. The hierarchical binaries of male/female, white/black, Christian/Jew,
heterosexual/homosexual, and human/animal are woven throughout the
text in variously overlapping and abutting matrices. As the novel opens,
the fabricated lineage of Felix Volkbein signals what will be the text's ongoing concern with such configurations of the powerful and the abject.
Felix's father, Guido Volkbein, was a Jewish man who invented for himself
an Austrian, Christian heritage of aristocratic lines. The father substantiated his false Christian identity to his Christian wife by laying claim to a
coat of arms and a list of nonexistent ancestors. Felix, who believes himself
a "pure" descendent of Christian, European aristocracy, is in fact a child of
miscegenation. Guido's "pretense to a barony" went undiscovered even by
his wife, Hedvig, but she remained suspicious of him throughout her life,
repeatedly asking her husband, "What is the matter?"[2] Hedvig's question
emphasizes the materiality of blood connections; according to the logic of
aristocratic power structures, one should only be named "baron" if one's
blood allows, so the linguistic signifier weds the material and immaterial,
the tissue and the title.

It is the physical make-up of the body here—bodily *matter*—that infuses aristocratic birthrights with value as cultural capital. Thus, aristoc-

racy is materialized or rendered powerful through bodies that are "purely" bred. Judith Butler explains such productions of "bodies that matter" with attention to the exclusions upon which they depend:

> This xenophobic exclusion operates through the production of ra-
> cialized Others, and those whose "natures" are considered less ratio-
> nal by virtue of their appointed task in the process of laboring to re-
> produce the conditions of private life. This domain of the less than
> rational human bounds the figure of human reason, producing that
> "man" as one who is without a childhood; is not a primate and so is
> relieved of the necessity of eating, defecating, living and dying; one
> who is not a slave, but always a property holder; one whose language
> remains originary and untranslatable.[3]

We will return to questions of animality and language. Here, Butler's discussion of racial abjection points out Felix's ironic position as he unknowingly invalidates his own assumed claim to aristocratic status.[4] In Žižekian terms, Felix operates as his own internal impediment in the "circuit" of racial purity and stable, normative identity. Žižek explains that in psychoanalytic theory, "even if the psychic apparatus is entirely left to itself, it will not attain the balance for which the 'pleasure principle' strives, but will continue to circulate around *a traumatic intruder in its interior*—the limit upon which the 'pleasure principle' stumbles is internal to it" (emphasis added).[5] Similarly, Felix's status as Jewish, which is materially inherent in his "blood" according to the logic of racial purity, functions as an inescapable impediment to his drive for European privilege and at the same time, of course, its alibi and *raison d'être*.

The "acculturation" of blood is manifested in the Volkbein's décor in the novel's opening scenes. Their pianos sit on "the thick dragon's-blood pile of rugs from Madrid," and the desks in their study are carved from "rich and bloody wood" (5–6). While the Volkbein's furniture seems to translate blood into breeding, their son suffers from the falsity of his father's claims. Felix's blood betrays him as one far removed from the fixity of an aristocratic heritage. Indeed, Felix is "the Jew that seems to be everywhere from nowhere" (7). He lacks place not only because his father has concealed Felix's actual lineage, but also because that Jewish heritage, according to the racial ideologies of the text, predisposes him to a life of wandering and homelessness. Such associations are found in a wide range of modernist texts—too wide to enumerate here—but particularly in the work of writers such as T. S. Eliot, Wyndham Lewis, and James Joyce.

The crucial point about Felix, the point that sets up the larger philosophical problems of the text as a whole, is that he suffers from what is essentially a desperate *desire for* identity—an identity that is fixed by language and culture, an identity whose meaning is guaranteed by the symbolic order, an identity that constitutes a stable subject-position in relation to humanist systems of value: in essence, a phallic identity. Felix's attempted identifications with aristocracy and hierarchy mirror, in psychoanalytic terms, his desire to "have" the phallus and, in the having, to be stabilized in relation to the Transcendental Signifier. As Judith Butler reminds us, however, such identifications are bound to fail: they are "vain striving[s] to approximate and possess what no one ever can have," and they therefore require rigorous and repeated citation:

> Identification is constantly figured as a desired event or accomplishment, but one which finally is never achieved; identification is the phantasmatic staging of the event. . . . Identifications are never fully and finally made; they are incessantly reconstituted and, as such, are subject to the volatile logic of iterability. They are that which is constantly marshaled, consolidated, retrenched, contested, and on occasion, compelled to give way. (105)

Felix's neurotic obsession with the past—and with *his* past—not only functions as a symptomatic marker of his false origins, but it also points to the more general unsustainability of identity as such. Felix is obsessed with "what he termed 'Old Europe': aristocracy, nobility, royalty . . . bowing searching, with quick pendulous movement, for the correct thing to which to pay tribute" (9). He also becomes "the 'collector' of his own past" (10), and the collector in this novel represents a distinct ideological position. Collectors meticulously gather singular objects in museums and galleries, objects which represent a particular style, culture, era, and so on. Each object in a museum has a quantifiable function; it *signifies* something specific and can be placed within an exacting narrative of "high" aesthetic and symbolic meaning.

Felix collects images of his own identity in an attempt to make it signify, to infuse it with a fixed meaning—or in Lacanese—with a symbolic plenitude. In fact, the "museums" in Barnes's text are often private residences arranged so that their furnishings and displayed objects represent a love relationship. The Volkbein's home, for instance, is "a museum of their encounter," (11) and this very phrase is used later to describe Nora's home and her attempted reification and control of her relationship with Robin. It is Robin, of course, who vigorously rejects the collector's penchant for fixing meaning and identity. But we will come to that.

For Felix, who has internalized racial, economic, and cultural distinctions,[6] and who vainly seeks to fill the void opened up in his subjectivity by his false lineage, nonidentity *functions as a lack*. Felix experiences nonidentity as a gapping void in his subjectivity which drives him to act out his desire to "bow down" to some proper cultural authority. In "Where the Tree Falls," Felix enters a café and believes he sees "the Grand Duke Alexander of Russia, cousin and brother-in-law of the late czar Nicholas" (125). On his way out that evening, Felix bows to this man in a ridiculous and shameful act of desperation meant to sustain his illusions of propriety and place. Robin's tendency to bow down will take on a much different valence in the novel.

While Felix is clearly marked by his need to create a phallic identity, Dr. Matthew O'Connor, the second primary character to emerge in Barnes's text, presents a more complicated relation to that desire. The doctor's introduction in the novel underscores the significance of language in Barnes's textual staging of the identity question. Matthew first appears at Count Altamonte's party, where everyone in attendance is listening to Matthew rant. "Once the doctor had his audience," we are told, "nothing could stop him" (15). Talking, it seems, is not only the doctor's habitual activity, but also his excessive compulsion. He speaks loudly, garishly, and endlessly. Matthew's linguistic excesses in the text are matched only— and conversely—by the surplus of Robin's silence.

Language and its absence are pivotal frameworks through which Barnes articulates the problematics of identity in *Nightwood*. When Matthew answers Felix's question about Vienna with rhapsodies on "young Austrian boys," instead of its "great names," Felix feels "that the evening was already lost . . . given over to this volatile person *who called himself a doctor*" (17; emphasis added). Felix's disappointment in Matthew turns centrally on the doctor's disinterest in the status conferred by great names and, most importantly, on the failure of a name to correspond accurately with its signified content. That is, Matthew seems to lay false claim to the title, "doctor," and the reader already senses that this "middle-aged 'medical student'" (14) is of questionable repute. This exchange, like much of the novel, exposes the arbitrary relationship between signifier and signified, putting particular emphasis on this disparity in matters of name and identity. Felix is also distressed by Matthew's dubitable claim to be a doctor because it ignites a subconscious confirmation that Felix's own claim to aristocratic lines is an equivalent sham.

Felix longs for what Derrida describes famously in "Speech and Phenomena" as the fullness of meaning as presence in speech and the correlative understanding of history as "the production and recollection of beings in presence, as knowledge and mastery."[7] Felix wants the term *baron* to correlate with a fullness of meaning, an originary power ascribed to his person through bloodlines. He would like for the term *doctor* to line up with Matthew's mastery of a body of knowledge. Felix desires a correspondence between the signifier and the self-presence and authority of humanist (phallic) identity. Both the word and the phallus are idealized in this wish-structure so apparent in Felix. Derrida helps us think about the specific connection between the idealized phallus and the spoken word in his well-known critique of Lacan's reading of *The Purloined Letter*. Addressing Lacan's claim that the letter in Poe's story is indivisible, Derrida argues that this indivisibility of the letter can be understood as an idealization of the phallus, an idealization upon which the whole ideological system of psychoanalysis depends. As Barbara Johnson explains in reference to Derrida's analysis, "With the phallus safely idealized and located in the voice, the so-called signifier acquires the 'unique, living, non-mutilable [*sic*] integrity' of the self-present spoken word, unequivocally pinned down to and by the *signified*."[8] This critique of Lacan underscores Derrida's ongoing skepticism toward meaning as univocal, circumscribed, and locatable in the metaphysics of presence, particularly as it is manifested in the spoken word. Accordingly, Felix's longing for a normative, phallic identity is tied to the "power" of words to express and embody the idealized plenitude of meaning that undergirds such identity, but this "power" is revealed by the text as a sham. The text insists that language is *opposed* to being or presence, that language, in fact, destroys being. Thus, I argue that the text displays a critique of the phallus and its derivatives, especially identity. This critique is specifically marshaled through the interrogation of language and the concomitant privileging of being as nonidentity, as something therefore beyond humanism. One might draw a parallel between Derrida's critique of Lacan's privileging of "full speech" in the psychoanalytic exchange and the novel's critique of "full speech" in the formation of identity. This parallel would, however, have to be tempered by the extraordinarily complex debate surrounding Derrida's critique of Lacan, which I cannot begin to outline here.[9]

Keeping in mind that Lacan's phallocentrism is a much contested topic that ranges well beyond the scope of this chapter[10]—and therefore leaving that question aside—we might posit Žižek's description of the Lacanian signifier as an initial parallel to the text's position on the word, a position I will continue to unpack:

> [Consider] the fundamental Lacanian notion of the signifier *qua* that power which mortifies/disembodies the life substance, "dissects" the body and subordinates it to the constraint of the signifying network. Word is murder of a thing, not only in the elementary sense of implying its absence—by naming a thing, we treat it as absent, as dead, although it is still present—but above all in the sense of its radical *dissection:* the word "quarters" the thing, it tears it out of the embedment in its concrete context. . . . The power of understanding consists in this capacity to reduce the organic whole of experience to an appendix to the "dead" symbolic classification. (51)

In this sense, then, the reign of the symbolic is the *"reign of the dead over life"* (54), and it is this reign of the symbolic that comes under vigorous attack in *Nightwood*. But I am getting ahead of myself: let us consider the novel's specific critique of language.

The distance or gap between the word and being, between the word and "the living," or what Žižek describes above as the signifier's radical dissection of experience, this distance is not only noted by Felix when he assumes that Matthew merely "calls" himself a doctor. The gap is also the subject of Nora Flood's first words in the novel, which come on the heels of Felix's misgiving. Addressing herself to Felix and Matthew, she boldly asks, "Are you both really saying what you mean, or are you just talking?" (18). The text repeatedly poses this question, particularly through the lens of Matthew's loquacity. Nora's first words set the stage for what becomes an inverse, exponential relationship between speaking and meaning in the novel: the more one says, the more divorced one becomes from meaning. Put another way, the more one uses language to capture experience, the further away one moves from that experience. Judith Lee confirms this dynamic when she writes that the "power of speech is associated with the experience of separation and difference" in the novel.[11]

Matthew, the novel's most excessive talker, already gestures toward self-rebuke in this opening scene when he describes Martin Luther as a man who "went wild and chattered like a monkey in a tree and started something he never thought to start." Matthew aligns Protestantism with prattle when he insists that in a Protestant church, one listens "to the words of a man who has been chosen for his eloquence . . . [whose] golden tongue is never satisfied until it has wagged itself over the destiny of a nation." Resurrecting the text's initial concern with the meaning and symbolism of blood, Matthew then contrasts this talkative faith to that of the Catholic Church, "Something that's already in your blood" (20). He aligns language with the noncorporeal and abstracted: blood and the body remain alien to excessive "chatter." The use of Catholicism to launch this distinction can be puzzling given the Catholic emphasis on ritual and liturgical symbolism. But the doctrine of transubstantiation probably underlies the comparison. That is, the Eucharist does not just *symbolize* the body and blood of Christ for Catholics; rather, it *is* the flesh of God. What Catholicism underscores by insisting on the sacramental fleshness of the body of Christ is precisely the link between "eating well" and the ethical bringing-into-being of the subject that Derrida outlines in his essay by the same name. Subjectivity in the West, Derrida suggests, operates most centrally through "cannibalisms" both real and symbolic. "Carnophallogocentrism," then, can be glossed as a certain "becoming-subject of substance" for which one must "take seriously the idealizing interiorization of the phallus and the necessity of its passage through the mouth, whether it's a matter of words or of things, of sentences, of daily bread or wine, of the tongue, the lips, or the breast of the other."[12] Becoming "human" is accomplished through the ingestion, incorporation, and interiorization of the other, the other both as object and as subject. Transubstantiation is indeed *the symbolic cannibalism* par excellence in which the ingestion of the flesh of God (the word that has become flesh) calls the subject into its highest relation to the ethical and the metaphysical. Thus Derrida's observation that

> The question is no longer one of knowing if it is "good" to eat the other or if the other is "good" to eat, nor of knowing which other. One eats him regardless and lets oneself be eaten by him. The so called nonanthropophagic cultures practice symbolic anthropophagy and even construct their most elevated socius, indeed the sublimity of

their morality, their politics, and their right, on this anthropophagy. ("Eating Well," 114)

Transubstantiation insists upon an interimbrication of the symbolic and material that performs a deconstruction of this most emblematic of binaries. What Matthew's discussion suggests, in a very Derridean way, is that the "highest" of symbolic spiritual discourses contains, indeed *is premised upon,* the "lowest" of physical economies which involves the intimate passage through—and we must not forget all the way through—the body. Such deconstructions characterize the novel, particularly through Matthew's discursive strategies (though not necessarily his performative ones, a distinction I discuss later), which are largely aimed at affirming the coincidence of high and low, clean and unclean.

Religion—particularly Catholicism—continues to be a significant discourse through which Barnes renders the entanglement or interimbrication of hierarchical opposites in the novel. The dissolution of oppositional boundaries serves as a meta-theme in the text, as Jane Marcus confirms in her discussion of tattooing as an activity that blurs the distinction between spirit and body. According to Marcus, "*Nightwood* is about merging, dissolution, and, above all, hybridization. . . . *Nightwood* makes a modernism of marginality" (223). Nikka, the "nigger who used to fight the bear in the *Cirque de Paris*" (Barnes, 16), embodies such hybridization in the text: his racially and culturally marginalized (and sexualized) body is covered with tattoos referencing high literary, architectural, and sacred "texts" that challenge his cultural assignation as "savage." Thus, while Nikka crouches nearly naked in the circus pit, locked in battle against an animal domesticated to act wild, his body references cultural discourses that challenge his cultural assignation as "savage." The linking of spiritual and bodily recurs later in the novel when Robin becomes pregnant and immediately takes the Catholic vow, when Matthew "masturbates" in an empty church, and of course, in the final scene in which Robin seemingly attempts to become dog, in whatever sense we might understand that becoming. In part, these linkages reflect the text's insistence upon the inclusion of animality as essential to human identity, as not separable from it. That inseparability explains Matthew's admonishments to embrace the "good dirt" (85), and Robin Vote will attempt such an embrace primarily through the suspicion of the usefulness of language and its counterpart, identity.

This usefulness is challenged as Felix and his friend Frau Mann are walking out of the count's *soirée;* Felix asks her, "Is he really a Count?" While this question is ostensibly concerned with the patrician bloodlines that are Felix's fixation, Frau Mann's reply constitutes the more radical interrogation of language and identity that underlies his query. She responds with knowing incredulity: "*Herr Gott!* . . . Am I what I say? Are you? Is the doctor?" (25). Thus one of the central problems of the novel is laid bare. One cannot *be* what one calls oneself: language cannot account for ontology. But this thesis is highly problematic since meaning, at least in the Western tradition, is almost always linked to symbolic systems, most often to linguistic ones. This linkage is what Derrida points out in his rigorous critique of Heidegger's concept of Being or spirit as an exclusively human phenomenon. Derrida explains that the fundamental difference Heidegger posits between man and animal is one of language; it is the human ability to name an entity, and recognize that entity in its individual entity-ness, that separates humanity from the rest of the "animal" world. In contrast, the animal is characterized by the inability to name, by the "properly *phenomenological* impossibility of speaking the phenomenon whose phenomenality as such, or whose very *as such*, does not appear to the animal and does not unveil the Being of the entity."[13] If identity cannot be posited through language, through what one says, then what of identity? Robin Vote produces the rejoinder to this, the text's deepest question.

Robin's introduction in the novel provides a marked divergence from the concerns with naming and placing that have characterized the text's first interactions between Felix and Matthew. She is not only silent in this introduction, she is wholly unconscious and utterly removed from the realm of social and civil distinctions. The first significant description of Robin highlights her odor as something "of the quality of that earth-flesh, fungi, which smells of captured dampness" (34). The emphasis on smell places Robin clearly in the realm of animality, for, later in the text, Matthew insists that "Animals find their way about largely by the keenness of their nose . . . [we] have lost ours in order not to be one of them" (119). A clear echo of Freud in his *Civilization and its Discontents,* this coupling of animality and the olfactory explains the "organic repression," to use Freud's term, that one must perform in order to stand upright, disavow one's animal nature, "become" and remain human.[14]

Robin is also figured as a prehuman organic body whose "flesh was the texture of plant life" and whose head is surrounded by "an effulgence as of phosphorus glowing about the circumference of a body of water" (34). She is a supremely primordial and elementary being whose subjectivity, rather than being crisp and distinct, is characterized by seepage and overlapping. Among other binaries, she confounds the typical separation between human and animal: she seems "to lie in a jungle trapped in a drawing room . . . [wherein] one expects to hear the strains of an orchestra of wood-winds render a serenade which will popularize the wilderness" (35). Thus Robin represents the refusal of organic repression as a necessary condition for the achievement of human subjectivity. Rather than abjecting animality, she seems to include it as a necessary part of her "humanity."

Robin is further described as one whose "life lay through her in ungainly luminous deteriorations—the troubling structure of the born somnambule, who lives in two worlds—meet of child and desperado" (35). The image of the sleepwalker suggests that Robin's primary subjectivity resides in her unconscious being, and that her "conscious" self is secondary. This is why Nora's eventual awakening of Robin from a deep sleep takes on such violent and devastating proportions later in the novel, for Robin is most at peace in the world of the unconscious. She will continue to defy and contest boundaries throughout the text because, in essence, she refuses to occupy a stabilized and locatable subjectivity.

Most interesting for my purposes is the text's description of Robin as "a woman who is beast turning human" (37). This crucial phrase refuses to place Robin firmly in either the animal or human realm. She is "turning" or becoming; she is both animal and human. As Kime Scott notes, Barnes "constructs a blurred middle ground between the bestial and the human, disrupting these categories, and the very practice of categorization" (43). It is thus through Robin's character that Barnes launches her most radical critique of humanism and its abjection of the animal. Robin's character insists that our connections to materiality must not be disavowed in order to produce the subject of humanism. The phrase—"beast turning human"—also emphasizes on the linguistic level that Robin cannot be described with one word or term. She defies the power of the signifier to represent its implied signified.

Robin's character undercuts the traditional notion that human and animal are separate realms at all and calls for an expanded definition of humanity that includes characteristics usually disavowed in Western culture. As the "infected carrier of the past," she represents what has been systematically repressed by centuries of civilization, and so "before her the structure of our head and jaws ache—we feel that we could eat her, she who is eaten death returning, for only then do we put our face close to the blood on the lips of our forefathers" (37). This opaque passage re-engages the question of cannibalism to emphasize Robin's connections to blood and corporeality. Infected by the past, she embodies our organic lineage, our ancestral connection to the animal, or as Karen Kaivola puts it, Robin offers "access to whatever aspects of ourselves we might ordinar-ily repress," personifying "the unconscious and the instinctual."[15] And, more importantly, the desire to eat her suggests an obscene cannibalis-tic drive that ignores the edicts of humanist ideologies that separate hu-man from animal by forbidding the consumption of human flesh. In this sense, Robin reminds us of some past organicism which destabilizes the most strident and humanist of boundaries, those against cannibalizing one another. Or, given Derrida's discussion of ingestion and incorpora-tion, Robin invites us into a transgressive *literalizing* of the symbolic can-nibalisms that structure our subjectivation.

Felix is ironically most compelled by Robin's ability to carry "the qual-ity of the 'way back' as animals do" (40). He naively believes that Robin's apparent link to the past will provide the stabilized identity he so des-perately seeks to inhabit. But their fundamental incompatibility begins to surface immediately and reaches its apex with the birth of their son, Guido. When the infant is a week old, Robin returns from a wandering spell, and, at Felix's approach, says "in a fury, 'I didn't want him!'" After striking Felix, Robin suggests that they deny Guido's existence: "'Why not be secret about him?' she said. 'Why talk?'" (49). The latter question re-sounds with Nora's opening query to Felix and Matthew. Why talk, she implies, when words are empty and meaningless? More to the point is the way this question characterizes Robin's implicit interrogation of phallic or symbolic identity.

In her dismay at not wanting to have given birth, Robin leaves Felix and Guido. After she reappears in a romantic relationship with Nora Flood, however, Robin refuses to provide an explanation for her disappearance: "She did not explain where she had been: she was unable or unwilling to give an account of herself" (49). Robin's *modus operandi* is to remain un-accounted for, unlocatable, particularly by avoiding language. Robin's few proclamations in the text insist that the word's ability to define and posi-tion one is false and undesirable. However, despite the fact that Robin has escaped from Felix and his loyalty to the signifier, she is now involved with Nora, who, "by temperament . . . was an early Christian; she believed *the word"* (51; emphasis added). But Nora, like Felix, seems attracted to Robin because Robin rejects the word and believes "the blood." Nora also wants to capture Robin and domesticate her within some Oedipalized framework, channeling Robin's wayward energies into a familial structure. As Dianne Chisholm argues, "For Nora ... Robin signals a primeval animism that Nora had not known she was missing and that she tries obsessively to domesticate and possess."[16] We might substitute the more specific term "animality" for Chisholm's "animism" here.

Robin's alliance with Nora is also marked by resistance and dissatisfaction, though it is less violent than her relationship with Felix. Nora and Robin meet at the circus, a carnivalesque setting traditionally associated with the disruption of hierarchies. Here, Robin is powerfully aligned with the circus animals *in their captivity:*

> A girl sitting beside Nora took out a cigarette and lit it; her hands shook and Nora turned to look at her; she looked at her suddenly because the animals, going around and around the ring, all but climbed over at that point. They did not seem to see the girl, but as their dusty eyes moved past, the orbit of their light seemed to turn on her. ... Then as one powerful lioness came to the turn of the bars, exactly opposite the girl, she turned her furious great head with its yellow eyes afire and went down, her paws thrust through the bars and, as she regarded the girl, as if a river were falling behind impassable heat, her eyes flowed in tears that never reached the surface. (54)

These animals do not rely on the humanized specular economy to "see" Robin; they rather seem to share her experience of imprisonment and her longing to escape. While there is an uncanny element of desire in the lioness's stance, it remains unclear whether that desire be for acknowledgment, release, or communion. The animal's going down parallels Robin's own prostration at the end of the novel and suggests surrender or abandon. The final image of a river "falling behind impassable heat" and tears that never reach the surface not only links the animal's and Robin's stultification by humanist power structures that repress animality, it also suggests that an animal's experience, though technically "untranslatable" into human language, is nonetheless powerful and clear. Indeed, the animal's experience/desire is so overwhelming that Robin "rose straight up" from her seat, and Nora insists they leave the circus immediately (54).

At this point, Robin is—typically—unable to articulate her desire to be positioned in relation to her surroundings. She "looked about distractedly. 'I don't want to be here.' But it was all she said; she did not explain where she wished to be" (55). This statement accurately condenses Robin's more general privileging of nonidentity and change: she does not want to be "here," to be specifically placed and marked, but she also does not express an alternative preference for another space/place from which to measure her relations to others. This childlike and animal-like resistance to self-definition elicits a parental or keeper function in Nora. As the two begin their life together, Robin "told only a little of her life, but she kept repeating in one way or another her wish for a home, as if she were afraid she would be lost again, as if she were aware, without conscious knowledge, that she belonged to Nora, and that if Nora did not make it permanent by her own strength, she would forget" (55). A few pages later, Robin's less-than-conscious "knowledge" is described as her "tragic longing to be kept, knowing herself astray" (58). This passage reinforces Robin's link to ("stray") animals and further constructs the relationship between Nora and Robin as one of keeper and pet. But Nora already senses that her "pet" will never be fully domesticated. While their home is a museum of their encounter, Nora obsessively keeps everything in its place because of "an unreasoning fear—if she disarranged anything Robin might become confused—might lose the scent of home" (56).

Inevitably, though the two women live together for years, Robin begins to stray. She refuses to be identified with one place or one person, so during her night "departures" Robin goes "from table to table, from drink to drink, from person to person." Even her thoughts, we are told, "were in themselves a form of locomotion" (59). These descriptions align Robin with continuous change and movement. Interestingly, her resistance to stable "positions" is foreshadowed the very moment she is introduced in the text, where she is figured as a dancer: "Her legs, in white flannel trousers, were spread as in a dance, the thick-lacquered pumps looking too lively for the arrested step" (34). While beginning dancers imitate positions, advanced dancers "move through" positions to create a seamless and continuously changing movement-event. Deleuze and Guattari address this phenomenon: "Movement has an essential relation to the imperceptible; it is by nature imperceptible. Perception can grasp movement only as the displacement of a moving body or the development of a form. Movements, becomings, in other words, pure relations of speed and slowness, pure affect, are below and above the threshold of perception."[17]

Robin is therefore appropriately figured as a dancer who functions within a continuous displacement of desire, a circuit of affect, and who in a certain sense cannot be *perceived*. This configuration of Robin as outside perception also explains the novel's repeated linkage of her character with the tactile sense. Felix is not only surprised by Robin's attraction to both the "excellent" and the "debased," but he also notices her peculiarly intense tactile proclivities:

> When she touched a thing, her hands seemed to take the place of the eye. He thought: "She has the touch of the blind who, because they see more with their fingers, forget more in their minds." Her fingers would go forward, hesitate, tremble, as if they had found a face in the dark. . . . At such moments Felix experienced unaccountable apprehension. The sensuality in her hands frightened him. (42)

This inversion of the Freudian privileging of the eye further removes Robin from the realm of the human.[18] Her radical refusal of identity and her consequent promiscuity are precisely what Nora cannot accept, despite Matthew's brutally accurate description of Robin as "outside the 'human type'—a wild thing caught in a woman's skin, monstrously alone, monstrously vain. . . . Every bed she leaves, without caring, fills her heart with peace and happiness. She has made her 'escape' again. That's why she can't 'put herself in another's place,' she herself is the only 'position'" (146).

Robin's compulsion to move, change, and resist symbolic forces that provide name, identity, and place, is torturous to Nora who respects the symbolic as a guarantor of meaning. But while Nora paces the floors awaiting Robin's return, she would "bend forward, putting her hands between her legs, and begin to cry, 'Oh, God! Oh, God! Oh, God!' repeated so often that it had the effect of *all words spoken in vain*" (61; emphasis added). This moment catalogues the failed appeal to Lacan's "big Other." Žižek explains that this "hidden agency" is typically construed as "a kind of meta subject (God, Reason, History, Jew)" (39). Nora's vain appeal "Oh, God!" reveals the emptiness of the meta-subject and the failure of words to fill out or correspond to this grand meaning. This moment, like the text as a whole, insists that the humanist, symbolic locus of power was always already evacuated, and that each performance of its power is in fact a staged feint which depends upon an "assumption" of privilege based on a retroactively posited origin that can never be substantiated. Moreover, each linguistic appeal to this meta subject is empty, vain, futile.

Words are vain for Nora because they fail to organize her relationship to Robin within a meaningful and recognizable narrative. Standard social markers like *husband* and *wife* mean nothing to Robin and are doubly insignificant for the couple since their relationship operates on the margins of a heteronormative culture. But one might argue that Nora's desire for a normative and monogamous relationship, and her maternal tendencies toward Robin, *mimic,* in some way, the standard hetero/Oedipal familial structures of Western culture. Some critics insist that the novel is just as skeptical about lesbianism as it is about heterosexual alliances; this is perhaps precisely because of Nora's need to mimic heteronormative relational frameworks. Chisholm maintains that "Instead of speaking out on lesbianism in cryptic modernism, *Nightwood* seriously challenges the epistemological and ontological claims of sexual discourse in general" (172). Moreover, it is the larger question of identity itself, and what abjections our identities require, that frames the deep ideological structure of the novel.

If Robin represents nonidentity as a privileged form of being in the text, Jenny Petherbridge provides another powerful foil to her. Jenny, like Felix, experiences nonidentity as an absence to be filled. With biting irony, the narrator indicates that Jenny's stories also fall into Nora's category of "just talking": "The stories were humorous, well told. She would smile, toss her hands up, widen her eyes; immediately everyone in the room had a certain feeling of something lost, sensing that there was one person who was missing the importance of the moment, who had not heard the story; the teller herself" (67). Jenny provides another affirmation in the text of the link between identity and language as repressive constraints: the narrator says of her, "She was master of the over-sweet phrase, the over-tight embrace" (68). In one of Robin's rare addresses to her, she snaps, "Shut up, you don't know what you are talking about. You talk all the time and you never know anything. It's such an awful weakness with you." Robin's rare speeches in the text often admonish others to give up talking. Here, violence erupts between the women. Jenny, jealous of Robin's attentions toward a young girl, strikes Robin and continues "scratching and tear-ing in hysteria, striking, clutching and crying." Robin, already bloody from the assault, does not resist the attack. Rather, she seems drawn to it: "as Jenny struck repeatedly Robin began to go forward as if brought to the movement by the very blows themselves, as if she had no will" (76).

Elaine Scarry's work on the phenomenology of pain helps to account for Robin's behavior. Scarry notes that physical pain "actively destroys [language], bringing about an immediate reversion to a state anterior to language, to the sounds and cries a human being makes before language is learned."[19] According to Scarry, the unspeakability of pain is due to its lack of referential content: pain "is not *of* or *for* anything. It is precisely because it takes no object that it, more than any other phenomenon, resists objectification in language" (5).

Robin seems partially drawn to violence because it is language-destroying. But Scarry also explains that losing the ability to speak corresponds to the destruction of identity. "It is intense pain," she claims, "that destroys *a person's self and world,* a destruction experienced spatially as either the contraction of the universe down to the immediate vicinity of the body or as the body swelling to fill the entire universe" (35; emphasis added). Jenny's beating assures, if for a moment, Robin's self-annihilation. The physical boundaries that usually demarcate a distinct "Robin" are destroyed as Jenny crosses them, and the symbolic order that creates and sustains the idea of "Robin" is therefore incapacitated.

Nora, who is made miserable by such self-obliterating behavior, decides to seek an explanation for it from Dr. O'Connor. In the labyrinthine section titled "Watchman, What of the Night?" Matthew explores the relationship between the night and identity in order to clarify Robin's mode of existence. He insists that Robin refuses to separate the clean and filthy; she serves as an organic repository that allows one to "trace himself back by his sediment, vegetable and animal, and so find himself in the odour of wine" (84). This tracing implies a dispersal of that which composes one's body. Materially speaking, what makes up the vegetable and animal, the particles of wine that enter one's nose to produce smell, these are all the same elements that compose human bodies. Thus, the hermetic separation of the human person from other objects required to produce the Cartesian subject, the "self"—or what Freud theorizes as the overcoming of "polymorphous perversity"—is troubled by Robin's mode of being.[20] We will return to the question of the polymorphous shortly, but first, a word about "the night." Žižek pays considerable attention to the Hegelian concept of "the night of the world" in his discussion of reality and the symbolic universe in *Enjoy Your Symptom.* To explain this "withdrawal of the subject into itself," this "experience of pure self *qua* 'abstract negativity,'" Žižek quotes from *Hegel's Recollection:*

The human being is this night, this empty nothing, that contains everything in its simplicity. . . . The night, the inner of nature, that exists here—pure self—in phantasmagorical presentations, is night all around it, here shoots a bloody head—there another white shape, suddenly here before it, and just so disappears. One catches sight of this night when one looks human beings in the eye—into night that becomes awful.[21]

Žižek goes on to gloss this moment as "the 'psychotic' withdrawal of the subject into itself" (50) and to point out that the symbolic order is only a temporary and momentary covering over of this fundamental negativity. In fact, while Hegel argues that language can transform this ephemeral confrontation with the night of the world, Žižek characterizes the power of language as momentary. This is his significant reversal: for Žižek, it is the night of the world that looms larger than spirit. And what Robin embodies is being *qua* "the night"—which does not require sublation through spirit because *it already is spirit,* in some post-Hegelian and post-Heideggerian sense. Indeed, in a rigorously post-human sense.

Hegel's night is an "empty nothing, that contains everything," a space of radical heterogeneity, multiplicity, and nondistinction where "phantasmagorical presentations" appear randomly and without reference to a meaningful narrative. Sleep and the unconscious also correspond with this night, explaining Robin's deep affinity for sleep and its connection to multiplicity and the nonsensical. Matthew tries to explain to Nora Robin's attraction to sleep and her own horror of that attraction:

The sleeper is the proprietor of an unknown land. He goes about another business in the dark—and we his partners . . . cannot afford an inch of it; because, though we would purchase it with blood, it has no counter and no till. . . . When she sleeps, is she not moving her leg aside for an unknown garrison? Or in a moment, that takes but a second, murdering us with an axe? Eating our ear in a pie, pushing us aside with the back of her hand, sailing to some port with a ship full of sailors and medical men? And what of our own sleep? We go to it no better—and betray her with the very virtue of our days. (87–88)

The sleeper, in her dreaming, obliterates all the commitments and promises she has made during her waking hours. In this way, sleep and the

night give the lie to social conventions, particularly monogamy and fidelity. That is, the night belies the symbolic in its foundation of the social.

Robin represents the kind of polymorphous "perversity" or multiplicity
that Deleuze and Guattari describe as "becoming-animal" in A *Thousand
Plateaus*. Animals that are nondomesticated, they explain, tend to experience themselves as packs or crowds, not as differentiated selves.[22] Robin's mode of being is rhizomatic, schizophrenic, and amorphous; it is the
practice of "deterritorializ[ing] oneself," of refusing an individuated identity (Deleuze and Guattari, 32). The essential critique that Deleuze and
Guattari level at Freud revolves around his penchant to reduce representations of multiplicity in psychotic episodes to the unifying Oedipal economy, to the "familiar themes of *the* father, *the* penis, *the* vagina, Castration
with a capital C" (27). Freud only finds "daddy" in the Wolf-Man's visions
of wolf packs: "he did not see that the unconscious itself was fundamentally a crowd" (29). Like Felix and Matthew, Freud relied upon language to
combat this frightening lack of differentiation in the psychotic mind:

When the thing splinters and loses its identity, the word is still there
to restore that identity or invent a new one. Freud counted on the
word to reestablish a unity no long found in things . . . *the* Signifier,
the devious despotic agency that substitutes itself for asignifying
proper names and replaces multiplicities with the dismal unity of
an object declared lost. (28)

Robin's character provides a similar, though implicit, critique of identity as necessarily unified by the signifier. She is indeed "psychotic" in
the sense that she refuses "to exchange enjoyment for the Name of the
Father" (77), and therefore inhabits a kind of plurality that Deleuze and
Guattari associate with the animal. Thus, the novel "affirms" psychosis,
or rather, it undoes the implied marginality of the term by insisting that
Robin's refusal of identity is, as Marcus puts it, the "more humane condition" (238). The novel also echoes Deleuze and Guattari's critique by
exposing a link between the tenets of psychoanalysis and authority that
borders on a fascist insistence on identity. Marcus says it forcefully: the
novel reveals "the collaboration of Freudian psychoanalysis with fascism
in its desire to 'civilize' and make 'normal' the sexually aberrant misfit"
(233). This normalizing function is precisely what Deleuze and Guattari
theorize in relation to animality and Freud's need to translate the Wolf-
Man's episodes into entirely humanized, Oedipalized narratives.

Robin also invites the retrieval of "filthiness" in oneself, particularly through sleep. Matthew belabors this point while Nora resists acknowledging his insights:

> A high price is demanded of any value, for a value is in itself a detachment! We wash away our sense of sin, and what does that bath secure us? Sin, shining bright and hard. In what does a Latin bathe? True dust. We have made the literal error. We have used water, we are thus too sharply reminded. A European gets out of bed with *a disorder that holds the balance*. The layers of his deed can be traced back to the last leaf and the good slug be found creeping. (89; emphasis added)

Matthew again privileges Robin's disorder as one that "holds the balance." This phrase suggests that the clean and civilized life, the Oedipalized and repressed life distant from animality, is conversely off balance. One is reminded of Judith Butler's discussion of the oppressive nature of coherent identities.[23] "The question here," she explains, "concerns the tacit cruelties that sustain coherent identity, cruelties that include self-cruelty as well, the abasement through which coherence is fictively produced and sustained. . . . if identity is constructed through opposition, it is also constructed through rejection" (115). Matthew suggests that we err by rejecting the unclean portions of ourselves—that we sustain a certain cruelty to that part of our "nature"—and that we should strive for a balance by refusing to abject the unclean. Julia Kristeva's discussion of abjection triggered by the improper and unclean in *Powers of Horror* only confirms the difficulty with which Nora, and Felix for that matter, confront Robin's embrace of the impure. According to Kristeva, objects like bodily excreta and corpses cause abjection because they disrupt "identity, system, order."[24] These objects destabilize boundaries and point out the falsity of purified identifications.

Matthew also explains that language cannot account for the night because the night's intimate alignment with death and mortality, with the inevitable reminder that humans are, despite everything, primates who must die alongside the rest of the animal world and whose languaging doesn't alter this inevitable fact. "Life, the permission to know death," Matthew continues: "We were created that the earth might be made sensible of her inhuman taste; and love that the body might be so dear that even the earth should roar with it. Yes, we who are full to the gorge with misery should look well around, doubting everything seen, done, spoken, precisely because we have a word for it, and not its alchemy" (83). The implicit desire here is for a direct experience of something, an experience that bypasses language.

But if Robin has mastered the art of bypassing language, Matthew certainly has not. He continues to be his own worst critic in this lengthy section, "Watchman, What of the Night?" After imploring Nora to doubt the things we have words for, he confesses to his self-betrayal in this regard. "I've given my destiny away by garrulity," he declares. This admission is immediately linked to Matthew's transvestitism. His compulsive self-disclosure soon reveals his truest desire, "to boil some good man's potatoes and toss up a child for him every nine months by the calendar" (91). These admissions come as no surprise given the section's opening image. In Matthew's cramped and squalid quarters he wears a woman's nightgown: "The doctor's head, with its over-large black eyes, its full gun-metal cheeks and chin, was framed in the golden semi-circle of a wig with long pendent curls. . . . He was heavily rouged and his lashes painted" (79). In fact, Matthew wants to be more than a woman; he wants to embody some archetypal femininity and betrays this desire by "taking the prominent features of one sex and inflating them with hyperbole."[25] To be sure, Matthew confesses to wanting "a womb as big as the king's kettle, and a bosom as high as the bowsprit of a fishing schooner" (91).

Ultimately, then, Matthew is the worst betrayer of his own advice to shun the "things we have words for." When he dons a woman's nightgown, he literalizes the very error of which he accuses Nora: "you have dressed the unknowable in the garments of the known" (136). Matthew seems unable to practice what he preaches. Despite his rejection of masculinity as a culturally normative identity marker, he desires its opposite. Matthew cannot enact a radical refusal of "false" identities and instead replaces one gendered identification with the desire for an exaggerated version of another. Matthew wants to be woman, and woman is indeed something that we have words for. The text implies that Matthew's profound desire to be barefoot and pregnant does not liberate him from the edicts of a heteronormative system, but rather tethers him more brutally to gendered modes of being that are constrained by the insidious binary "boy/girl." Thus, while Matthew's *mind* wanders and changes, and while he repeatedly speaks the text's privileging of nonidentity as being, Matthew himself does not necessarily accomplish this undifferentiated mode in its phenomenality. But according to the logic of the text, he could in no way begin to accomplish it unless he *stopped speaking* about it.

Matthew himself, then, has more in common with Felix than with Robin—despite the fact that he voices the text's radical critique of identity—because he remains a slave to the masculine/feminine distinction. His adoption of excessive femininity reinscribes a symbolic system that operates fundamentally upon difference. Matthew says of himself, "I am a doctor and a collector and a talker of Latin" (92). And though his discursive values tend toward the polymorphous, he places himself in an exacting narrative of gendered meaning, becoming a kind of masterpiece on display in the museum of transvestitism.

Matthew makes his last appearance in the "Go Down Matthew" section, which serves as the novel's final comment on the link between language and identity. As this section opens, Matthew finds Nora writing a letter and admonishes her in a manner that suggests she is speaking rather than writing: "Can't you be quiet now?" he asks, "Can't you be done now, can't you give up?" (124). Matthew's pleading appears to be directed more at himself than at Nora, and his redundant revision of the question emphasize his inability to comply, and, at the same time, his frustration with that inability. He begs Nora to abandon words by saying, "put the pen away," "lay down the pen," and finally "put down the pen" (125–27). The pen is an all too obvious metaphor for the phallus in this section, but the comparison warrants our attention. If the novel stages a critique of phallic identity and its residue in language, then Matthew's request that Nora put down the pen serves as his final plea—to self and other—to abandon the desire for such identity. Indeed, images of the phallus in this novel are either flaccid or accursed. When Matthew exposes himself—exposes Tiny O'Toole—inside an empty church, the only overt image of his penis is that of Tiny "lying in a swoon" (132). And as Marcus points out, at the center of the novel are the *pissoir* episodes that "condemn the upright. A woman curses her lover in the toilet: 'May you die standing upright! May you be damned upward! . . . May it wither into the grin of the dead, may this draw back, low riding mouth in an empty snarl of the groin'" (238). The novel seems to insist that the phallus is never really turgid and therefore does not provide ontological plenitude; rather, it robs us of a certain fullness of being.

Matthew's continued pleading with Nora to lay down the pen results only in his own verbal surplus, and as the scene continues he becomes exponentially hysterical. Soon he is cataloguing his own fanatical belief in the word. He asks Nora, "Haven't I eaten a book too? Like the angels and prophets? And wasn't it a bitter book to eat?" This striking image suggests that Matthew has forfeited a physical or material sustenance for the "ingestion" of words and images. Explaining his own entrapment does not release him from it, for he keeps talking: "Jenny without a comma to eat, and Robin with nothing but a pet name. . . . But does that sum her up? Is even the end of us an account?" (127).

As if in response to his question about Robin, Matthew gives an account of himself that is clearly doomed to inconsequence. The image of the book is again central to the broad philosophical question Matthew poses about human experience. This question turns on the constitutive disjunction between animality and consciousness or "spirit" in the human person. Matthew explains that a priest once gave him this advice: "Be simple, Matthew, life is a simple book, and an open book, read and be simple as the beasts in the field" (131). This dual objective—to be within language and simultaneously outside it, to be bard and beast—is precisely what Matthew cannot accomplish. It is ultimately impossible to be "like and animal, and yet think" (131). More importantly, Matthew *despairs of this impossibility,* while Robin relinquishes and almost celebrates it by variously rejecting the symbolic and embracing animality.

After instructing those in his favorite café to listen, Matthew insists, "To think is to be sick" (158). Though he cries out for a permanent escape from all explanations—"God, take my hand and get me up out of this great argument" (162)—he begins to blame others for his damned condition. "I've done everything and been everything that I didn't want to be or do," he exclaims, "and I wouldn't be telling you about it if I weren't talking to myself. I talk too much because I have been made so miserable by what you are keeping hushed" (162–63). Matthew suggests in this moment that the forces of repression or disavowal that people like Nora and Felix employ to deny their own connection to the "good dirt"—to animality and organicism—suffocate him. The weight of such repressions compels him to speak what others keep "hushed." John Forrester might argue that this moment reveals a Derridean infiltration of an analytic space by the nonanalytic.[26] Perhaps Matthew's speech becomes inhabited by the animality that others reject, but this particular infiltration into language is one the novel does not seem to recommend.

Matthew's explanations are complex and sometimes contradictory. While he claims that he talks because of what others refuse to speak, he also insists that he talks because he is talked to. When his soliloquies become excessively hysterical, he finally begins to "scream with sobbing laughter. 'Talking to me—all of them—sitting on me as heavy as a truck horse—talking!'" (165). Language takes on the properties of a physical weight, bearing down heavily upon Matthew. Before his final descent into raving, Nora forces Matthew to hear her: "Listen," she insists, "You've got to listen!" (155). Despite his requests for Nora to "put down the pen," literally and figuratively, she narrates her disappointment in Robin to its bitter and unsatisfying end, telling Matthew that a mutual deathbed would have been her only happiness with Robin. At that point, Matthew seems obliterated by the force of her language and stands "in confused and unhappy silence" (18).

In his last, pathetic moments in the text, an extremely drunk Matthew falls "upon the table with all his weight, his arms spread, his head between them, his eyes wide open and crying" (165). Though he only whispers, he manages to address the crowd around him, begging for release: "'Now that you have all heard what you wanted to hear, can't you let me loose now, Let me go? I've not only lived my life for nothing, but I've *told it for nothing*'" (165; emphasis added). Matthew's sense of being trapped by the words he speaks is acute. He seeks release from the lure of a language that promises meaning through stable identifiers but does not deliver, and he notes in the end that his words, like Nora's before him, have all been spoken in vain: "'Now,' he said, 'the end—mark my words—now *nothing, but wrath and weeping!*'" (166).

The final and much contested section in the novel, "The Possessed," provides a complicated and ambiguous foil to the various excesses of language that precede it. While Matthew seems paralyzed at his café table by his reliance on words, Robin is anything but stationary. After arriving with Jenny in New York, she "began to haunt the terminals, taking trains to different parts of the country, wandering without design" (167). Unable or unwilling to be fixed, Robin must wander, move, and change. She then gravitates toward Nora's home, mostly walking in the open country, "pulling at the flowers, speaking in a low voice to the animals. Those that came near, she grasped, straining their fur back until their eyes were narrowed and the teeth bare, her own teeth showing as if her hand were upon her own neck" (168). In this brief and final chapter, the novel's deep engagement with the discourse of species surfaces most clearly. Robin grasps the animals *as if she grasps herself*. The boundaries of her subjectivity lapse out toward animals and a kind of animal consciousness that rejects strictly humanist identifications.

Jenny becomes hysterical. Robin's "desperate anonymity" is unacceptable to her, so Jenny "accused Robin of a 'sensuous communion with unclean spirits.'" Robin's desire for anonymity is figured as her absorption into the nonhuman world: "Sometimes she slept in the woods; the silence that she had caused by her coming was broken again by insect and bird flowing back over her intrusion, which was forgotten in her fixed stillness, obliterating her as a drop of water is made anonymous by the pond into which it has fallen" (168). In this passage Robin can stop moving, and become "fixed," only when she is deeply subsumed into a nonhuman milieu, and, in this rare moment of stillness, human language is replaced by animal sound or noise. This often overlooked description is crucial to recognizing the redeeming nature of Robin's subjectivity as nonidentity. To be obliterated as human and self by becoming nonself, by becoming an anonymous drop of water in the greater ontological pond—a pond that exceeds Being as merely human, as merely *Dasein*—this is Robin's reverie. And to frame the "merely human" here, to deflate the self-importance of humanism by privileging the nonhuman, the undecidable, the nonlinguistic, the animal, this is the posthumanist triumph of Barnes's novel, a triumph that ultimately *revises* the category "human."

The ambiguity of Robin's final encounter with Nora's dog in a chapel near a "contrived altar" begins to make sense in light of this radical posthumanism. This last scene, so highly contested in critical readings of the novel, obliterates distinctions between sacred and profane, human and animal, fear and desire, play and aggression. When Robin goes down on all fours, she renounces Freud's upright humanity in all its cruelty, abandoning the exclusionary edicts of identity; she swings her head against the dog's body, seeming at times to play with him, but having become animal so fully that the dog "reared as if to avoid something that troubled him to such agony that he seemed to be rising from the floor." And in her final renunciation of the symbolic, Robin "began to bark also, crawling after him—barking in a fit of laughter, obscene and touching" (170).

The fundamental undecidability proffered by this final scene echoes the larger tenets of the novel, which declare the impossibility of choosing between rigid binaries. Unlike Matthew, who supplants one culturally constructed identity with another, or Felix who attempts to reinforce his false identity with signs from the past, Robin challenges the symbolic at its core, asserting that the outside of symbolization is not a radical absence but rather a kind of ontology, a plenitude experienced as anonymity, self-obliteration, movement, and change, or perhaps as communion with alterity, especially with the nonhuman. *Nightwood,* then, is striking among its contemporaneous texts in the radicalness of its posthumanism. Perhaps more than any other modernist character, Robin provides a powerful gesture away from being as identificatory, humanist, exclusionary, and sustained within a matrix of abjection. Robin's life is said to have "no volition for refusal" (43), and it is this openness toward alterity that defines her, and in my reading, redeems her, while those around her are doomed to suffer the disappointments of symbolic systems that repress, constrict, and ossify experience.[27] And, in the end, it is Robin's refusal to abject animals and animality that saves her from the perils of such reification in the human. Indeed, Robin seems to be modernism's clearest realization of Matthew's hypothesis: "'Ah,' he added, 'to be an animal, born at the opening of the eye, going only forward, and, at the end of the day, shutting out memory with the dropping of the lid'" (135).

Conclusion

Animal Studies, Ethics, and the Humanities

The last two years have marked the "mapping" of animal studies on an unprecedented level, and I am partly playing on the simple colloquialism, to be "on the map." In literary and cultural studies, we have witnessed the likes of special issues on the animal in the British journal, *Parallax*, and in the interdisciplinary Canadian journal *Mosaic*, whose editors received so many submissions in the field that they put out two volumes dedicated to the subject. Essay collections are underway on the animal in literary signification and in postcolonial theory. "H-Animal" has appeared on the web as a discussion and networking site for scholars in this broadly interdisciplinary subfield. And for the first time, MLA sessions dedicated expressly to the question of the animal have begun to appear regularly on the annual convention program. Margot Norris notes, as other scholars have, that literary studies has been slow to enter this interdisciplinary discussion. But on the heels of poststructuralism and recent debates in posthumanism, she maintains, the shift toward entertaining the animal problem as a serious theoretical nexus has begun for literature scholars as well: "In the process of reorienting the human subject within its metaphysical and ethical cosmos, these theoretical resources have begun to recuperate the human *qua* animal from ideological repression, marginalization, and demonization. The cultural climate seems propitious, then, for expanding the methodological tools for exploring the appearance and status of the human animal in literary genres."[1]

This study, then, contributes to that exploration as it refines our understanding of the British subject in modernism. But, I want to emphasize, it does so in a way that radically destabilizes the terms under which that subject has almost always been understood. Indeed, Norris's mention of the posthuman is crucial in locating a study such as this amid emerging works, some of which only look at the animal in literature from what we might call a neohumanist perspective—leaving the human essentially uninterrogated—and others that want to challenge that cordoning off of the human at its very core. Cary Wolfe helps us think through such distinctions when discussing the "commitment to [a] distinctly posthumanist way" of examining these questions when he notes that such a commitment "will enhance our understanding of the embeddedness and entanglement of the 'human' in all that it is not, in all that used to be thought of as its opposites or its others."[2] Entanglement is an especially apt word for the complexities of the dance between human and animal subjectivities in modernism that these pages have outlined and probed.

On some level, a study such as this lines up with the "turn to ethics" that has been heralded as characterizing the movement of recent political, philosophical, and humanistic theory. But ethics itself, typically understood as involving rational subjects who can propositionally agree to the terms of a moral community, usually remains embedded within a proscriptive "human" grid. As I note in chapter 1, Levinas's work is frequently cited as a foundation for the deepening of our inquiries into who counts as the neighbor, and what our obligations are to such subjects. Yet all too often scholarly claims about suffering, disavowal, and inequity ignore these dynamics when they cross species lines. On another level, then, this study asks us to radically reconsider the terms of ethical inquiry, the contours of the "other," and the assumptions about subjectivity that are often profoundly embedded in our vision of what constitutes legitimate theoretical and scholarly work.

At a recent committee meeting, I listened to several of my colleagues who teach philosophy at universities nationwide lament the sometimes automatic dismissal of questions pertaining to animal theory and ethics by their peers, despite the impressive strides made in this area of philosophy. It occurred to me that this kind of stalwart "protectionism" in our thinking and analytical practice is one powerful tendency that depletes and hardens our intellectual habits. At the 2005 School of Criticism and Theory, several of the prominent scholars working and presenting there were concerned with what they called "the exhaustion of the humanities." This set of apprehensions seemed focused around the rehashing of specific theories that take on a dogmatic and predictable quality. Indeed, this phrase and the concept of "exhaustion" became something of a subtheme that those of us in residence as fellows began to worry over and puzzle through. The anecdotal resistance of certain philosophy scholars to interrogate their species assumptions seems to be a useful example of such dogmatism, of the way in which our intellectual practices become unidimensional and outmoded. Perhaps one of the promises of animal studies as a subfield lies in confronting the mysterious animal other as a way to reinvigorate the humanities, to move beyond the "exhaustion" of various human-centered rhetorical modes. As we look at a creature that is both our kin and our most confounding "alien" being, we find new ways to understand our humanness and the way that humanness participates in and should be contextualized alongside the nonhuman world.

One compelling recent example of a broadly posthuman theoretical perspective that reframes the human in this manner can be found in Elizabeth Grosz's work on art and creativity. Building off of a number of theories ranging from Deleuze to French feminism and her own rereading of evolution, Grosz maintains in an interview with Julie Copeland that we need to understand art as "the revelry in the excess of nature, but also a revelry in the excess of the energy in our bodies."[3] Grosz removes art from the humanistic realm to which it has classically been ascribed, claiming that "we're not the first artists and we're perhaps not even the greatest artists, we humans; we take our cue from the animal world. So what appeals to us? It's the striking beauty of flowers, it's the amazing colour of birds, it's the songs of birds" (2). Rather than being fundamentally about concepts or representation, art's "fundamental goal is to produce sensations," and "it's about feeling something intensely [while] there may be the byproduct of a kind of understanding" (3). Grosz goes on to emphasize the way that her ideas decenter the traditional attribution of art to an elevated, human function:

> I think what's radical about what I'm saying is that art isn't primarily or solely conceptual, that what it represents is the most animal part of us rather than the most human part of us. Frankly, I find it

really refreshing, in a way, that it's not man's nobility that produces art, it's man's animality that produces art, and that's what makes it of potential interest everywhere. (3)

One of the most fascinating and instructive moments in this interview occurs when the interviewer, during a discussion of the frame and framing, wants to draw a hard and fast distinction between humans who "are aware" of the role of the frame, and other creatures who "of course" are unaware of the frame's meaning (5). Grosz responds, "I'm not sure that we're any more aware than they are, and I'm quite sure, at a certain extent, when the bird is undertaking a courtship dance that it's aware that there's something intense and special about this activity which is very different to gathering food and so on" (5). It is this real resistance to the rote privileging of human abilities that provides a sweeping challenge to our thinking about the nature of the aesthetic. Here, I would suggest, is the kind of intellectual and ethical model that may be able reinvigorate the humanities by taking it beyond and outside of itself, by reimagining what the human really participates in and constitutes. Again, my aim in the previous pages is to provide a similar perspective on literary modernism.

As I approach the end of this project, which situates itself among various theoretical and literary discourses, I want to return to the ethical or material animal by invoking Derrida's work once again. In "The Animal That Therefore I Am," Derrida resuscitates Jeremy Bentham's classic question about animal sentience: "Can they suffer?" He goes on to link our own mortality and contingency to the "experience of compassion" and the "anguish" of our shared vulnerability with other animals.[4] A struggle, he claims, has been and continues to be waged "between those who violate not only animal life but even and also this sentiment of compassion and, on the other hand, those who appeal to an irrefutable testimony to this pity." It is just after this moment that Derrida signals the unique timeliness of the animal question:

This war probably has no age but, and here is my hypothesis, it is passing through a critical phase. We are passing through that phase and it passes through us. To think the war we find ourselves waging is not only a duty, a responsibility, an obligation, it is also a necessity, a constraint that, like it or not, directly or indirectly, everyone is held to. Henceforth and more than ever. And I say "to think" this war, because I believe it concerns what we call "thinking." The animal looks at us, and we are naked before it. Thinking perhaps begins there. (397)

In this critical phase, then, by attending to the question of the animal on a discursive and a material level, we might begin to reshape our vision not only of modern literatures, but also of the human and the humanities themselves. In doing so, we also answer our obligation to animals, who are looking at us now more than ever.

Notes

Note to readers: The first citation of a work in each chapter is listed in full as a note. Subsequent references in the text use only the parenthetical page number.

1. The Animal Among Others

1. Noel Annan, "Science, Religion, and the Critical Mind: Introduction," in *1859: Entering an Age of Crisis,* ed. Philip Appleman, William A. Madden, and Michael Wolff (Bloomington: Indiana University Press, 1959), 35.

2. Howard Mumford Jones, "1859 and the Idea of Crisis: General Introduction," in *1859: Entering an Age of Crisis,* ed. Philip Appleman, William A. Madden, and Michael Wolff (Bloomington: Indiana University Press, 1959), 17.

3. Peter J. Bowler, *Charles Darwin: The Man and His Influence* (Cambridge: Basil Blackwell, 1990), 177.

4. Elizabeth Grosz, *The Nick of Time: Politics, Evolution, and the Untimely* (Durham: Duke University Press, 2004), 21.

5. Charles Darwin, *The Origin of Species* (New York: Gramercy, 1979), 107.

6. Charles Darwin, *The Descent of Man* (London: Penguin, 2004), 105.

7. Harriet Ritvo, *The Animal Estate: The English and Other Creatures in the Victorian Age* (Cambridge, MA: Harvard University Press, 1987), 40.

8. Quoted in Lucille B. Ritvo, *Darwin's Influence on Freud: A Tale of Two Sciences* (New Haven: Yale University Press, 1990), 76.

9. Emanuel Garcia, "Reflections on Death, Phylogeny, and the Mind-Body Problem in Freud's Life and Work," in *Understanding Freud the Man and His Ideas,* ed. Emanuel Garcia (New York: New York University Press, 1992), 151.

10. Cynthia Marshall, "Psychoanalyzing the Prepsychoanalytic Subject." *PMLA* 117, no. 5 (2002): 1211.

11. Thomas Docherty, *Alterities: Criticism, History, Representation* (Oxford: Clarendon Press, 1996), 26.

12. Akira Mizuta Lippit outlines theories of animality in Western philosophy near the beginning of *Electric Animal: Toward a Rhetoric of Wildlife.* His analysis includes such major figures as Aristotle, Descartes, Kant, Hegel, and Heidegger. Heidegger's problematic treatment of animal being is treated with particular rigor by Derrida, especially in *Of Spirit.*

13. Emmanuel Levinas, *Totality and Infinity: An Essay on Exteriority,* trans. Alphonso Lingis (Pittsburgh: Duquesne University Press, 1969), 207.

14. Bernhard Waldenfels, "Levinas and the Face of the Other," in *The Cambridge Companion to Levinas,* ed. Simon Critchley and Robert Bernasconi (Cambridge: Cambridge University Press, 2002), 63.

15. John Llewelyn, "Am I Obsessed by Bobby? (Humanism of the Other Animal)," in *Re-reading Levinas,* ed. Robert Bernasconi and Simon Critchley (Bloomington: Indiana University Press, 1991), 241.

16. Richard Beardsworth, *Derrida and the Political* (New York: Routledge, 1996).

17. Cary Wolfe, *Critical Environments: Postmodern Theory and the Pragmatics of the "Outside,"* (Minneapolis: University of Minnesota Press, 1998), 43.

18. Marjorie Perloff, "Modernist Studies," in *Redrawing the Boundaries: The Transformation of English and American Literary Studies,* ed. Stephen Greenblatt and Giles Gunn (New York: MLA, 1992), 166.

19. Marianna Torgovnick, *Gone Primitive: Savage Intellects, Modern Lives* (Chicago: University of Chicago Press, 1990), 3.

20. Jacques Derrida, "'Eating Well,' or The Calculation of the Subject: An Interview with Jacques Derrida," in *Who Comes After the Subject?,* ed. Eduardo Cadava, Peter Connor, and Jean-Luc Nancy (New York: Routledge, 1991), 98.

21. Derrida notes that the same sacrificial operation occurs for the subject in a symbolic relation to other humans.

22. Nick Fiddes, *Meat: A Natural Symbol,* (London: Routledge, 1991), 2.

23. Judith Butler, *Bodies That Matter* (New York: Routledge, 1993), 38.

24. Robert McKay, "'Identifying with the Animals': Language, Subjectivity, and the Animal Politics of Margaret Atwood's *Surfacing,*" in *Figuring Animals: Essays on Animal Images in Art, Literature, Philosophy, and Popular Culture,* ed. Mary Sanders Pollock and Catherine Rainwater (New York: Palgrave Macmillan, 2005), 211.

25. Jacques Derrida, *Of Spirit: Heidegger and the Question,* trans. Geoffrey Bennington and Rachel Bowlby (Chicago: University of Chicago Press, 1989), 50.

26. Cary Wolfe and Jonathan Elmer, "Subject to Sacrifice: Ideology, Psychoanalysis, and the Discourse of Species in Jonathan Demme's *Silence of the Lambs,*" *Boundary 2* 22, no. 3 (1995): 145.

27. Georges Bataille, *Theory of Religion,* trans. Robert Hurley (New York: Zone Books, 1992), 22.

28. Deleuze and Guattari discuss the habit of making a pet part of the family in *A Thousand Plateaus* where they explain, "individuated animals, family pets, sentimental, Oedipal animals each with its own petty history, 'my' cat, 'my' dog. These animals invite us to regress, draw us into a narcissistic contemplation" (240). Gilles Deleuze and Félix Guattari, *A Thousand Plateaus: Capitalism and Schizophrenia,* trans. Brian Massumi (Minneapolis: University of Minnesota Press, 1987).

29. I should emphasize that this does not imply that animals do not engage in linguistic modes at all. Rather, I am noting their inability to participate *fully* in human languages, an inability that emphasizes their otherness *for us.*

30. Jean-François Lyotard, *The Differend: Phrases in Dispute* (Minneapolis: University of Minnesota Press, 1988), 28.

31. It is instructive to remember here that what seems a progressive posthuman opening toward otherness in Lyotard's work has been shown to redouble itself finally into a familiar humanism that excludes animals' ethical consideration. See Cary Wolfe in *Animal Rites,* where he discusses how Lyotard's concept of the "inhuman" is not extended to animal others. Cary Wolfe, *Animal Rites: American Culture, the Discourse of Species, and Posthumanist Theory* (Chicago: University of Chicago Press, 2003).

32. Jacques Derrida, "The Animal That Therefore I Am (More to Follow)," *Critical Inquiry* 28, no. 2 (2002): 417.

33. Akira Mizuta Lippit, *Electric Animal: Toward a Rhetoric of Wildlife* (Minneapolis: University of Minnesota Press, 2000), 33.

34. Jacques Derrida, "Force of Law: The Mystical Foundation of Authority," *Cardozo Law Review* 11, no. 919 (1990): 953.

35. Cary Wolfe, "Faux Post-Humanism, or, Animal Rights, Neocolonialism, and Michael Crichton's *Congo,*" *Arizona Quarterly* 55, no. 2 (Summer 1999): 118.

36. As I explain in chapter 3, I refer via Žižek to the "official" image of the Enlightenment, to the strain of rationalism most prominent in Kant and Descartes. Not all thinkers in this period subscribed to such an extreme view of the human subject. Nonetheless, this position was very powerful and influential.

37. Slavoj Žižek, *Looking Awry: An Introduction to Jacques Lacan through Popular Culture* (Cambridge, MA: MIT Press, 1991), 142.

38. Max Horkheimer and Theodor W. Adorno, *The Dialectic of Enlightenment,* trans. John Cumming (New York: Continuum, 1944), xi.

2. Imperialism and Disavowal

1. Marjorie Spiegel, *The Dreaded Comparison: Human and Animal Slavery* (New York: Mirror Books, 1996), 21.

2. Patrick Brantlinger, *Rule of Darkness: British Literature and Imperialism, 1830–1914* (Ithaca: Cornell University Press, 1988). Brantlinger contextualizes his

discussion of the "Imperial Gothic" Victorian text by describing racial theories that were used to justify domination.

3. Robert M. DeGraaff, "The Evolution of Sweeney in the poetry of T. S. Eliot," in *Critical Essays on T. S. Eliot: The Sweeney Motif,*" ed. Kinley E. Roby (Boston: G. K. Hall, 1985), 222.

4. T. S. Eliot, "Sweeney Among the Nightingales," *Collected Poems, 1909–1962* (New York: Harcourt Brace, 1963), 49.

5. John Ower, "Pattern and Value in 'Sweeney Among the Nightingales,'" in *Critical Essays on T. S. Eliot: The Sweeney Motif,*" ed. Kinley E. Roby (Boston: G. K. Hall, 1985), 73.

6. Stephen Clark, "Testing the Razor: T. S. Eliot's *Poems 1920,*" *Engendering the Word: Feminist Essays in Psychosexual Politics* (Urbana: University of Illinois Press, 1989),1 67–89.

7. Kinley E. Roby, ed., "Introduction," in *Critical Essays on T. S. Eliot: The Sweeney Motif* (Boston: G. K. Hall, 1985), 10.

8. Nancy Hargrove, "The Symbolism of Sweeney in the Works of T. S. Eliot," in *Critical Essays on T. S. Eliot: The Sweeney Motif,*" ed. Kinley E. Roby (Boston: G. K. Hall, 1985), 151.

9. In the tradition of Ovid, Philomela, who was raped by her brother-in-law, was changed into a nightingale. For further discussion of Eliot's use of Greek mythology in this poem, see Ower, "Pattern and Value."

10. Bryan Cheyette, "Neither Excuse nor Accuse: T. S. Eliot's Semitic Discourse," *Modernism/Modernity* 10, no. 3 (2003): 431–37.

11. I refer to the discovery of Eliot's correspondence with Horace M. Kallen that Ronald Schuchard elucidates in his apologetic essay on Eliot and critical charges of anti-Semitism. See *Modernism/Modernity* 10, no. 1 (2003) for Shuchard's discussion and the six scholarly responses to his essay. See also the debate's continuation, especially by Freedman and Cheyette, in *Modernism/Modernity* 10, no. 3 (2003).

12. Jonathan Freedman, "Lessons Out of School: T. S. Eliot's Jewish Problem and the Making of Modernism," *Modernism/Modernity* 10, no. 3 (2003): 421.

13. Anthony Julius cites this anti-Semitic stereotype. See Anthony Julius, *T. S. Eliot, Anti-Semitism, and Literary Form* (Cambridge: Cambridge University Press, 1995), 27.

14. Rachel Blau DuPlessis, "Circumscriptions: Assimilating T. S. Eliot's Sweeneys," in *People of the Book: Thirty Scholars Reflect on Their Jewish Identity,* ed. Jeffrey Rubin-Dorsky (Madison: University of Wisconsin Press, 1996), 141.

15. See Hargrove, "The Symbolism of Sweeney," 151.

16. Sigmund Freud, *Civilization and its Discontents* (London: Hogarth Press, 1930), 29.

17. Anne McClintock's study *Imperial Leather* contains illustrations of this type that show profiles of the head through evolutionary progression. McClintock, *Imperial Leather: Race, Gender, and Sexuality in the Colonial Conquest* (New York: Routledge, 1995), 38–39.

18. Stephen Clark discusses Sweeney Todd as a possible source for Eliot's Sweeney. See also Rachel Blau DuPlessis's consideration of the ethnic references in the name Sweeney in "Circumscriptions: Assimilating T. S. Eliot's Sweeneys."

19. See Judith Butler, *Bodies That Matter* (New York: Routledge, 1993), 12–16, on performativity as citationality.

20. T. S. Eliot, "Burbank with a Baedeker: Bleistein with a Cigar," *Collected Poems, 1909–1962* (New York: Harcourt Brace, 1963), 33.

21. T. S. Eliot, "Sweeney Agonistes: Fragments of an Aristophanic Melodrama," *Collected Poems, 1909–1962* (New York: Harcourt Brace, 1963), 119–20.

22. Richard Sheppard, "The Crisis of Language," in *Modernism: A Guide to European Literature,* ed. Malcolm Bradbury and James McFarlane (London: Penguin, 1976), 323.

23. Frederick R. Karl, "Introduction to the *Danse Macabre:* Conrad's *Heart of Darkness,*" in *Heart of Darkness: A Case Study in Contemporary Criticism,* ed. Ross C. Murfin (New York: St. Martin's Press, 1989), 134.

24. C. T. Watts, "*Heart of Darkness:* The Covert Murder Plot and the Darwinian Theme," *Conradiana* VII (1975): 139.

25. Joseph Conrad, *Heart of Darkness,* ed. Robert Kimbrough, 3rd ed. (New York: Norton, 1988), 9.

26. Stephen Kern, *The Culture of Time and Space* (Cambridge: Harvard University Press, 1983), 42.

27. Chinua Achebe, "An Image of Africa: Racism in Conrad's *Heart of Darkness,*" *The Massachusetts Review* 18 (1977): 782–94. Rpt. in *Heart of Darkness,* ed. Robert Kimbrough, 3rd edition (New York; Norton, 1988), 257.

28. As I discuss in chapter 1, Emmanuel Levinas in *Totality and Infinity* privileges the human face as the impetus for ethical relations: "the Other faces me and puts me in question and *obliges* me by his essence qua infinity" (207).

29. Hugh Mercer Curtler, "Achebe on Conrad: Racism and Greatness in *Heart of Darkness,*" *Conradiana* 29, no.1 (1997): 33.

30. Edward W. Said, *Culture and Imperialism* (New York: Vintage, 1993), 14.

31. Carl G. Jung, *Man and His Symbols* (New York: Dell Publishing, 1964), 6.

32. Jeffrey Moussaieff Masson and Susan McCarthy, *When Elephants Weep: The Emotional Lives of Animals* (New York: Delacorte Press, 1995), 24.

33. Georges Bataille, *Theory of Religion,* trans. Robert Hurley (New York: Zone Books, 1992), 39–40.

34. Bette London, "Reading Race and Gender in Conrad's Dark Continent," *Criticism: A Quarterly for Literature and the Arts* 31, no. 3 (1989): 249.

35. Johanna M. Smith, "'Too Beautiful Altogether': Patriarchal Ideology in *Heart of Darkness,*" in *Heart of Darkness: A Case Study in Contemporary Criticism,* ed. Ross C. Murfin (New York: St. Martin's Press, 1989), 184.

36. Jacques Derrida, *Speech and Phenomena And Other Essays on Husserl's Theory of Signs,* trans. David B. Allison (Evanston: Northwestern University Press, 1973), 7–8.

37. Georges Bataille, *Visions of Excess: Selected Writings, 1927–1939* (Minneapolis: University of Minnesota Press, 1985), 59.

38. Slavoj Žižek, *Enjoy Your Symptom* (New York; Routledge, 1992), 181.

39. Cary Wolfe and Jonathan Elmer. "Subject to Sacrifice: Ideology, Psycho-analysis, and the Discourse of Species in Jonathan Demme's *Silence of the Lambs*," *Boundary 2* 22, no. 3 (1995): 156–57.

40. Carole Stone and Fawzia Afzal-Khan, "Gender, Race and Narrative Structure: A Reappraisal of Joseph Conrad's *Heart of Darkness*," *Conradiana* 29, no. 3 (1997): 229.

41. Carol Adams, *The Sexual Politics of Meat: A Feminist-Vegetarian Critical Theory* (New York: Continuum, 1990), 40.

42. Jacques Derrida, "'Eating Well,' or The Calculation of the Subject: An Interview with Jacques Derrida," in *Who Comes After the Subject?*, ed. Eduardo Cadava, Peter Connor, and Jean-Luc Nancy (New York: Routledge, 1991), 112.

43. Friedrich Nietzsche, *The Birth of Tragedy* (New York: Russell and Russell, 1964), 25.

44. Friedrich Nietzsche, *On the Genealogy of Morals*, trans. Walter Kaufmann (New York: Vintage, 1989), 58–59.

45. L. D. Clark, *Dark Night of the Body: D. H. Lawrence's "The Plumed Serpent"* (Austin: University of Texas Press, 1964), 52.

46. D. H. Lawrence, *The Plumed Serpent (Quetzalcoatl)*, ed. L. D. Clark (Cambridge: Cambridge University Press, 1987), 16.

47. Marianna Torgovnick, *Gone Primitive: Savage Intellects, Modern Lives* (Chicago: University of Chicago Press, 1990).

48. Gilles Deleuze and Félix Guattari, *A Thousand Plateaus: Capitalism and Schizophrenia*, trans. Brian Massumi (Minneapolis: University of Minnesota Press, 1987), 238.

49. D. H. Lawrence, "Reflections on the Death of a Porcupine," *Reflections on the Death of a Porcupine and Other Essays*, ed. Michael Herbert (Cambridge: Cambridge University Press, 1988), 358.

50. Thomas McCarthy, "Introduction," in *The Philosophical Discourse of Modernity*, Jürgen Habermas (Cambridge: MIT Press, 1987), viii.

51. Thomas Lyon, "Introduction" in *D. H. Lawrence: Future Primitive*, Dolores La Chapelle (Denton: University of North Texas Press, 1996), xvi.

52. Dolores La Chapelle, *D. H. Lawrence: Future Primitive* (Denton: University of North Texas Press, 1996), 32.

53. Max Horkheimer and Theodor W. Adorno, *The Dialectic of Enlightenment*, trans. John Cumming (New York: Continuum, 1944), xi.

54. John Humma, "The Imagery of *The Plumed Serpent*: The Going-under of Organicism," *The D. H. Lawrence Review* 15, no. 3 (1982): 201.

3. Facing the Animal

1. Wells's relationship to science and to Darwinism in particular has been examined by a number of scholars in light of his tutelage under T. H. Huxley. R. D. Haynes has written that "Evolutionary theory then seemed to Wells, and may

still be regarded as, the nearest approach to a unifying factor in contemporary thought." See Haynes, *H. G. Wells: Discoverer of the Future* (New York: New York University Press, 1980), 16.

2. Slavoj Žižek, *Enjoy Your Symptom*, (New York: Routledge, 1992), 136, 181.

3. H. G. Wells, *The Island of Dr. Moreau* (New York: Bantam, 1994), 2.

4. Cyndy Hendershot, "The Animal Without: Masculinity and Imperialism in *The Island of Dr. Moreau* and 'The Adventures of the Speckled Band,'" *Nineteenth Century Studies* 10 (1996): 7.

5. Cary Wolfe and Jonathan Elmer, "Subject to Sacrifice: Ideology, Psychoanalysis, and the Discourse of Species in Jonathan Demme's *Silence of the Lambs*," *Boundary 2* 22, no. 3 (1995): 156.

6. Carl G. Jung, *Man and His Symbols* (New York: Dell Publishing, 1964), 57.

7. Anne Simpson, "The 'Tangible Antagonist': H. G. Wells and the Discourse of Otherness," *Extrapolation: A Journal of Science Fiction and Fantasy* 31, no. 2 (Summer 1990): 135.

8. In fact, in *Totem and Taboo*, Freud notes, "Children show no trace of the arrogance which urges adult civilized men to draw a hard-and-fast line between their own nature and that of other animals. Children have no scruples over allowing animals to rank as their full equals. Uninhibited as they are in the avowal of their bodily needs, they no doubt feel themselves more akin to animals than to their elders, who may well be a puzzle to them." Freud, *Totem and Taboo* (New York: Norton, 1950), 157.

9. Friedrich Nietzsche, *On the Genealogy of Morals*, trans. Walter Kaufmann (New York: Vintage, 1989), 85.

10. Max Horkheimer and Theodor W. Adorno, *The Dialectic of Enlightenment*, trans. John Cumming (New York: Continuum, 1944), 6.

11. Judith Butler, *Bodies That Matter* (New York: Routledge, 1993), 107.

12. Cyndy Hendershot discusses the Victorian equation of feminine sexuality and the animal. See note 4.

13. Jacques Derrida, "The Animal That Therefore I Am (More to Follow)," *Critical Inquiry* 28, no. 2 (2002): 396.

14. Jill Milling, "The Ambiguous Animal: Evolution of the Beast-Man in Scientific Creation Myths," in *The Shape of the Fantastic* (New York: Greenwood, 1990), 108.

15. H. G. Wells, *The Croquet Player* (New York: Viking, 1937), 9.

16. Sigmund Freud, *The Interpretation of Dreams* (New York: Avon Books, 1965), 587.

17. Akira Mizuta Lippit, *Electric Animal: Toward a Rhetoric of Wildlife* (Minneapolis: University of Minnesota Press, 2000), 16.

18. Stephen Kern, *Culture of Time and Space* (Cambridge: Harvard University Press, 1983), 38.

19. See William Scheick, "Exorcising the Ghost Story: Wells's *The Croquet Player* and The Camford Visitations," *Cahiers: Victoriens et Edouardiens* 17 (April 1983): 53–62. Scheick agues that Frobisher's ineffective will functions as the central horror of the novel and that the reader is invited to "participate in the collective 'mind

of Man'" (59). I suggest that this very participation is unveiled as an impossibility in Wells's text.

20. Sandra M. Gilbert, *Acts of Attention: The Poems of D. H. Lawrence* (Carbondale: Southern Illinois University Press, 1990), 142.

21. D. H. Lawrence, *Birds, Beasts, and Flowers* (Santa Rosa: Black Sparrow Press, 1995), 127.

22. Christopher Pollnitz, "'I Didn't Know His God'": The Epistemology of 'Fish,'" *The D. H. Lawrence Review* 15, no. 1–2 (1982): 1–50.

23. D. H. Lawrence, *Birds, Beasts, and Flowers* (Santa Rosa: Black Sparrow Press, 1995), 105.

24. Georges Bataille, *Theory of Religion,* trans. Robert Hurley (New York: Zone Books, 1992), 17.

25. Georges Bataille, *The Accursed Share,* trans. Robert Hurley (New York: Zone Books, 1991), 19.

26. Deborah Slicer, "Your Daughter or Your Dog? A Feminist Assessment of the Animal Research Issue," *Hypatia* 6, no. 1 (Spring 1991): 112.

4. Recuperating the Animal

1. D. H. Lawrence, *Women in Love,* ed. David Farmer, Lindeth Vasey, and John Worthen (Cambridge: Cambridge University Press, 1987), 9.

2. Michael Bell, *D. H. Lawrence: Language and Being* (Cambridge: Cambridge University Press, 1991), 7.

3. George J. Zytaruk discusses Lawrence's belief in the need for spontaneity for the development of individuality in his essay "The Doctrine of Individuality: D. H. Lawrence's 'Metaphysic,'" in *D. H. Lawrence: A Centenary Consideration,* ed. Peter Balbert and Phillip Marcus (Ithaca: Cornell University Press, 1985), 237–53.

4. Diane S. Bonds, *Language and the Self in D. H. Lawrence* (Ann Arbor: UMI Research Press, 1987), 21.

5. Michael Bell, "Lawrence and Modernism," in *The Cambridge Companion to D. H. Lawrence,* ed. Anne Fernihough (Cambridge: Cambridge University Press, 2001), 184.

6. See David Parker, "Into the Ideological Unknown: *Women in Love,*" *The Rainbow and Women in Love: Contemporary Critical Essays,* ed. Gary Day and Libby Di Niro (New York: Palgrave MacMillan, 2004).

7. Carola M. Kaplan, "Totem, Taboo, and *Blutbrüderschaft* in D. H. Lawrence's *Women in Love,*" in *Seeing Double: Revisioning Edwardian and Modernist Literature,* ed. C. M. Kaplan and Anne B. Simpson (New York: St. Martin's Press, 1996), 115.

8. Barbara Ann Schapiro, *D. H. Lawrence and the Paradoxes of Psychic Life* (Albany: State University of New York Press, 1999), 9.

9. Max Horkheimer and Theodor W. Adorno, *The Dialectic of Enlightenment,* trans. John Cumming (New York: Continuum, 1944), 20.

10. Kenneth Inniss, *D. H. Lawrence's Bestiary: A Study of His Use of Animal Trope and Symbol* (Paris: Mouton, 1971), 24.

11. As is so often the case with symbolic uses of animality, it is important to note here Lawrence's easy and oversimplified association between animality and detachment.

12. Michael Bell, *D. H. Lawrence: Language and Being* (Cambridge: Cambridge University Press, 1991), 100.

13. D. H. Lawrence, *St. Mawr* (New York: Vintage, 1960), 6.

14. Carol Siegel, "*St. Mawr:* Lawrence's Journey Toward Cultural Feminism," *D. H. Lawrence Review* 26, no. 1–3 (1995–96): 279.

15. Marjorie Garber, "Heavy Petting," in *Human, All Too Human,* ed. Diana Fuss (New York: Routledge, 1996), 32.

16. In *Adam's Task: Calling Animals by Name* Hearne argues that we have a duty to train animals such as horses and dogs because they are "so generous" in answering our call. Hearne suggests that humans call creatures into a more noble context by facilitating their partial participation in human symbolic systems. She insists that such animals have a right to "freedom of speech" and, at the same time, believes that humans have something to learn from animals' nonhuman phenomenological modes. See Vicki Hearne, *Adam's Task: Calling Animals by Name* (New York: Knopf, 1986), 265.

17. John Haegert, "Lawrence's *St. Mawr* and the De-Creation of America," *Criticism* 34, no. 1 (Winter 1992): 75.

5. Revising the Human

1. Bonnie Kime Scott, "Barnes Being 'Beast Familiar': Representation on the Margins of Modernism," *The Review of Contemporary Fiction* 13, no. 3 (Fall 1993), 41.

2. Djuna Barnes, *Nightwood* (New York: New Directions, 1937), 3.

3. Judith Butler, *Bodies That Matter* (New York: Routledge, 1993), 48.

4. I am leaving aside the larger question of the text's treatment of Jewishness as such. It seems possible that despite the text's privileging of abjected positions and discourses (such as animality and sexual deviation) Jewishness remains marginalized to a greater extent than these.

5. Slavoj Žižek, *Enjoy Your Symptom* (New York: Routledge, 1992), 48.

6. For another discussion of Felix's embodiment of racial "purity" tainted by false claims to ancestry see Jane Marcus, "Laughing at Leviticus: *Nightwood* as Woman's Circus Epic," in *Silence and Power: A Reevaluation of Djuna Barnes,* ed. Mary Lynn Broe (Carbondale: Southern Illinois University Press, 1991).

7. Jacques Derrida, *Speech and Phenomena And Other Essays on Husserl's Theory of Signs,* trans. David B. Allison (Evanston: Northwestern University Press, 1973), 102.

8. Barbara Johnson, "The Frame of Reference: Poe, Lacan, Derrida," in *The Purloined Poe: Lacan, Derrida and Psychoanalytic Reading,* ed. John P. Muller and William J. Richardson (Baltimore: Johns Hopkins University Press, 1988), 225.

9. For an introduction to some of the primary critical issues at stake in the disagreements between Derrida and Lacan, see Barbara Johnson, "The Frame of Reference."

10. See, for instance, Jane Gallop's *Reading Lacan* (Ithaca: Cornell University Press, 1985), especially 133–46.

11. Judith Lee, "*Nightwood:* 'The Sweetest Lie,'" *Silence and Power: A Reevaluation of Djuna Barnes,* ed. Mary Lynn Broe (Carbondale: Southern Illinois University Press 1991), 216.

12. Jacques Derrida, "'Eating Well,' or The Calculation of the Subject: Interview with Jacques Derrida," interview by Jean-Luc Nancy, in *Who Comes After the Subject?*, ed. Eduardo Cadava, Peter Connor, and Jean-Luc Nancy (New York: Routledge, 1991), 113.

13. Jacques Derrida, *Of Spirit: Heidegger and the Question,* trans. Geoffrey Bennington and Rachel Bowlby (Chicago: University of Chicago Press, 1989), 53.

14. Sigmund Freud, *Civilization and its Discontents,* trans. Joan Riviere (London: Hogarth Press, 1930), 30.

15. Karen Kaivola, "The 'Beast Turning Human': Constructions of the Primitive in *Nightwood," The Review of Contemporary Fiction* 13, no. 3 (Fall 1993), 175.

16. Dianne Chisholm, "Obscene Modernism: *Eros Noir* and the Profane Illumination of Djuna Barnes," *American Literature* 69, no. 1 (March 1997), 181.

17. Gilles Deleuze and Félix Guattari, *A Thousand Plateaus: Capitalism and Schizophrenia,* trans. Brian Massumi (Minneapolis: University of Minnesota Press, 1987), 280–81.

18. Freud figures our transition from animal to human as an organic repression and a developing shift from the olfactory to the specular; see *Civilization and Its Discontents,* 29–30.

19. Elaine Scarry, *The Body in Pain* (New York: Oxford University Press, 1985), 4.

20. Sigmund Freud, "Lecture II Parapraxes," in volume 15 of *The Standard Edition of the Complete Psychological Works of Sigmund Freud,* trans. James Strachey (London: Hogarth, 1953–74), 209.

21. Donald Philip Verene, *Hegel's Recollection: A Study of Images in the Phenomenology of Spirit* (Albany: State University of New York Press, 1985), quoted in Žižek, *Enjoy Your Symptom,* 50.

22. It is important to note that Deleuze and Guattari err in characterizing animal consciousness as nondifferentiated because, in fact, we know that animals have complex experiences of self and other that cannot be so simplistically categorized; see, for example, Paola Cavalieri and Peter Singer, eds., *The Great Ape Project: Equality beyond Humanity* (New York: St. Martin's, 1993); and Donald R. Griffin, *Animal Minds* (Chicago: University of Chicago Press, 1992).

23. Given my reliance on Žižek in this essay, it is necessary to note that Butler, and for that matter Kristeva, finally disagree with Žižek's privileging of the real, which they and other feminists interpret as a potential reification of castration and the Oedipal scenario. In *Bodies That Matter,* Butler raises the possibility that Žižek understands these classic psychoanalytic mechanisms as existing outside cultural and political contingencies, and she suggests that Žižek's work therefore valo-

rizes the real as "a token of a phallus" (197), as a doctrine closed to interrogation that secures the correlative links between man-phallus and woman-lack. See also Žižek's rejoinder to Butler's critique in the appendix to his *Metastases of Enjoyment* where he reiterates the Lacanian insistence that the phallic signifier is defined by difference and lack.

24. Julia Kristeva, *Powers of Horror,* trans. Lion S. Roudiez (New York: Columbia University Press, 1982), 4.

25. Andrea L. Harris, "The Third Sex: Figures of Inversion in Djuna Barnes's *Nightwood,*" in *Eroticism and Containment: Notes from the Flood Plain,* ed. Carol Siegel and Ann Kibbey (New York: New York University Press, 1994), 233–59.

26. John Forrester, *The Seductions of Psychoanalysis: Freud, Lacan, and Derrida,* (Cambridge: Cambridge University Press, 1990), 235.

27. My understanding of Robin's "redemption" from the human differs significantly from readings that interpret her assumption of nonhuman identity as pathological or regressive. Dana Seitler's classification of *Nightwood* as a "degeneration narrative," for instance, frames the novel in such a register, though Seitler's reading understands this kind of narrative through a complex analysis of scientific culture. See Dana Seitler, "Down on All Fours: Atavistic Perversions and the Science of Desire from Frank Norris to Djuna Barnes," *American Literature* 73, no. 3 (2001): 525–62.

Conclusion

1. Margot Norris, "The Human Animal in Fiction," *Parallax* 12, no. 1 (2006): 9.

2. Cary Wolfe, *Animal Rites: American Culture, the Discourse of Species, and Posthumanist Theory* (Chicago: University of Chicago Press, 2003), 193.

3. Elizabeth Grosz, "The Creative Impulse," interview by Julie Copeland, *Sunday Morning Radio National,* August 14, 2005, 2, http://www.abc.net.au/rn/arts/sunmorn/stories/s1435592.htm.

4. Jacques Derrida, "The Animal That Therefore I Am (More to Follow)," *Critical Inquiry* 28, no. 2 (2002): 396.

Works Cited

Achebe, Chinua. "An Image of Africa: Racism in Conrad's *Heart of Darkness.*" *The Massachusetts Review* 18 (1977): 782–94. Rpt. in *Heart of Darkness,* edited by Robert Kimbrough, 3rd edition, 251–62. New York: Norton, 1988.

Adams, Carol. *The Sexual Politics of Meat: A Feminist-Vegetarian Critical Theory.* New York: Continuum, 1990.

Annan, Noel. "Science, Religion, and the Critical Mind: Introduction." In *1859: Entering an Age of Crisis.* Edited by Philip Appleman, William A. Madden, and Michael Wolff. Bloomington: Indiana University Press, 1959.

Appleman, Philip. *1859: Entering an Age of Crisis.* Edited by Philip Appleman, William A. Madden, and Michael Wolff. Bloomington: Indiana University Press, 1959.

Barnes, Djuna. *Nightwood.* New York: New Directions, 1937.

Bataille, Georges. *The Accursed Share.* Translated by Robert Hurley. New York: Zone Books, 1991.

——. *Theory of Religion.* Translated by Robert Hurley. New York: Zone Books, 1992.

——. *Visions of Excess: Selected Writings, 1927–1939.* Minneapolis: University of Minnesota Press, 1985.

Beardsworth, Richard. *Derrida and the Political.* New York: Routledge, 1996.

Bell, Michael. *D. H. Lawrence: Language and Being.* Cambridge: Cambridge University Press, 1991.

——. "Lawrence and Modernism." In *The Cambridge Companion to D. H. Lawrence,* edited by Anne Fernihough, 179–96. Cambridge: Cambridge University Press, 2001.

Bonds, Diane S. *Language and the Self in D. H. Lawrence.* Ann Arbor: UMI Research Press, 1987.

Bowler, Peter J. *Charles Darwin: The Man and His Influence.* Cambridge: Basil Blackwell, 1990.

Brantlinger, Patrick. *Rule of Darkness: British Literature and Imperialism, 1830–1914.* Ithaca: Cornell University Press, 1988.

Butler, Judith. *Bodies That Matter.* New York: Routledge, 1993.

Cavalieri, Paola and Peter Singer, eds. *The Great Ape Project: Equality beyond Humanity.* New York: St. Martin's, 1993.

Cheyette, Bryan. "Neither Excuse nor Accuse: T. S. Eliot's Semitic Discourse." *Modernism/Modernity* 10, no. 3 (2003): 431–37.

Chisholm, Dianne. "Obscene Modernism: *Eros Noir* and the Profane Illumination of Djuna Barnes." *American Literature* 69, no. 1 (March 1997): 167–206.

Clark, L. D. *Dark Night of the Body: D. H. Lawrence's "The Plumed Serpent."* Austin: University of Texas Press, 1964.

Clark, Stephen. "Testing the Razor: T. S. Eliot's *Poems 1920.*" In *Engendering the Word: Feminist Essays in Psychosexual Politics,* edited by Temma Berg, 167–89. Urbana: University of Illinois Press, 1989.

Conrad, Joseph. *Heart of Darkness.* Edited by Robert Kimbrough, 3rd ed. New York: Norton, 1988.

Curtler, Hugh Mercer. "Achebe on Conrad: Racism and Greatness in *Heart of Darkness.*" *Conradiana* 29, no. 1 (1997): 30–40.

Darwin, Charles. *The Descent of Man.* London: Penguin, 2004.

——. *The Origin of Species.* New York: Gramercy Books, 1979.

DeGraaff, Robert M. "The Evolution of Sweeney in the Poetry of T. S. Eliot." *Critical Essays on T. S. Eliot: The Sweeney Motif,* edited by Kinley E. Roby, 220–26. Boston: G. K. Hall, 1985.

Deleuze, Gilles, and Félix Guattari. *A Thousand Plateaus: Capitalism and Schizophrenia.* Translated by Brian Massumi. Minneapolis: University of Minnesota Press, 1987.

Derrida, Jacques. "The Animal That Therefore I Am (More to Follow)." *Critical Inquiry* 28, no. 2 (2002): 369–418.

——. "'Eating Well,' or The Calculation of the Subject: An Interview with Jacques Derrida." in *Who Comes After the Subject?,* edited by Eduardo Cadava, Peter Connor, and Jean-Luc Nancy, 96–119. New York: Routledge, 1991.

——. "The Force of Law: The Mystical Foundation of Authority." *Cardozo Law Review* 11, no. 919 (1990): 921–1045.

——. *Of Grammatology.* Baltimore: Johns Hopkins University Press, 1974.

——. *Of Spirit: Heidegger and the Question.* Translated by Geoffrey Bennington and Rachel Bowlby. Chicago: University of Chicago Press, 1989.

——. *Speech and Phenomena And Other Essays on Husserl's Theory of Signs.* Translated by David B. Allison. Evanston: Northwestern University Press, 1973.

Docherty, Thomas. *Alterities: Criticism, History, Representation.* Oxford: Clarendon Press, 1996.

DuPlessis, Rachel Blau. "Circumscriptions: Assimilating T. S. Eliot's Sweeneys." In *People of the Book: Thirty Scholars Reflect on Their Jewish Identity*, edited by Jeffrey Rubin-Dorsky, 135–52. Madison: University of Wisconsin Press, 1996.

Eliot, T. S. *Collected Poems, 1909–1962*. New York: Harcourt Brace, 1963.

Fiddes, Nick. *Meat: A Natural Symbol*. London: Routledge, 1991.

Forrester, John. *The Seductions of Psychoanalysis: Freud, Lacan, and Derrida*. Cambridge: Cambridge University Press, 1990.

Freedman, Jonathan. "Lessons Out of School: T. S. Eliot's Jewish Problem and the Making of Modernism." *Modernism/Modernity* 10, no. 3 (2003): 419–29.

Freud, Sigmund. *Civilization and its Discontents*. Translated by Joan Riviere. London: Hogarth Press, 1930.

——. *The Interpretation of Dreams*. New York: Avon Books, 1965.

——. "Lecture II Parapraxes," in volume 15 of *The Standard Edition of the Complete Psychological Works of Sigmund Freud*. Translated by James Strachey. London: Hogarth, 1953–74.

——. *Totem and Taboo*. New York: Norton, 1950.

Garber, Marjorie. "Heavy Petting." In *Human, All Too Human*, edited by Diana Fuss, 11–36. New York: Routledge, 1996.

Garcia, Emanuel. "Reflections on Death, Phylogeny, and the Mind-Body Problem in Freud's Life and Work." In *Understanding Freud the Man and His Ideas*, edited by Emanuel Garcia. New York: New York University Press, 1992.

Gilbert, Sandra M. *Acts of Attention: The Poems of D. H. Lawrence*. Carbondale: Southern Illinois University Press, 1990.

Griffin, Donald R. *Animal Minds*. Chicago: University of Chicago Press, 1992.

Grosz, Elizabeth. *The Nick of Time: Politics, Evolution, and the Untimely*. Durham: Duke University Press, 2004.

Habermas, Jürgen. *The Philosophical Discourse of Modernity*. Cambridge, MA: MIT Press, 1987.

Haegert, John. "Lawrence's *St. Mawr* and the De-Creation of America." *Criticism* 34, no. 1 (Winter 1992): 75–98.

Hargrove, Nancy. "The Symbolism of Sweeney in the Works of T. S. Eliot." In *Critical Essays on T. S. Eliot: The Sweeney Motif*, edited by Kinley E. Roby, 147–69. Boston: G. K. Hall, 1985.

Harris, Andrea L. "The Third Sex: Figures of Inversion in Djuna Barnes's *Nightwood*." In *Eroticism and Containment: Notes from the Flood Plain*, edited by Carol Siegel and Ann Kibbey, 233–59. New York: New York University Press, 1994.

Haynes, Roslynn D. *H. G. Wells: Discoverer of the Future*. New York: New York University Press, 1980.

Hearne, Vicki. *Adam's Task: Calling Animals by Name*. New York: Knopf, 1986.

Hendershot, Cyndy. "The Animal Without: Masculinity and Imperialism in *The Island of Dr. Moreau* and 'The Adventures of the Speckled Band.'" *Nineteenth Century Studies* 10 (1996): 1–32.

Horkheimer, Max, and Theodor W. Adorno. *The Dialectic of Enlightenment*. Translated by John Cumming. New York: Continuum, 1944.

Humma, John. "The Imagery of *The Plumed Serpent: The Going-under of Organi-cism." The D. H. Lawrence Review* 15, no. 3 (1982): 197–218.

Inniss, Kenneth. *D. H. Lawrence's Bestiary: A Study of His Use of Animal Trope and Symbol.* Paris: Mouton, 1971.

Johnson, Barbara. "The Frame of Reference: Poe, Lacan, Derrida." In *The Pur-loined Poe: Lacan, Derrida, and Psychoanalytic Reading,* edited by John P. Muller and William J. Richardson, 213–51. Baltimore: Johns Hopkins University Press, 1988.

Julius, Anthony. *T. S. Eliot, Anti-Semitism, and Literary Form.* Cambridge: Cam-bridge University Press, 1995.

Jung, Carl G. *Man and His Symbols.* New York: Dell Publishing, 1964.

Kaivola, Karen. "The 'Beast Turning Human': Constructions of the Primitive in *Nightwood." The Review of Contemporary Fiction* 13, no. 3 (Fall 1993): 172–85.

Kaplan, Carola M. "Totem, Taboo, and *Blutbrüderschaft* in D. H. Lawrence's *Women in Love."* In *Seeing Double: Revisioning Edwardian and Modernist Literature,* ed-ited by C. M. Kaplan and Anne B. Simpson, 113–30. New York: St. Martin's Press, 1996.

Karl, Frederick R. "Introduction to the *Danse Macabre:* Conrad's *Heart of Darkness."* In *Heart of Darkness: A Case Study in Contemporary Criticism,* edited by Ross C. Murfin, 123–38. New York: St. Martin's Press, 1989.

Kern, Stephen. *Culture of Time and Space.* Cambridge, MA: Harvard University Press, 1983.

Kristeva, Julia. *Powers of Horror.* Translated by Leon S. Roudiez. New York: Colum-bia University Press, 1982.

LaChapelle, Dolores. *D. H. Lawrence: Future Primitive.* Denton: University of North Texas Press, 1996.

Lawrence, D. H. *Birds, Beasts, and Flowers.* Santa Rosa: Black Sparrow Press, 1995.

——. *The Plumed Serpent (Quetzalcoatl).* Edited by L. D. Clark. Cambridge: Cam-bridge University Press, 1987.

——. "Reflections on the Death of a Porcupine." *Reflections on the Death of a Por-cupine and Other Essays.* Edited by Michael Herbert. Cambridge: Cambridge University Press, 1988.

——. *St. Mawr.* New York: Vintage, 1960.

——. *Women in Love.* Edited by David Farmer, Lindeth Vasey and John Worthen. Cambridge: Cambridge University Press, 1987.

Lee, Judith. "*Nightwood:* 'The Sweetest Lie.'" In *Silence and Power: A Reevaluation of Djuna Barnes,* edited by Mary Lynn Broe, 207–18. Carbondale: Southern Il-linois University Press, 1991.

Levinas, Emmanuel. *Totality and Infinity: An Essay on Exteriority.* Translated by Al-phonso Lingis. Pittsburgh: Duquesne University Press, 1969.

Lippit, Akira Mizuta. *Electric Animal: Toward a Rhetoric of Wildlife.* Minneapolis: University of Minnesota Press, 2000.

Llewelyn, John. "Am I Obsessed by Bobby? (Humanism of the Other Animal)." In *Re-reading Levinas,* edited by Robert Bernasconi and Simon Critchley, 234–45. Bloomington: Indiana University Press, 1991.

London, Bette. "Reading Race and Gender in Conrad's Dark Continent." *Criticism: A Quarterly for Literature and the Arts* 31, no. 3 (1989): 235–52.

Lyotard, Jean-François. *The Differend: Phrases in Dispute.* Minneapolis: University of Minnesota Press, 1988.

Marcus, Jane. "Laughing at Leviticus: *Nightwood* as Woman's Circus Epic." In *Silence and Power: A Reevaluation of Djuna Barnes,* edited by Mary Lynn Broe, 221–50. Carbondale: Southern Illinois University Press, 1991.

Marshall, Cynthia. "Psychoanalyzing the Prepsychoanalytic Subject." *PMLA* 117, no. 5 (2002): 1207–16.

McClintock, Anne. *Imperial Leather: Race, Gender, and Sexuality in the Colonial Conquest.* New York: Routledge, 1995.

McKay, Robert. "'Identifying with the Animals': Language, Subjectivity, and the Animal Politics of Margaret Atwood's *Surfacing.*" In *Figuring Animals: Essays on Animal Images in Art, Literature, Philosophy, and Popular Culture,* edited by Mary Sanders Pollock and Catherine Rainwater, 207–27. New York: Palgrave Macmillan, 2005.

Milling, Jill. "The Ambiguous Animal: Evolution of the Beast-Man in Scientific Creation Myths." *The Shape of the Fantastic.* New York: Greenwood, 1990.

Moussaieff Masson, Jeffrey and Susan McCarthy. *When Elephants Weep: The Emotional Lives of Animals.* New York: Delacorte Press, 1995.

Mumford Jones, Howard. "Introduction." In *1859: Entering an Age of Crisis,* edited by Philip Appleman, William A. Madden, and Michael Wolff. Bloomington: Indiana University Press, 1959.

Nietzsche, Friedrich. *The Birth of Tragedy.* New York: Russell and Russell, 1964.

——. *On the Genealogy of Morals.* Translated by Walter Kaufmann. New York: Vintage, 1989.

Norris, Margot. "The Human Animal in Fiction." *Parallax* 12, no. 1 (2006): 4–20.

Ower, John. "Pattern and Value in 'Sweeney Among the Nightingales.'" In *Critical Essays on T. S. Eliot: The Sweeney Motif,* edited by Kinley E. Roby, 67–75. Boston: G. K. Hall, 1985.

Parker, David. "Into the Ideological Unknown: *Women in Love.*" In *The Rainbow and Women in Love: Contemporary Critical Essays,* edited by Gary Day and Libby Di Niro, 209–34. New York: Palgrave MacMillan, 2004.

Perloff, Marjorie. "Modernist Studies." In *Redrawing the Boundaries: The Transformation of English and American Literary Studies,* edited by Stephen Greenblatt and Giles Gunn, 154–78. New York: MLA, 1992.

Pollnitz, Christopher. "'I Didn't Know His God': The Epistemology of 'Fish.'" *The D. H. Lawrence Review* 15, no. 1–2 (1982): 1–50.

Roby, Kinley E., edited Introduction to *Critical Essays on T. S. Eliot: The Sweeney Motif.* Boston: G. K. Hall, 1985.

Ritvo, Harriet. *The Animal Estate: The English and Other Creatures in the Victorian Age.* Cambridge, MA: Harvard University Press, 1987.

Ritvo, Lucille B. *Darwin's Influence on Freud: A Tale of Two Sciences.* New Haven: Yale University Press, 1990.

Said, Edward W. *Culture and Imperialism.* New York: Vintage, 1993.

Scarry, Elaine. *The Body in Pain*. New York: Oxford University Press, 1985.

Schapiro, Barbara Ann. *D. H. Lawrence and the Paradoxes of Psychic Life*. Albany: State University of New York Press, 1999.

Scheick, William. "Exorcising the Ghost Story: Wells's *The Croquet Player* and The Camford Visitations." *Cahiers: Victoriens et Edouardiens* 17 (April 1983): 53–62.

Schuchard, Ronald. "Burbank with a Baedeker, Eliot with a Cigar: American Intellectuals, Anti-Semitism, and the Idea of Culture." *Modernism/Modernity* 10, no. 1 (2003): 1–26.

Scott, Bonnie Kime. "Barnes Being 'Beast Familiar': Representation on the Margins of Modernism." *The Review of Contemporary Fiction* 13, no. 3 (Fall 1993): 41–52.

Sheppard, Richard. "The Crisis of Language." In *Modernism: A Guide to European Literature*. Edited by Malcolm Bradbury and James McFarlane, 323–36. London: Penguin, 1976.

Siegel, Carol. "*St. Mawr:* Lawrence's Journey Toward Cultural Feminism." *D. H. Lawrence Review* 26, no. 1–3 (1995–1996): 275–86.

Simpson, Anne. "The 'Tangible Antagonist': H. G. Wells and the Discourse of Otherness." *Extrapolation: A Journal of Science Fiction and Fantasy* 31, no. 2 (Summer 1990): 134–47.

Slicer, Deborah. "Your Daughter or Your Dog? A Feminist Assessment of the Animal Research Issue." *Hypatia* 6, no. 1 (Spring 1991): 108–24.

Smith, Johanna M. "'Too Beautiful Altogether': Patriarchal Ideology in *Heart of Darkness*." In *Heart of Darkness: A Case Study in Contemporary Criticism*, edited by Ross C. Murfin, 179–95. New York: St. Martin's Press, 1989.

Spiegel, Marjorie. *The Dreaded Comparison: Human and Animal Slavery*. New York: Mirror Books, 1996.

Stone, Carole, and Fawzia Afzal-Khan. "Gender, Race and Narrative Structure: A Reappraisal of Joseph Conrad's *Heart of Darkness*." *Conradiana* 29, no. 3 (1997): 221–34.

Torgovnick, Marianna. *Gone Primitive: Savage Intellects, Modern Lives*. Chicago: University of Chicago Press, 1990.

Waldenfels, Bernhard. "Levinas and the Face of the Other." In *The Cambridge Companion to Levinas*. Edited by Simon Critchley and Robert Bernasconi. Cambridge: Cambridge University Press, 2002.

Watts, C. T. "*Heart of Darkness:* The Covert Murder Plot and the Darwinian Theme." *Conradiana* VII (1975): 137–43.

Wells, H. G. *The Croquet Player*. New York: Viking, 1937.

——. *The Island of Dr. Moreau*. New York: Bantam, 1994.

Wolfe, Cary. *Animal Rites: American Culture, the Discourse of Species, and Posthumanist Theory*. Chicago: University of Chicago Press, 2003.

——. *Critical Environments: Postmodern Theory and the Pragmatics of the "Outside."* Minneapolis: University of Minnesota Press, 1998.

——. "Faux Post-Humanism, or, Animal Rights, Neocolonialism, and Michael Crichton's *Congo*." *Arizona Quarterly* 55, no. 2 (Summer 1999): 115–53.

Wolfe, Cary, and Jonathan Elmer. "Subject to Sacrifice: Ideology, Psychoanalysis, and the Discourse of Species in Jonathan Demme's *Silence of the Lambs*" *Boundary 2* 22, no. 3 (1995): 141–70.

Žižek, Slavoj. *Enjoy Your Symptom*. New York; Routledge, 1992.

———. *Looking Awry: An Introduction to Jacques Lacan through Popular Culture*. Cambridge, MA: MIT Press, 1991.

———. *The Metastases of Enjoyment: Six Essays on Woman and Causality*. New York: Verso, 1994.

Zytaruk, George, J. "The Doctrine of Individuality: D. H. Lawrence's 'Metaphysic.'" In *D. H. Lawrence: A Centenary Consideration,* edited by Peter Balbert and Phillip Marcus, 237–53. Ithaca: Cornell University Press, 1985.

Index